Given A Chance

Given A Chance

The Success Story of
A Killing Fields Survivor

Hong L. Net

PALMETTO
P U B L I S H I N G
Charleston, SC
www.PalmettoPublishing.com

Second Edition

www.givenachance.life

Editor: Philip Turner

Hardcover ISBN: 979-8-8229-4474-9
Paperback ISBN: 979-8-8229-4475-6
eBook ISBN: 979-8-8229-4476-3

This book is dedicated to my beloved father
Richard A. Johnson, who devoted all his time to
teaching and providing me the opportunity to
grow up to become who I am today.

Contents

"No one saves us but ourselves.

No one can and no one may.

We ourselves must walk the path."

— Buddha

Based on the United Nations map.

Preface

The person who asked me if I would write a book about thirty years ago, was one of my classmates, after I told my story to my world history class at the University of Massachusetts in Amherst. Many students, including my professor, cried. She approached me and encouraged me to tell my story to the world and offered her assistance in writing it.

I was reluctant because I did not think that it was important at the time. However, during my travels to many different places, people continued to ask the same questions. As questions persisted, I started to think that it would benefit other people who were in my situation to come out to tell their stories as well. The opportunity to write this book began in November 2018 after my election for state legislature. I began to organize in my mind with a frightening confidence to how the book would proceed.

When I decided to sit down and begin to write, I gathered my memories, went through some of my diaries, and put them into my computer. I tried to remember the stories of the family my mother and her parents told me as a child. I also tried to recall my years as a child working in labor camps in Cambodia and living in refugee camps in Thailand. In addition, I remembered the stories my father's cousin told me when we were riding in my cousin's taxi from my village to Phnom Penh, describing the grandfather I had never known and the mother I hardly remember.

This book started in January 2019 and finished in July 2021. Most events that I put in this book, occurred for the first time. As you go through the pages of this book, I trust you will find something that you can relate to, because it is just a story of mine.

Acknowledgements

T'he greatest blessing in my life is having a loving family, wonderful friends, and understanding colleagues. I have been fortunate to have all of that, and they all helped me tremendously to write this memoir. I am thankful to have met them, known them, and worked with them. Some of them are mentioned in this book and some are not because I could not recall the memories correctly.

To those whom I failed to mention or mistakenly recalled their names and statuses, please accept my apologies. Some of them were good to me and some were not. A few have died, but most are still alive. Some of them thrived, but some of them were not so lucky. Those who were mean to me, I wholeheartedly forgive them. Those who were good to me, I thank them from the bottom of my heart. Those who trusted me by giving me jobs and allowing me to serve the community, I thank them profoundly for the opportunity to live the American dream.

A special thanks to Richard, Michaela, Nicholas, and Patrick for opening up their hearts by trusting me and taking me into their lives. They love me and treat me as their son and brother. Their beautiful home in South Hadley, Massachusetts was my birthplace of freedom. I have no records of my biological family because everything was destroyed.

I learned a lot from my colleagues at the council, state government, federal government, and nonprofit circles, which benefited enormously from their expertise, advice, and friendships. My aunt Nadyne Millar fed me information about Grandpa J, my uncles, and my cousins' information. My mother Michaela Johnson fed me about Grandfather and Baba's information. They both worked hard to gather all my family's photos and old articles that were written about me when I first came to America. My sister-in-law Sem Phomadin fed me information about Thavra's childhood and her family's background. My father-in-law Chun Lun told me about the political situations that took place during Norodom Sihanouk, Lon Nol, and Heng Samrin's regimes. My biological father Neth Uok and my aunt Cheng Yong fed me information about my childhood and the background of our family. My uncle Hai Cheng helped me to recall some of the events that took place in refugee camps.

My beloved wife, Thavra Net, is a wonderful advisor. She asked me hard questions about my past experiences as far as I could remember to bring back my memories. My amazing children, Anna and William Net offered critical comments on the manuscript. My friends, Stella-Mae Seamans and Marge Nix, and my editor Phillip Turner read everything diligently and edited my memoir meaningfully. All have contributed in their way to make this book what it is. My sharp-minded brothers Nicholas August Johnson and Patrick Michael Johnson gave useful feedback and great ideas. Thank you all so much for undertaking this project together.

Introduction

One night, I followed fellow refugees across a river into Thailand to steal corn, tomatoes, cassava roots, and peanuts from Thai farms near the border. We assigned some people as lookouts and spread around the gardens. We were all determined to stay alive and to find food. We often heard the farmers shoot their rifles in the air, but we did not stop. This worked for months and no one was caught. Sometimes, the farmers outsmarted us. They would hide in their huts or behind bushes waiting for us to sneak into their gardens and then they would start to shoot at us, but they always missed.

One evening under a full moon in January 1980, I got caught while digging for roots in an open field on a peanut farm. I saw a shadow under me and was scared because I thought that it was an ogre coming to eat me alive. I was about to run, but wanted to see what it was. When I turned my head around and looked up, a man was standing above me, pointing his shotgun at me. He pulled me up by the hair and was ready to pull the trigger. I kneeled and begged for mercy then closed my eyes. At the same time, I asked my mother's spirit for protection. I was shaking from fear. I heard the farmer sigh. He put down his shotgun and pulled me up to a standing position. This was a moment in my life that I could never have expected in my dreams.

He hugged me and then led me to his tiny thatched hut at the edge of his farm. He fed me cooked cassava root and an ear of corn. He put his shirt on while looking at me, but I was too afraid to look up. I could barely eat because I was still shaking with fright.

PART I

My Childhood

CHAPTER 1

Blessings

I was born in the small village of Chi Kha in the province of Koh Kong in southwestern Cambodia, in the district known as Sre Ambel. It lies between high hills to the north and rice fields to the south. It was beautiful with rolling hills, valleys, ponds, lakes, streams, and rivers.

No one in Chi Kha owned a vehicle. No scholars, government officials, or military generals came from there. It was a peaceful community. There were no paved roads, running water, or electricity. People fetched water from ponds, lakes, streams, rivers, or wells for drinking, cooking, and washing. They used candles, lamps, and torch flames to brighten their homes at night. The main road was gravel, running between the mountains and rice fields.

In the rainy season, from May to October, the green rice fields with dikes divided up the area in a checkerboard pattern. During the harvest, the dry season in December and January, the temperature was perfect and the rice fields turned brilliant green and gold. There were white, pink, and purple lotuses and water lilies in the ponds and lakes. The wind blew cool breezes making coconut leaves dance back and forth or up and down under clear blue skies. Little naked boys swam in the wide streams and small lakes, while little girls covered

3

their eyes giggling. Fishermen went to the rivers and lakes in groups with fishnets, traps, and fishing poles on their shoulders. Everyone lived peacefully and was free to move around.

The majority of Chi Khans were farmers and peasants. Families planted crops twice a year, during the dry and rainy seasons. During the dry months, they farmed in the hilly forest area, and in the rainy season on their farmlands. People were pleasant and kind toward each other. When hearing the morning bell at the Buddhist temple and the monks chanting, the villagers would prepare food offerings for the monks to earn spiritual merits. When hearing the first crow of roosters, farmers would leave their homes and go to plow their fields, to plant their rice plants, or to harvest their crops. Sellers would get ready to bring their products to the market. Small children would get ready to go to school; while herdboys would go and let out the cattle and buffalos from the barns and take them to nearby fields, hills, and valleys where they ate grasses, weeds, and leaves. By sunset, everyone would return home to their families.

My father Neth Uok (Cambodians put their family name first) was born during the rainy season of 1942 in Koh Kong, a capital town of Koh Kong province, in southwestern Cambodia near the border with Thailand. Everyone in Chi Kha called him *Gu Uok* (Uncle Uok) in Chinese. In our family, we called him *Pak* (father). My mother, Cheng Kim-muoy, was born sometime in the year 1946 in the town of Kampong Trach in the province of Kampot in southeastern Cambodia near the border with South Vietnam. Everyone called her *Je Muoy*

(Sister Muoy) in Chinese. In our family, we called her *Maek* (mother). Our parents called us *kon* (child).

I was born sometime in October 1967 in a good wooden home high on stilts that my parents had built. A midwife from the village delivered me. My parents were grateful to have a boy. I was their first baby, a fat little boy. Our house was in the middle of a rice field. A walkway ran from the front door to the main road, dividing our farmland in two. Half of our house was walled up for a bedroom. We all slept on mats in the bedroom. The other half of our house was a hall-like room, with one piece of furniture, a big teak wood, rectangle table-bed pushed up against a wall. In the hall room, we all ate seated on the floor in a circle. Sometimes we had a big bowl of vegetable stew or a big bowl of soup in the middle for us to share. The mixed stew *(samlaw kawko)* had fish, pork, and chicken and the mixed vegetable sour soup *(samlaw machou sre)* had tamarind leaves with crabs, baby shrimp, and small fish.

In our house, the wooden floors were always shiny. Once a month, my mother or grandmother Kuoy would clean and smear the floors with wax to keep them shiny and slippery. The kitchen was on the far back part of the house. Our rice storage room was next to the kitchen. Our house was easy to spot from a distance because it was built in an open space.

Villagers believed that monsters called the *(arb)* would wander at night searching for new mothers' placentas, and hide under people's houses waiting to eat whatever came out of mothers who had just given birth. My father placed thorny branches around a fire pit to keep away the *arb*. We had a family altar high on one wall, where he placed burning incense sticks, asking our ancestors to bless the newborn. My grandmother on my mother's side chewed sticky and sour leaves *(sleuk trakeab kdam)* and placed these on my head's soft fontanel hoping to hasten its hardening. And since there were no modern medications to help ease the pain of the new mother, my grandmother made *(sra thanam)*, a mixture of Chinese herbs with wine and gave this to my mother to drink to keep her healthy and to clean out her insides.

Soon after I was born, some Cambodian-Chinese families in my village came to look at me and started making arrangements for me to marry one of their daughters when I grew up. A family that lived close by convinced my parents that I should marry their daughter. This baby girl, whom it was arranged I would marry, had been born a few months before me. Her name was Jik. When we got a little older, we were told that we were reserved for each other. We became good friends and played together. Our families always shared things, especially various foods. Many families in my village, and throughout Cambodia, had a tradition of arranging marriages for their children. They would be matched from infancy. Although brides and grooms might hardly know each other before their marriage, they would have an obligation to fulfill their parents' wishes. It was believed that eventually the couples would fall in love after marriage and live happily together.

My parents had met in the village of Cham Bak, where my father's cousin lived, and heard of a beautiful young Cambodian-Chinese girl living there. Right away, my father asked my mother to marry him. My mother's godfather, Dek, proposed to my mother's parents asking for my mother to marry my father. A year later my parents were married and the ceremony took place in Chi Kha, in January 1965. My mother was 19 years old and my father was 23 at the time of their marriage. After their marriage, my mother moved into my father's family home. Because my father was an only child, he and his new wife inherited all the lands and farms from my grandmother, Kuoy.

Though my father did not have a formal education, he spent most of his childhood learning precepts and scriptures in the monastery. He was five feet eight inches tall and slender. He was quiet, always with a smile on his face. As far as I remember, he never yelled or hit any of his children. His father died when he was two years old. His mother was deaf and widowed until she died in 1976.

My mother had received some education in Kampot, the capital city of Kampot province. She was the oldest and had two younger siblings. Her mother, my grandmother, was a gentle-hearted, loving person. Her father, my grandfather, was strict. My mother was lively, kind, and beautiful. She was short, about five feet two inches tall. She kept her shiny black hair long and was her parents' favorite child. She sang at school. She joined the national youth movement that was similar to Girl and Boy Scouts. This youth movement, formed by Prince Norodom Sihanouk in 1955, was to serve his political organization called Sangkum Reastr Niyum, the community of common people.

My mother often reminded us children not to accept anything from anyone. She arranged everything for our family, while my father was always in the fields with his hoe and machete, breaking grounds and clearing bushes for farming and gardening. He would leave home at dawn and come home at dusk. My mother was strict like her father. She ran her home with rules and discipline. Both of her younger siblings were afraid of her. My mother had gotten special permission from her parents to discipline her siblings when they were young.

I remember hearing that my mother had whipped my aunt, her sister—who was ten years younger—so hard for skipping school that her legs bled. My mother always warned me not to make my sister cry. Although I loved my sister unconditionally, I did often make her cry. I remember one day I did something unforgivable to her, which I still regret to this day. I mixed thorny berries with tree wax and poured it on my sister's head. It was very sticky and she panicked. My grandmother Kuoy tried to wash it off, but it could not be washed away. So my grandmother cut off most of my sister's hair to get rid of it. I was so scared and felt so ashamed that I hid for hours in the rice storage room behind the kitchen.

When my mother came home from working in the fields and found out what I had done, she began looking for me. When she found me, she asked me to come out to receive my punishment. Instead, I ran away. When I looked back, my mother was right behind me. The faster I ran, the closer she got to me. She chased after me from our house to the end of the village. Unfortunately, I was caught and dragged home by the hand while she yelled to everyone watching, "This is a very naughty child, don't ever look up to him as your role model."

I received a few hard hits with a rattan stick on my legs for having run away from her. After that incident, I realized that I was never going to get away from her. She had so much energy and was a very fast runner. From then on, I voluntarily went to her to be disciplined and I can say that the future punishments were much lighter.

I was the oldest of five siblings. My sister Suon was born in June 1969. She resembled my mother, slim with fair skin. My brother Mouch was born in November 1971. He had beautiful long eyelashes, talked nonstop, and was close to me and my mother. My brother Kun was born in October 1973. He was the cutest and had very light skin. He was born small. But he was a special baby because he was born with two hair crowns in the center of his head and a swirl of hair above his forehead.

I remember that my mother was very sick after giving birth to Kun. She could not provide enough milk. He cried all the time. I took care of my mother and Kun while my father and his mother worked. I cooked porridge, salted eggs, and dried fish for my mother every day. Also, I made soup for her, so she could produce milk for her newborn son. I spent a lot of time with my mother. I would build fires in the fire pit to keep her warm and I ate with her. My mother appreciated my assistance and she always fed me before taking her first bite.

In September 1975, my youngest brother Hing was born. My mother did not have time to nurse him because she was forced to work in the rice fields right after giving birth to him. This was during the beginning of Pol Pot's atrocious regime in

Cambodia. My mother had no milk to feed him. She gave Hing only the water from rice porridge. Hing had very dark skin and a big round belly like a balloon. He never had a proper name. He was called Hing because he was dark, and round, and cried a lot, just like toads do.

My sister, my first two brothers, and I all had Chinese first names. Our first names were given by our grandfather, my mother's father. My name was Liang-hong. My sister was Siv-suon and my two younger brothers were Liang-mouch and Liang-kun. No one ever called us by our full names. I was the eldest child in the family, and my mother expected much from me. She looked upon me to carry on all our various family traditions if our father was absent. Also, being a boy and the oldest, I was my grandparents' favorite.

My family lived a middle-class life in the countryside. We owned land and had a farm with animals such as water buffaloes and pigs. During the dry season, we cultivated land in the nearby hilly area, planting rice, corn, and black pepper. Because no one had a car or motorcycle, people in our village used oxcarts and bicycles to transport goods to market. In our village, there was a small grocery store (owned by my father's cousin Chao), a school, and a Buddhist temple. The village chief was another cousin of my father. When the villagers had issues, they would go to him for advice or solutions to all their problems. He also was a traditional healer. His wife was a midwife.

With no hospitals or modern medicines, a healer treated the sick and his wife delivered babies. Many adults believed in spirits and were superstitious. When children became sick, their parents would invite a traditional healer to come to their house. The healer would chant, take a sip or a mouthful of wine, and then spit it out gently onto the sick child's head. The drummers would beat their drums and the healer would dance around the sick child to scare the devil away.

My grandfather was against all Khmer/Cambodian traditional healers because he was a Chinese spiritual healer himself. I was told that once when I was sick lying on the floor, a healer came to our house. He chanted and then spit the wine out of his mouth onto my face and my head. However, my symptoms got worse. The healer was called again. Somehow, the news got to my grandfather. One night while the healer was engaged in his practice, my grandfather came into the house and screamed so loud and jumped so high that my grandfather cut his tongue until it was bleeding. The poor healer was scared and took off. My grandfather said that our ancestors disapproved of the practices of the Khmer traditional healers. He apologized to our ancestors. To make amends, he cooked a whole chicken including the head.

In the village, my friends and I used whatever we found such as clay, bamboo sticks, banana branches, and tin cans, turning them into toys, make-believe cows, elephants, buffaloes, cars, trucks, bicycles, trains, airplanes, and hot-wheels. My favorite toy was a push hot-wheel. I used a tin can for a car body, a wooden stick for a handle, and thorny fruits *(phle rolu-os)* for wheels. Usually, we boys played among ourselves, but sometimes we allowed girls to join us. Boys and girls would play games like hide-and-seek, touch-and-run, and hopscotch.

When I completed my chores, I immediately took off my shirt and wearing only my shorts, dashed off to play with my hot wheels pushing it along the road while making the sound of a car engine. Some of my friends would run out of their homes to join me. We raced along the dirt and gravel roads.

Another favorite toy was my slingshot. Friends and I would go into the woods and aim at birds, but we never hit one. We also used it to shoot at fruits such as mangoes, cashews, guavas, and other kinds. I remember my parents gave me a jumping plastic frog toy. It was the only real toy I ever owned. I had to share it with my sister. It was the best thing I ever had. We played together and screamed with joy as we squeezed the toy frog making it jump off the floor.

Once or twice a week, I would see a logging truck hauling timber driving fast on Route 48, the gravel road that ran through our village. The truck threw up a lot of red dust and smoke. The children would run and follow the truck and inhale the fumes. I loved the smell of the fumes mixed with dust because it was different and new. Whenever I heard the sound of the engine of a logging truck in the distance, I would race to the road and wait for it to pass. Then, I would chase behind it as far as I could, take a deep breath, and inhale the fumes mixed with the red dust from the road. The dust mixed with fumes smelled, especially good to me after a recent rain.

* * *

One day our mother told us about a big trip we were going to make. It was the only vacation that my family had ever planned, before what became our country's civil war. She told us a few days ahead that we would be going to her hometown somewhere far away from Chi Kha. She said that it would be a magical trip. All we had to do just sit and a big machine would take us there. I bragged to my friends for days that I was going on a trip, but they seemed not to either care or comprehend what I was saying. I could hardly wait for the day to come. I tried to imagine the big machine that would take us to the places that my mother talked about, but I could not think of anything.

One day in April 1971, before the Cambodian New Year, we went on our big trip. Cambodians, Thais, Laotians, Burmese, and other Theravada Buddhists celebrate the new year in April, with festivities lasting three days. I was the first of the family to awake the morning of our departure. I wandered around the house and waited impatiently for everyone else to wake up. I did not know what time it was exactly, but I knew that it was still dark outside. By dawn, everyone was up and packing. We left on a popular two-wheel carriage pulled by a motorcycle *(remauk)* to Sre Ambel, east of Chi Kha. Along the road to Sre Ambel, there were miles and miles of rice fields and countless small lakes filled with beautiful colored water lilies and lotuses. I could not take my eyes off the unfamiliar scenery.

After about thirty minutes, we were dropped off at the river port of Ta Ben and took a ferry across the salt river to the town of Sre Ambel. The river widened and opened up to the Gulf of Thailand at one end. At the other end, were the forests of Sre Ambel. Our ferry went up the river from the woody area into open water. As we sailed along, I saw boats of many different sizes in the open water. It was noisy on the ferry with many travelers, but I did not mind because I was focused on the scenery. I enjoyed seeing the different-sized cargo boats, fishing boats, and commercial boats all sharing the same body of water. My heart beat in excitement. About fifteen minutes later, we reached the port of Sre Ambel, where there was a busy outdoor market.

Sre Ambel was a big, busy town compared to Chi Kha. There were stucco buildings, wooden houses on stilts, and hills with amazing views of the rolling countryside and of the wide open river. On the narrow roads, bicycles, motorcycles, and automobiles competed with people on foot. It was very noisy, but I found it all very exciting. There seemed to be more ethnic Chinese living in Sre Ambel than Cambodians. It was one of the major trading ports in Koh Kong province. There was a big outdoor market by the river, where people could buy fresh fish and crabs from fishermen and all kinds of products such as cooked and raw foods from other sellers. People could buy food at the food stalls such as breakfast foods, beef noodles soup *(kuy teav sach ko)*, and pork rice porridge *(bawbaw sach chrouk)*. Then they could sit on plastic or wooden stools and eat their meals. I enjoyed watching and was fascinated by how people bargained for everything.

Everyone seemed to mind their own business. Taxi and bus attendants chased after travelers asking them to ride with them. Each vehicle was packed with people, while bags and baskets were piled on the roof. Around eight or nine o'clock, we squeezed into an already crowded taxi van. The driver placed us in the far back with two strangers. I sat on my father's lap and my sister on my mother's. There were six passengers including us four sitting in the back row. At least fifteen passengers were sitting on top of each other in the van.

National Route 48 linked at Chamkar Luong with National Highway 4, which continued west toward Koh Kong and the Thai border. It was a nice ride on a gravel road snaking through beautiful green mountains and rolling valleys. About half an hour later, we reached the smooth, newly paved asphalt of National Highway 4, which had been built by the United States in the 1950s. Highway 4 connected the capital city of Phnom Penh with the seaport of Sihanoukville in southwest Cambodia. The highway crossed through the provinces of Kampong Speu, Koh Kong, Kampot, and Sihanoukville. Now, our van picked up speed and went much faster. I looked back and there was no dust only diesel smoke from our vehicle. I felt so lucky and privileged to ride in a nice vehicle on a smooth highway going on a vacation with my family. Life was magical. I did not talk or ask questions. I was taking in everything: the inside of the van, the green fields, the mountains, and the magnificent new highway.

However, after a while, as I looked outside trying to see everything, I got quite dizzy because the vehicle was traveling so fast. I came close to throwing up on my father's lap. But my father quickly put his scarf in front of my mouth, so that I could throw up into it. We crossed a couple of small bridges and about an hour later stopped at the town of Veal Renh. In the bus station there, many people were selling all kinds of things to eat and drink, more than in Sre Ambel's taxi depot. People were selling palm and coconut juices, sugarcane, stuffed frogs, grilled chickens, many kinds of vegetables and fruits, and much more. My parents bought some chopped sugarcane on sticks for me and my little sister. The sugarcane was sweet and juicy. For me, just a farm boy, traveling to cities was quite fascinating—seeing the bus station, ferry crossings, and river ports, smelling new smells, and trying new foods.

In Veal Renh, we got on a city bus. I had my seat by the window, and I was no longer sick to my stomach. I was so excited. We went east on National Highway 3. I enjoyed the great diversity of scenery—green rice fields, green mountains, tall palm trees, ferry crossings, river ports, seashore, a railroad track, villages, colorful roofs of Buddhist temples above treetops, and the famous Bokor Mountain. I stuck my head out of the window to get fresh air and loved it.

National Route 3 had been built in the 1930s by the French *(Barang)*. Cambodians referred to all white people, Europeans, and Americans, as *Barang* because they all looked the same. They were tall and had white skin, blue eyes, long noses, and blond hair. If a Cambodian child was born with white skin, a long nose, and light eyes, their family would name them *Barang*. Historically, the French came to Cambodia in response to the invitations of King Ang Duong and his eldest son Norodom for protection because they feared that their kingdom would be invaded by their two powerful neighbors, the Annamese (Vietnamese) and Siamese (Thais). However, this protection agreement gave the French extensive rights in Cambodia such as the right to explore and exploit Cambodia's mineral and forest resources, rights to own businesses, villas, vast land holdings, and rubber plantations. They turned many Cambodian people into their servants. The French also deeply influenced Cambodia's language, culture, and government until the country gained its independence in 1953.

Around noon, we reached Kampot, east of Veal Renh, and stopped at the bus depot there. I saw a thin, handsome, smiling young man, approach us. My mother introduced me and my sister to him. She told us that this was her cousin Deth. My sister and I greeted him with the common gesture called *sampeah*, in which we raised both hands in front of our noses. Deth rubbed my head gently. Then, he handed me and my sister each a half of a baguette, a French bread, that had been spread with condensed milk inside.

My mother gave us a signal to accept it. The baguette was crispy, sweet, and delicious. Deth worked as a bus attendant servicing Kampot and Sihanoukville; the latter was a seaside resort town renowned for its beaches. Deth seemed like a happy man. I thought that when I grew up, I wanted to be like him, to work like him, and to eat French bread like him.

Everything in Kampot was amazing to me, the buildings, restaurants, paved roads, and street lights. We ate our lunch at one of the food stalls in the *Phsa Chas* (Old Market) which had been built in the 1930s, art-deco-style. There was no wall. The market had shops, cafes, and food stalls. My father ordered a plate of grilled chicken with steamed rice on the side *(buy chamhoy sach moan chean)*. My mother ordered her favorite dish of Khmer noodles with chicken curry *(nom banh chok kari sach moan).* I ate chicken rice porridge *(bawbaw sach moan)* and my sister ate a sandwich of meat and vegetables *(nom pang pa-te).* It was hot and noisy in the market, but this did not bother me. It was a great experience for me to be a city boy for a day. I tried to take everything in because I had never been anywhere beyond the market in Sre Ambel.

After a brief visit with my mother's relatives in Kampong Trach, we went to see Kep, a beach resort in southern Cambodia. The town of Kep was established in the 1900s and served as a thriving resort town for both the French and Cambodian elite until 1975 when the Khmer Rouge took over the country. The thirty-minute bus ride to Kep went by very quickly. The views were breathtaking, with green fields on one side and mountains, and on the other side was the beautiful blue water of the Gulf of Thailand.

When we arrived at the beach, we went swimming in the warm and crystal clear water, then ate seafood and sweets. After lunch, we crossed over the *Spean Chas* (Old Bridge) of Kampot and went sightseeing in Teuk Chou, a very beautiful place. I saw a lot of children swimming in the river. I wanted to go and swim, but my mother said it was too dangerous because there was a strong current. Besides, none of us in our family knew how to swim very well. Instead, my mother decided that all of us should try Kampot's famous fruit, durian. Durians are slightly oval, about a foot wide, covered in formidable-looking spikes, and have a strong smell.

Most Asians considered durians the king of fruit. It was the first time that I had eaten this exotic fruit. It smelled bad and

I did not like it. I thought it smelled like chicken poop. My father and my sister did not like it either. My mother kept trying to convince us it was good. She said only city people could afford to buy this kind of fruit. On this short trip, we also visited the famous zoo at Teuk Chou. My sister and I ate a lot of ice cream. It was a most memorable trip and it would be the only vacation that our family ever enjoyed together. Little did we know that our calm, peaceful lives, and the memory of those special days by the seashore, would soon be disrupted by bombs and bullets.

* * *

I remember my father built a small thatched hut on stilts at the edge of the nearby forest after we harvested the rice in the field near our house in 1973. Everyone worked slashing and burning an area to plant crops. It was a very quiet and lonely place. I missed my friends and all the activities back in the village. At night, I was scared of wild animals, ghosts, and big birds. We children slept between our parents. I often heard tigers roaring in the distance and night owls crying on the rooftop of our hut. We always kept a fire going all night, every night.

Before my father and other villagers could do the farming, they took turns clearing and cutting down trees, letting them dry, and then burning them to prepare the fields for growing crops. After the area was cleared, my father cleared out the unburned wood, then my mother poked holes in the ground with a wooden pole and my grandmother and I put a few grains of rice, corn, and other seeds in the holes before covering them up. Then we would pray for the rain to wet the land so that the seeds would sprout. Most of the time, my father would carry water from the river to water the land. This was hard work and it took him hours each day to carry water in tin buckets to water the seeds.

I loved the farm when everything started to sprout. It smelled so sweet to me. It was a perfect time to catch snails, hunt for turtles, and collect wild mushrooms. I also loved to chase after the rabbits and deer that would try to eat our young plants.

One day sometime in May, when my parents and my grandmother were harvesting our rice, they left me alone to babysit my little sister Suon and my little brother Mouch in our hut. At around noontime, I saw a spy plane flying above us, which then vanished. About ten minutes later two fighter planes flew very low over us and then disappeared. I was scared. A few minutes later, another pair of fighter jets flew very low at very high speed over us and then they turned around. They started shooting at our hut while dropping two bombs. Fortunately, the bombs missed us and instead landed on our neighbor's farm. In an instant, the jets were gone, but the air was filled with plumes of white smoke.

I grabbed my sister's hand who was pretending a corn cob was a baby doll and was combing the doll's silky hair. In my other arm, I carried my brother who began to cry. We ran to the nearby river and hid there. When the smoke cleared a little bit, I saw my grandmother standing by the riverbank looking around. I yelled for her to come into the river, but she could not hear me. I remembered my grandmother was deaf, so I pointed up to the sky, but she still stood there.

Minutes after the fighter jets flew away, my parents ran to look for us at the hut. I heard my mother cry and yell our names, "Hong! Suon! Where are you, child?" Then, the fighter jets came back and flew very low. I believe that the pilots could see my grandmother standing on the riverbank, but they did not shoot at her. My parents ran toward us. My father pulled on his mother's hand and ran into the river taking shelter under a tree. My mother began praying for our safety. She reached her hand into the riverbed and pulled out a handful of dirt that she put on our heads. She called on Mother Earth's protection. The fighter jets continued dropping bombs and shooting for about twenty minutes all around where we were. Most of our crops were destroyed, but somehow our hut was still standing.

Later, we heard a rumor that the Khmer Republic in Phnom Penh received information through the government's central intelligence that the Vietcong guerrillas were taking shelter somewhere in the forests of Chi Kha.

CHAPTER 2

War and Peace

*M*y mother's parents lived in a small mud house under a big gooseberry tree in the place called Kampong Trach where they raised their two daughters. Life was difficult for them due to unemployment and financial insecurity, as well as the Vietnam War, which affected them greatly. The North Vietnamese and Vietcong forces frequently crossed into Cambodia across its eastern border seeking a haven from the South Vietnamese and American armies. At night, the North Vietnamese and Vietcong soldiers would shoot people's dogs. During the day, they abducted Cambodian children and sent them to Hanoi in North Vietnam to be educated about communist ideology so that they could return to Cambodia one day to rule the country. The abductors *(Bramat Bramong)* were Vietminh guerrillas, who painted their teeth pitch black. Cambodian children feared them, and the villagers dubbed them *Yuon Thmenh Khmao*, black-teeth Vietnamese.

Some of these former children returned to Phnom Penh in 1979 when the Socialist Republic of Vietnam armed forces invaded Cambodia in December 1978. They were installed as high-ranking officials within the puppet government of the People's Republic of Kampuchea (PRK). Pen Sovann was the PRK general secretary and later became prime minister.

Chan Sy was defense minister and then became prime minister. Keo Chenda became governor of Phnom Penh; Lim Nay
became governor of Kompong Som; Nov Samam became ambassador to Laos; Meas Samnang became minister of energy
and mines; Chea Suth became minister of planning, and Nou
Peng became minister of health. Some of them had married
Vietnamese women during their long exile in North Vietnam,
and their wives worked as spies for communist Vietnam from
inside Cambodia.

For the safety of their two daughters and to search for a
job opportunity, my grandparents moved to the western part
of the country in the early 1960s. They traveled by boat in the
Gulf of Thailand and settled in a remote village called Cham
Bak. My grandfather found a job working in a black pepper
plantation for a Cambodian-Chinese man, named Dek. Everyone called him *thawke* (a business owner or wealthy individual)
in Chinese, a term that is also widely used in the Cambodian
language. My grandfather and Dek quickly developed a mutual
friendship because they spoke the same language. Since Dek
began to trust my grandfather, he allowed him to run the business as his own.

Because Cham Bak was so remote, a group of Khmer-
Thai communist recruiters came to recruit the villagers to join
the Khmer Communist Party (KCP) using the popularity of
Prince Sihanouk's name to lure the villagers into joining them
in the forests fighting against the Khmer Republic of Lon Nol.
The KCP's leader was Pol Pot and its followers were known
as *Khmer Kraham* (Red Khmer) in Cambodian. The party was

formed in the mid-1950s when the two factions of the Khmer People's Revolutionary Party the "Urban Committee" and "Rural Committee" merged. The party was underground for most of its existence, but took power in April 1975, and established the state known as Democratic Kampuchea. I remember some of the women in the village came to recruit my aunt, but she refused to join them.

When I turned five years old, I began to feel lonely because most of my friends had started school. Although they only went to school in the morning, it was five days a week, and I felt I had been abandoned. I came up with a solution. For me to be near my friends, I decided to herd my water buffaloes close to where the school was located. I let them eat grass near the schoolyard and watched my friends learn and play. I often repeated the Khmer alphabet after the teacher and sang along with my friends and other students in the class while sitting on the back of my buffalo. At night, I would show off my skills by reciting the alphabet and singing to my parents about what I had learned during the day. My mother praised my talent. "You have a lovely voice, my dear," she proclaimed with a smile.

Soon enough I began my formal education, entering first grade in my village. It was in October 1973. That morning I woke up early. Taking a cold shower and combing my hair, I ate my usual breakfast of leftover rice with shrimp paste. I had my school uniform on and was ready to join my friends at school. My mother was proud to know that her oldest child was old enough to go to school. Around 6:45 a.m., she walked me to school, a ten-minute walk. I was proudly walking and clinging to my mother's hand asking her about her first day of school from when she was young. She told me that her parents sent her off to school in a town far away from home, and it had been scary for her. She said that I was lucky to live close to school and had a supportive mother like her. I giggled and thanked my mother for walking me to school on my first day.

That morning we went straight to the school building, which was built from wood with a lot of windows and a tin roof. We stood by the doorway waiting for the teacher to come in. Soon, a middle-aged slender man in a nicely pressed long-sleeved-white shirt tucked inside his khaki pants with dress shoes walked into the classroom. All the students rose from their seats and greeted him, shouting in unison *"Som chum reab suo lok krou"* (Hello teacher) then they sat down at their long tables. We walked up to the teacher and greeted him with our *sampeah* and he returned his *sampeah* with a nice smile. He looked like a million-dollar man. I wanted to look like him and dress like him.

My mother introduced me to him, and he was happy to accept me in his class and assured my mother that he would make me learn. He pointed to one of the students sitting in a front-row seat to tell us what his name was. The boy bravely stood up and said, *"Bart lok krou Deap"* (Yes, teacher Deap). "Teacher, he is yours now," my mother said. "You have my permission to discipline him, just save me his bones and eyeballs." I asked myself, "What was that supposed to mean?" I was terrified by my mother's words. The teacher assigned me to sit in a front-row seat in the corner next to the brave boy. Before I took a seat, my eyes were scanning the room and I noticed that there was a rattan stick on the teacher's desk. I immediately knew what it was for. There were fifteen long tables, five in each row, a total of three rows in the classroom facing the big blackboard.

My mother left after thanking the teacher, but I started to cry and ran after her. The teacher ordered me to return to my seat. After seeing I was still crying, the teacher hit the table with his stick very hard. Bang. I was frightened and started to pee in my pants. I did not realize it until the boy next to me jumped up and yelled, "The seat is wet!" He looked at me from top to bottom and stood up, pointing to me and calling out, "A pee boy!" Suddenly, all the boys burst into laughter and the girls covered their faces giggling. "Nay, you clean it up!" the teacher demanded that the shouting boy clean up my pee. Somehow, I got past that difficult first day of school.

In the mornings before class started, we saluted the Cambodian flag in the middle of the schoolyard. We stood straight with our hands down and sang the national anthem while the flag of the Khmer Republic was raised. The colors of the flag had great significance. Red represented bravery; blue stood for liberty; and white was a depiction of Angkor Wat, plus three stars for the nation, the religion, and the Republic of Cambodia. The three stars also represented the power of state including executive, legislative, and judicial.

The teacher selected two of his favorite students, usually older ones, a boy and a girl, to lead our class. The leaders were responsible for tidiness in the classroom, including the blackboard, the teacher's table and chair, as well as the floor.

Our class started at 7:15 a.m. and ended at 11:45 a.m. We went to school on Monday, Tuesday, Wednesday, Friday, and Saturday. Before we were dismissed from class, we would sing a farewell song to our classmates, *"Mit euy yeung bek khnea heuy..."* When the song ended, we gave the teacher our *sampeah* again, shouting goodbye to the teacher *"Som chum reab lea lok krou."* It was our routine throughout the school year. After school, I helped my parents in the fields or herded our buffalos. Sometimes my parents allowed me to play with my friends pushing my favorite toy, the hot-wheels, along the road.

We sometimes had a female teacher *(neak krou)*. She was young, petite, and attractive with shoulder-length hair. She was in her early twenties and newly trained as a teacher. She was a good teacher, but strict. I remember one day, one of the boys put poison ivy powder *(khnhe)* on her chair. The poor *neak krou* sat down on it. Then, I noticed that she kept walking down the aisle scratching herself. The boys who sat two tables down behind me started to giggle. She was embarrassed and left the building covering her face and crying softly. I felt terrible for her. But I could feel that punishment was coming.

Sure enough, the principal stormed into the classroom with a stern look on his face. As soon as my eyes met his angry eyes, I was terrified and about to run, but I was afraid that he might think it was I who put the poison ivy on the teacher's chair.

I looked down trying to avoid eye contact. He demanded to know who had done it. But there was silence. "Who did it?" he called out again. Silence again. Everyone's face turned pale. He knew exactly that only the boy students had done this terrible thing. He made all the boys stand on one leg by the flagpole for fifteen minutes. I had no problem with standing on one leg for that long.

For the first few months, we learned the Khmer alphabet. When the teacher called out a letter, we wrote it down on a small chalkboard and then, turned the chalkboard over. When he asked us to show it to him, we held up the chalkboard to let him see what we had written. He would walk down the aisle to take a closer look at everyone's chalkboard. When we made mistakes, he would ask us to extend our palms for him to strike. I got hit a few times, but I managed all right compared to some of my classmates. Some of them cried for getting hit so often, for misbehaving, or poor academics. As time went on, we learned numbers and basic arithmetic.

By the end of my first year, I knew how to spell words and do simple math. I felt proud of my accomplishments. However, at the beginning of my second year, I began to get bored with school because I was learning nothing new. I started to skip school. This angered my mother badly. She pulled me back to the classroom by yanking my ears and sometimes she even hit me. One day, I told her that I did not need to go back to school because I knew it all. Boy, that angered her even more. But I proved to her by telling her all that I had learned. Finally, she realized that I was not being taught anything new and that was the end of my formal schooling.

During that time, between 1974 and early 1975, I began to see our village changing. The government's soldiers abandoned their garrison. Weekly outdoor movies at the schoolyard, which had been shown regularly, were stopped. During the "golden age" of Cambodian cinema of the 1960s and early 1970s, people in my village loved movies that featured traditional legends. My parents would find a perfect spot for us to sit and enjoy the movies. Among the classic films of that period were *Puthi Sen Neang Kang Rey* (the Cambodian myth of the twelve sisters whose heroine is Lady Kang Rey), *Pos Keng Kang* (the snake king's wife), and *Kon Euy Madai Arb* (my mother is a monster). These movies featured many of our beloved actors and actresses such as Kong Samoeun, Virak Dara, Vichara Dany, Chea Yuthorn, Dy Saveth, and Som Van Sodany. I remember my mother and many other women cried when the bad guys attempted to hurt the main female characters. And they cheered when the main male characters rescued them and defeated the bad guys in the battles.

At this time, government airplanes started to shoot at us randomly because they had received information from the central intelligence that the Khmer Rouge guerrillas were taking shelter in our village. The fighter jets dropped bombs often. People began to fear for their safety. At mealtimes, our parents asked us to eat quickly just so that we would not flee on an empty stomach if an emergency occurred. We also started to sleep with our clothes on, just in case we needed to dive into the bunker in the middle of the night. In addition, villagers and my parents could not farm as we used to and a food shortage broke out in our village. Sometimes we faced hunger and were forced to drink a lot of water to fill our stomachs.

We saw the government's spy planes fly high above us very often, and sometimes they fired at us, making us run for cover. We hid behind small hills and sometimes lay flat by the edge of rice fields or by the dikes. We spent all afternoon and sometimes all day herding our buffaloes in the fields and deep water in the woods. We sat on the backs of our water buffaloes when they went deep into the water eating weeds. Before I became an expert in riding on the backs of buffaloes, I fell off many times and got hurt often.

During the rainy season, we went frog catching. The best time to catch them was after the rain had stopped. We used torch flames or flashlights to look for frogs in the night and caught them alive with a net and our bare hands. When the water rose, we would use a net to trap small fish and baby shrimps in the rivers to make pastes for cooking. We called them *(mam)* and *(kee),* respectively. We could see schools of small fish and baby shrimps traveling in rivers against the current. People who did not have cash would barter with their rice grains for our pastes. I remember that my family collected lots of rice grains from traders.

Since the government's planes continued to fly above our village regularly, my father built an in-ground bunker between our house and my grandparents' house. At night, we would see the blinking red light of a military spy plane flying high above us. During the day it would circle above the village, and sometimes it fired at us causing the villagers to panic.

There was a company of soldiers that was commanded by Captain Sun under the division of Khmer National Armed Forces (FANK). Starting in the early 1970s, I saw Captain Sun's men try to recruit my father and other villagers to join

FANK. Many young men in my village joined them, but men with families, like my father, refused to join them because they felt an obligation to take care of their families. I believe my father made the right choice when he declined to join FANK because many of the men who joined them either disappeared or were murdered by the Khmer Rouge when they came to power in 1975.

CHAPTER 3

Black Clothes

$\mathcal{S}$tarting in 1973 and 1974, I began to see young men and women fighters in black clothing recruiting the villagers to their ranks. They were attractive people who acted very nice. Some of them slept in their hammocks under villagers' homes talking to them and volunteering as their protectors. They also were self-disciplined and seemed honest.

I remembered adults in my villagers talking about the voice of Prince Sihanouk calling through a radio broadcast from China urging young Cambodians living in the countryside to join the communist Khmer Rouge in the jungle, known as (*prey maquis)* fighting against the government of Lon Nol to liberate the country from his rule. Sihanouk also cursed the United States for killing Cambodian civilians by bombing the countryside, while praising the friendly stance of communist China and the Soviet Union toward Cambodia. The bombing in Cambodia was an effort to support the new regime of the Khmer Republic to root out communists, Khmer Rouge, and Vietcong fighters. However, this had served mostly to increase sympathy for the communist guerrilla movement.

The country's civil war began when Prince Sihanouk was removed from power in 1970. After many weeks of anti-communist rioting in the capital city of Phnom Penh, the Cambodian National Assembly unanimously passed a no-confidence vote against Sihanouk. On March 18, 1970, the tension led to a coup against the prince while he was on a foreign visit to the Soviet Union. The uncle of my wife Thavra, Ieng Kunsaky, then a young Cambodian diplomat representing Cambodia in Paris, France accompanied the prince to Moscow, Soviet Union on the day he was deposed. Kunsaky had studied in Paris on a government scholarship and later was appointed to represent Sihanouk's National United Front for an independent, peaceful, and neutral Cambodia (FUNCINPEC, a French acronym), at the United Nations in the late 1980s and early 1990s. Ambassador Kunsaky lived in New York City and Massachusetts from the early 1990s to 2008. He took his own life, to join his wife, the late Cambodian Senator Keo Bun Tuok, in heaven, or so he may have believed.

It was widely believed that the coup against Sihanouk was masterminded by the prince's pro-western Defense Minister Lon Nol, with support from America's Central Intelligence Agency (CIA). The coup was bloodless, though the absence of violence did not last long. At the time the prince was deposed, his Royal Khmer Armed Forces, soon to be renamed the Khmer National Armed Forces had 35,000 to 40,000 personnel, ground forces for the most part. The prince's popularity had mobilized young peasants and farmers to leave their families joining the Khmer Rouge guerrillas in jungles fighting against the pro-western government forces.

My parents warned me not to talk to these recruiters in black clothes. They said that they were the *Bramat Bramong,* people who would kidnap children, cut their stomachs open, and place their bodies under bridges. I did not fully believe them because these people seemed very nice, but I listened to my parents' advice.

Among the young men of the village who had not been seen since this group began to enter the village was Kou. He decided to leave his family and join the communist Khmer Rouge guerrillas. At the urging of his Chinese patrons, Prince Sihanouk allied himself with the Khmer Rouge, giving the Cambodian communists his prestige and enormous popularity. The Khmer Rouge victory in 1975 brought the ruthless dictator Pol Pot to power. In exchange for the prince's help in achieving victory over Lon Nol's regime, the prince served for the first year as the figurehead head of state until the Khmer Rouge placed him under house arrest. Over the next four years, the murderous conduct of the Khmer Rouge regime led to the deaths of more than two million Cambodians, a period that became known as the Killing Fields.

Within a week or two after celebrating the Khmer New Year of 1975, I was aware that some people had disappeared from my village; Captain Sun and government soldiers were nowhere to be seen. I saw Kou and his comrades carrying AK-47s on their shoulders and pistols on their hips. Some of them I had never seen before. We were told that the war was over and the country was at peace. People in the village, including my parents and grandparents, were happy with the news.

However, I noticed that everything had changed. The village was now run by the people in black clothes. They went to the Buddhist temple demanding that monks disrobe and they destroyed all the statues of Buddha. They also demanded that the school be closed and the national flag be replaced with the bright red communist banner with a yellow sickle and hammer. I heard a song from loudspeakers at the schoolyard: *Dob brampi mesa Kampuchea rom dos...* (17 of March, Kampuchea was liberated...), the day the Khmer Rouge armed forces entered the capital city of Phnom Penh.

Now, the Khmer Rouge Pol Pot regime was in charge and started to establish a social division between the politically suspect and other Cambodians. The New People *(Bracheachon Thmei)* were those who had been driven out of the towns and cities. They were those who owned land, were business people, and were more educated. The Old People *(Bracheachon Chas)* were the poor, middle-lower class, and peasants who remained in the countryside. The Khmer Rouge trusted the Old People. Everyone's activities were more closely watched in small groups of ten to fifteen people *(krom)* by working group leaders *(mekrom).* This grassroots leadership was required to note the backgrounds of people and to report to persons higher up in the hierarchy *(Angka Leu).* The New People were constantly moved around the countryside. They were forced to do the hardest physical labor and worked in the most inhospitable areas such as forests, upland areas, and swamps.

Within weeks, I began to see refugees coming to our village looking for places to stay. I saw the people in black clothes separate families and take children away to live in another place.

Families with small children were allowed to stay together. These refugees were classified as the New People. The people in black clothes with pistols on their hips and checkered *krama* (scarves) around their necks went around telling everybody to dye their clothes black. Everyone was confused. I heard my grandmother Khan tell my mother not to challenge these people's orders and to avoid eye contact with them. She said they were Khmer Communists or *Khmer Kraham.* She also said that these people were trained by the Vietnamese Communists and were very cruel. She told my mother to tell us not to say anything if they asked about our backgrounds.

My grandfather was nervous because he was not fluent in Khmer. He spoke mostly Chinese to us before the Khmer Rouge came to power. The Khmer Rouge told him to stop speaking Chinese and to speak only Khmer if he wanted to live. He did whatever he was told and tried very hard to be proficient in the Khmer language. However, we were proud of him that his stubbornness and hot temper had changed. He was patient and willing to adapt to the new environment. At this time, we also learned that the pro-western government of Lon Nol had been overthrown and the communist guerrillas, the Khmer Rouge, had seized the capital Phnom Penh on the morning of April 17. The Khmer Rouge immediately began a bloody war on their opponents. The Khmer Rouge's leader, Pol Pot, announced that Cambodia was to be safe from Western decadence by being turned back to an agrarian society. The cities and towns were emptied and the country was cut off from the outside world.

At first, my mother gathered all our clothes and covered them with mud to make them black. Later on, my father discovered a new way to dye our clothes black, or at least get rid of colors. He boiled the bark of blackberry trees *(daem pring)* with our clothes. It worked to some degree. The Khmer Rouge demanded that we give them all of our belongings. They began to confiscate people's homes, lands, farms, and animals claiming that they were no longer ours. We had to leave our home, and my father built a much smaller house on the other side of my grandparents' home. The Khmer Rouge announced that from this time forward, everything belonged to *Angka* (government organization). They also said that everyone was equal. They sarcastically proclaimed that the rich did not need to be happy while the poor needed not to worry, *neak mean kom aw neak kraw kom phei.* They further claimed, "All workers and peasants are masters of their factories and fields." The Khmer Rouge started to assign people to work in groups; the work began at dawn and ended at dusk.

My grandfather was assigned to grow vegetables, which was something at which he excelled. He worked very hard and the Khmer Rouge were satisfied. Despite the ideological commitment to radical equality, the Khmer Rouge members and armed forces were the elite. They did not work or go hungry like the New People and workers. They took everything away from us for their benefit. They lived in nice houses, while workers lived in huts. They made up their laws and executed people without due process. The Khmer Rouge formed their cult to brainwash peasants and children to turn against their friends and families.

My mother was assigned to work in the rice fields with a group of ten or fifteen people even though everyone knew that she was pregnant. I remember that my mother was exhausted every day after coming home from work. My sister and I would give her a massage every night. Each day, I noticed that my mother's health got worse and her belly got bigger. She cut her hair short and did not care how she looked.

One day, I heard my mother ask my aunt to adopt her unborn child when she died. My aunt agreed and assured her older sister that her baby girl Hech would be happy to have a sibling. I thought that it was a joke between the two loving sisters. My aunt was assigned to work in a different group but always came to our house to spend quality time with my mother. She lived next door with her parents, brother, and daughter. Although the fieldwork was very hard, our family felt blessed to be able to see each other every day. My father's job was to find rattan vines and cut wood for the government organization to build homes for the New People. He got up at dawn and walked to the forests with a small group of men and would come back at sunset. My uncle and I were assigned to dig holes and plant coconut trees by the side of the road near the communal dining hall. Everyone in my family was assigned to do some work except my younger siblings and my cousin, Hech.

Soon, I began to see men building new wooden and bamboo homes *(phteah komrou)* in a row, and a new communal dining hall, while other adults dug irrigation canals and built a

dam. It seemed like fun at first because everyone had to work
and we all worked in groups. My father's cousin, Chao, had a
stucco home that was turned into a children's center. Before it
had been used as a grocery store. It was the only store in the
village at that time. Very often my mother would ask me to
buy sugar palm at Chao's store. I would eat it while walking
back home without realizing that I would be punished. Sure
enough, my mother struck my butt with a rattan stick and I
had to run back to purchase some more.

At this time, the Khmer Rouge began to separate children
from their families and put them in Chao's stucco home. The
so-called New and Old children lived together doing the same
kind of work. The New and Old people were also forced to
work side by side. The children were assigned to cut *kantreang
khet* (a type of bush that has soft leaves and fragile stalks and
branches) and to chop them for compost.

After coming back from work in the rice field one evening, my mother complained that she was exhausted and felt
dizzy. She asked me to help her to make a fire to cook our dinner. After putting a rice pot on an outdoor cooking tripod, she
wanted to lie down. I helped her to get inside the house and
I laid her down on a mat, then she asked me to get my aunt. I
ran quickly to get my Aunt Yong, who was nursing her baby.
As soon as Yong entered the house, my mother needed to go
to the bathroom. She was taken by her sister to the bathroom,
but she was not able to poop or pee.

While lying on a mat, I noticed that my mother tried to
say something to me, but I saw that she could not speak. All of

a sudden, her eyes turned gray and her fingers and toes turned blue. I was frightened. "Are you all right, *Maek?*" I asked my mother. She was silent, but gazing at me. I noticed that she was trying to open her mouth, but no sound came out. "Please answer me, *Maek,*" I continued trying to get her to respond. Still silence. My sister started to cry. Suon shook our mother's body violently to rouse her, but she still could not move or make a sound. Her eyes fixedly stared at the ceiling. I sat on my mother's right side and Suon sat on her left continuing to ask our mother if she was all right, while shaking her body gently with great concern. When I reached my fingers to touch her feet, they were cold like ice.

Finally, she was able to raise her right hand to touch my face and then turned to Suon, touching hers, I felt relieved. At the same time, I saw my mother's tears rolling down her cheeks. There were lots of tears. She tried to look around the room and opened her mouth, but again no sound came out. I wiped our mother's tears with my fingers and told her that she would be all right. I saw she tried to smile, which made me hopeful.

At the same time, she tried to lift her right knee and with her arms, she attempted to sit up. "Okay *Maek,* let us help you," I assured our mother. My sister and I tried to assist her, but her knee and both arms fell together. Our mother's head fell against my left shoulder, and she was gone without saying a word of goodbye. She left this cruel world hungry and exhausted. She left her newborn baby and all of us behind. It was not fair. She was too young and we were too young to be motherless. Our beloved mother died in my sister's arms and mine.

To me, she looked like *"Sleeping Beauty"* who fell asleep in our arms, but the only difference was that her eyes were open. We refused to let her go. We kept holding her halfway up shaking her body and pleading for her to come back to us. "Please come back, *Maek,"* my sister cried. "Please don't leave us, *Maek,"* I begged while crying.

It was in October 1975 that my beloved mother passed away. She died from overwork and exhaustion. She was forced to work in the rice paddies just a few days after she had delivered her baby. Her body was quickly wrapped in a straw mat to be buried. My aunt, who was watching the rice that was boiling in the pot outside, ran to tell our grandparents. They ran from their home panicking. We gently and carefully laid our mother down.

My grandmother Khan threw herself on our mother's body hugging her and crying and begging for angels and gods to bring back her beloved daughter. *Tevoda euy preah euy chuoy kon khnhom oy ros venh mork* (Please angels, please gods help to bring my child back to life). All of a sudden, my grandfather screamed and jumped up shaking the whole house, saying something, and then sat down breathing heavily. He said it was too late. He hit his chest and his head and continued doing this until his son Hai stopped him. My grandmother cried even louder, shaking her head and screaming desperately, *te kon khnhom men slab te* (No, my child will not die).

When our father came back from working in the forests, he knew something was wrong and rushed into the house. He gently lifted his wife's head onto his lap ran his fingers over her eyes to close them and said, "I'm so sorry that I didn't come on time." He said that he wished to meet her in the next life. We all cried, but our father did not. Cambodian men believed that crying was a sign of weakness. I clung to our mother's legs. I did not want to let her go. My sister and I kept pleading with our mother to wake up. Soon, I saw two middle-aged men come carrying a pole on one of the men's shoulders. I knew that they had come to take our mother away. My sister and I continued crying and asked them to go away. I noticed that Hai and his sister Yong were crying together for the unexpected loss of their oldest sister.

My mother's body was wrapped in a straw mat that she was sleeping on and tied on both ends and in the middle with ropes. The two men carried her with a wooden pole from each end. My father went with them. There was no proper memorial ceremony allowed to honor our mother's death. My aunt asked us to have dinner, but we could not eat. We went to sleep with empty stomachs that night missing our mother terribly. My aunt put a little rice in a small bowl asking my mother to eat. "Ah Je (an older sister in Chinese), please come back to eat rice." My aunt kept blaming herself for not being able to help. "I know that you're hungry and exhausted," she continued. I remember that my grandmother cried every day for weeks over the loss of her beloved daughter.

A few weeks after the passing of my mother, we were forced to move to a different place. We relocated to the western part of the village. There, my father built a bamboo house on stilts with a straw roof between bushes. My father was still going to the forests chopping wood, cutting rattan vines, and gathering straws for the new government to build homes. My job was to take care of my younger siblings. I spent a lot of time in the rice fields catching crabs, collecting snails, and digging for wild potato roots at the nearby bushes to feed my sister and brothers.

Under my care were my sister Suon who was almost bald with head lice, my brother Mouch, who had a bloated belly from hookworms, and my brother Kun who continually cried from the pain caused by skin infections. My baby brother Hing, who had just been born, lived with my aunt in a different village. Both my brothers Mouch and Kun were very sick and always crying from hunger. Sometimes they cried for our mother. Every day my sister went to the communal kitchen to get our food rations, and I had to look for crabs and snails for our dinners. Mouch was sick from diarrhea and malnutrition, so ill that he could not walk. He looked like a skeleton with a huge belly. Very often he asked us to bring him to our mother. The night before he died, Mouch was craving rice field crab *(kdam sre)*. That night I slept next to him and hugged him all night. I did not mind his smelly skeletal frame. I loved him and cared so much about my beautiful, little brother. I tried to recall all the wonderful things that we did together and prayed for his speedy recovery. However, no one knew that he was dying.

The next morning, I went to look for crabs in the rice fields on the other side of the village. The crabs lived in holes by the edge of fields, rivers, and lakes. I caught five or six crabs. I was so happy. I could not wait to bring them home to my brother. I ran back home so fast to cook them for him. "Mouch is going to be so appreciative and remember the delicious taste of these fatty crabs," I imagined with a smile on my face. "He is going to feel better soon, so we all can go to get our rice rations at the commune kitchen together." I was so hopeful that my brother would stay with us until we all got old together.

On the way home, I ran into a girl who lived close to us and she motioned me to stop running. She approached me and said that she saw some people take my brother's body away. She continued that she saw his body was wrapped in an old blanket that he had been sleeping with. I asked her to repeat it, but still, I refused to believe her. "That can't be true, I don't believe that," I almost convinced myself. I was shocked. I stood still, not crying. I just stood there letting all the crabs crawl out of my wet black shirt. I could not walk. Suddenly, a burst of tears came out and I blamed myself for not getting home on time. I also blamed myself for letting him die hungry. I did not want to go home. I did not want to see anyone. I wanted to run away, but I could not because I knew that I had the responsibility of taking care of two more siblings. My heart was broken over the fact that I did not have a chance to see my brother for one last time.

The villagers forced my father to take Mouch away for burial for fear of spreading disease. I remember our father did not talk to us for days. I knew how he felt. He had had to bury two of his loved ones in less than two months. I loved my brother Mouch so much because he was the smartest of all of us, children. He was sharp and quick.

Soon after my brother Mouch died, the Khmer Rouge separated me from my father, sister Suon, and brother Kun to live in a group with other children in Chao's stucco home at the foot of a new dam. My uncle Hai also joined me. A huge crowd of children lived in a small home near a wetland. At night, we slept pretty much on top of each other. I lived with a group of boys ranging in age from ten to fifteen. The children were from the New and Old families. We were all treated equally. We did the same work and ate the same amount of food.

During the day, we collected *kantreang khet* and in the evening, we helped the adults build a dam and dig irrigation canals. The Khmer Rouge used *kantreang khet* for fertilizer. They would toss the chopped *kantreang khet* into the rice fields to let them compost and fertilize the grounds. Sometimes, *kantreang khet* was mixed with cow or buffalo dung for better fertilizing. We got up at dawn and would march in a big group to work and then later, march back to the stucco home for dinner. Sometimes, we worked between thirteen to sixteen hours a day. After dinner, we marched to the nearby dam and irrigation canals to help adults at work. We would pass the baskets of dirt from one person to the other. Every day, the Khmer Rouge blasted a revolutionary song through loudspeakers high up on tall poles on top of the dam. This was to encourage people to work under a blazing sun or in the soaking rain.

Before going to sleep, we had to listen to the revolutionary leaders preach to us about the new government organization, the new life, and the revolution. At night, we slept on the cement floor in pitch-black darkness. Every night, frightened children peed in their sleep and some pooped everywhere around the house. It smelled unbearable. I, too, peed in my sleep sometimes. The fresh warm pee that soaked my body would make me sleep comfortably. But, when it turned cold, I would jump up from my deep sleep in the middle of the night.

Kou, the village neighbor who had joined the revolutionary forces a couple of years earlier, was in charge of all the inhabitants in our house. He broke us into small groups of ten or fewer. About sixty children live in that tiny stucco home. One day, within a week or two of living there, he lined us up and announced that I was to be one of the group leaders *(mekrom),* the lowest rank of leadership during the cruel Pol Pot rule. Hai also was appointed *mekrom,* and Kou himself was *(mekorng),* overseeing all sixty-plus in one big working team of children. Kou was in his early twenties. He had a Chinese background with light skin and was tall. He was not mean. He was nice. I believe I was eight years old at the time. Kou called us comrades *(mit)* and he expected us to address him the same way. We were asked to call each other *mit.* The word *mit* means friend in Khmer.

Kou loved music, talk shows, and DJs. He did not live with the rest of us, but in another place, a small house. He would invite me to his house often to listen to his radio and record player. We first listened to the revolutionary songs on his radio, and then, we would lower the volume and listen to the Old Society *(sangkum chas)* music and DJ music, which were prohibited by the New Society *(pakdavat)* of Khmer Rouge. Kou asked me if I ever had owned a radio or record player.

I told him that I never had. He told me that his radio and record player were special because real people were singing inside them, but I was not convinced. I had seen the posters of the popular artists: Sin Sisamouth, Huy Meas, Ros Serey Sothea, Pen Ran, and others. There was no way these people could fit in such a tiny portable device. He let me listen to Sin Sisamouth's songs and the DJ of Huy Meas. Among other great artists, Sisamouth and Meas were Kou's favorites.

Sin Sisamouth was an influential and highly prolific Cambodian singer and songwriter from the 1950s to 1975. He was Cambodia's most popular singer and widely considered the king of Khmer music. His crooning voice, which has been likened to that of Nat King Cole, and his stage presence has been compared to that of Frank Sinatra. Huy Meas was another famous Cambodian singer and radio announcer from 1960 to 1975. Until the Khmer Rouge took control of Cambodia in April 1975, she was the most popular female radio DJ in Cambodia, working for the national radio station and keeping alive the Cambodian rock and roll scene. Sisamouth and Meas, along with many other Cambodian artists, were tortured and killed by the Khmer Rouge during the evacuation from Phnom Penh on April 17, 1975. Many of their unbelievable, beautiful master recordings were destroyed by the Khmer Rouge in its efforts to eliminate foreign influences from Cambodian society.

Out of curiosity, one night I took Kou's radio apart. I wonder if I could see those people inside which he claimed lived there. Afterward, I tried to put the pieces back together, but I was not able to do it. I was panicked, so I ran off quickly hoping that he would not notice it. When he found out what I had done, he was so angry and took my ranked position away and punished me harshly. He put me to work in the harshest conditions. He would toss me a hoe and baskets and would demand that I complete a section of the dam alone. I dug the earth and carried the dirt to fill the dam under the scorching sun. Also, he ordered the cook lady to reduce my food rations. I was so tired and hungry. I could hardly lift the hoe and baskets. After three days of hard work, I decided to run away. I went home, but my father told me to return to the camp. He feared that I would receive a much more severe punishment.

CHAPTER 4

The Separation

*O*ne day in December, one of the men in black from the Khmer Rouge authority told me that I would have to move. I was worried because I feared it would be somewhere far away from my family. The man was dressed in the garb worn by Chinese communists, with a Mao-type hat and rubber-tire sandals. He told me and some other children that we would go to live in Sre Ambel, a town I knew well. I flashed back to when I was a much smaller boy and had gone shopping with my parents at the market. I felt a little bit of relief knowing that it was not going to be too far away. The man assured us that there would be less work and more food. I was very happy to hear that. But I was very sad because I did not know if I would ever see my uncle again. At least ten of us were selected to leave the tiny stucco home.

Among the selected ones were me, Man, Bith, Sith, and Seak, whom I knew well. Sith, Bith, and Seak were distant relatives and Man was my best friend. We were taken by oxcarts to Sre Ambel. I kept thinking sadly about my uncle whom I was leaving behind. Three years later, I found out that my uncle had also been selected to live and work in Sre Ambel in a Khmer Rouge base camp there. He was in Sre Ambel until

1979, but I did not know that at first. Sadly, the tiny stucco home I had lived in was left to decay.

My friends and I traveled east. Unlike previous trips with my parents, I noticed that the road had deteriorated and that bridges along the way had been destroyed by bombs. It was a very bumpy ride and noisy. The poor cows pulling the cart on the dusty road sent red dust back into our eyes, onto our clothes, and into our hair. It was a muggy morning. The road was quiet with just us passing along. People were working in the fields, but they did not look at us. They were concentrating on their work because they had guns pointed at their backs, guns held by Khmer Rouge soldiers.

To me, the scene was somewhat unchanged. There were still beautiful water lilies and lotuses blooming everywhere in the lakes and ponds along the road. On the way to Sre Ambel, we did not talk much to each other. Our eyes were fixed on the road and its surroundings. It took us about two hours to get to the west bank of the Sre Ambel River. Then we were ferried by a Khmer Rouge boat across the river to the other side and from there we walked for half an hour to an abandoned building. There, the Khmer Rouge soldiers told us to go in and stay. It was a very quiet and scary place with no walls, nothing. There was an open space in front and a driveway in the back of the building. There were no people or markets around us. There were only some small empty houses, a banana farm, and some coconut trees.

There were about twenty to thirty children already there before us. For the first two days, we were not assigned to do any work. Twice a day we were fed solid rice porridge and soup with water lily stalks *(daem prolit)* and small fish. At nighttime, we slept on plastic sheets on the dirt floor. We slept in small groups of five. The building had some electricity. "This is great," I told Man. He agreed. I hoped that we could stay there forever, but my wishful thinking was not granted. We were told to move on. I was saddened by the announcement.

One cloudy morning, the third day, I saw a military truck come to a stop in the front yard. Some Khmer Rouge soldiers, carrying AK-47s and rocket-propelled grenade (RPG) launchers jumped out of the truck. I was frightened. I had never seen such serious-looking soldiers with big guns before. They walked like ducks but came toward us fast. I peed in my pants. "I'm going to die," I thought. I immediately started to think of Nay, my former classmate, a Cham Muslim whose ancestors had come from Champa, presently in the central part of Vietnam. Poor Nay had to run around the classroom looking for something to wipe off my pee from our long stool. All of a sudden, I started to feel bad for him. Back while living in the stucco home, I had heard that Nay and his family had disappeared soon after the Khmer Rouge occupied his village. Soon after they came to power, the Khmer Rouge began an execution of Muslim village elders and a full-scale mass killing of the Muslim population throughout the country. Under the reign of Pol Pot, the Khmer Rouge had a policy of state atheism. All religions were banned, including Islam, Christianity, and Buddhism. According to sources, it is estimated that up to 50,000 Buddhist monks were murdered by the Khmer Rouge.

However, I tried to convince myself that it was not true. "No, that can't happen," I told myself. "We are just children, innocent children. We also had served *Angka* (government organization)." I continued with my wishful thinking in my head. I saw one of the soldiers pull out a sheet of paper and he started to read our names. They did not smile or greet us. He began calling, "Comrade Sith, Comrade Bith, Comrade Hong" and about ten to fifteen other names. They told us to get on the truck. I did not hear Man's and Seak's names. They told us that this building was only for a temporary stay, and everyone needed to be transferred to different places to serve the new government organization. I saw the worries in Man's face. Besides being my best friend, Man had been my neighbor. Seak was the eldest among us five. When we were small boys, Seak taught me how to make a slingshot. I always followed him to the woods for bird hunting and to pick wild fruits. He was my second cousin. Only Man, Seak, and I survived the genocide.

After hearing the demanding voice of a Khmer Rouge soldier, I was a little hesitant to climb into the vehicle. I was also frightened and saddened by the look in Man's and Seak's eyes. Like them, I did not trust these Khmer Rouge soldiers. For the first time, I prayed to my ancestors and my mother, asking them to look after me. I said to myself if mother's milk was dear, I would be all right *(beu teuk dos madai thalai khnhom men ey te).* I placed trust in my ancestors and mother's spirits. I chose to let my fate decide my destiny. Many Cambodians believe that their mothers and fathers are the living gods at home. When one drinks a mother's milk, it is a blessing from a living god. Traditionally, one would offer food to the monks, after making sure parents are offered something first. Buddhist monks expected this before they accepted food from any laypersons.

After having seen that most of the children were already on the truck, I forced myself to climb up into the back of the military truck and then waved goodbye to my friends. No one told us where we were going. The truck's diesel engine started and shook. It spat out foul-smelling black smoke which made some of the children cough. The truck rolled away and my heart started to rise. When it got on the road, it started to pick up speed and my heart beat faster. Soon, we found ourselves on Route 48 heading east. The truck threw out red dust behind it. I tried to look at my friends for one last time, but the dust blocked the view. "Goodbye Man, goodbye Seak, and goodbye everyone," I said while the truck picked up speed.

The driver drove like a drunk, hitting bumps as if he was aiming for them, and the truck swayed noisily all over the road making us bump into each other like pigs or sheep taken to be slaughtered. We were tossed around, and lost our balance, falling on top of each other. I was very scared. It was the first time I rode in an army convoy truck. I got nauseous from being swung around, side to side, up and down, and banging into each other. Despite the bruising ride, we all were patient, and no one dared complain.

I remembered the road well. I had been on it with my family four years earlier when we went on vacation to Kampot. It was a smooth ride back then. The road was new and in perfect condition, but this time there were deep potholes and wreckage everywhere. When we reached the National Highway 4, the truck turned left toward the northeast. Like National Route 48, National Highway 4 looked new and had been in perfect condition four years earlier. Sadly, now I saw that there were potholes the whole way and it was very quiet. Our truck was the only vehicle on the crumbled highway. The once modern and beautiful highway built by Americans had been destroyed by the Khmer Rouge and Vietcong rockets, and American bombs during the five years of the country's civil war. After going through a few Khmer Rouge checkpoints, the truck stopped near some abandoned military barracks. I saw the writing on the gate, "Kampong Seila Military Base" in the Khmer language.

As soon as we got off the truck, we were led to the fields and immediately put to work. There was no warning of what we should expect, nor did anyone tell us what we were supposed to do. It was around noontime and hot. We worked through lunch with no breaks that day. We collected *kantreang khet* that had been slashed earlier and put them in piles to chop up for compost. The Khmer Rouge gave us machetes to chop them. The soldiers told us to work fast. I asked one of the boys if he thought they were ever going to give us lunch. The boy complained to me that he was starving. I responded that I was hungry, too. Then, one of the Khmer Rouge soldiers heard our conversation and came over to us yelling, "No talking, work faster, no eating today." I shut my mouth and continued working quietly, but my stomach was crawling. It was hard to adjust from having two meals a day to none. It was an abrupt change for a hungry boy like me. Soon, fear and intimidation overcame my desire for food and drink.

After work, a little before sunset, they told us to go to the nearby pond and wash ourselves. I was happy with this announcement and quickly washed myself and drank a lot of water to fill up my stomach that day. The water tasted so sweet and delicious because I was so thirsty and hungry. Then, we were lined up and directed back to where we had been dropped off. The Khmer Rouge soldiers led us inside an almost destroyed former military compound. This compound had been where a battalion of Khmer National Armed Forces had been stationed; Colonel Sar Man had commanded the post. From inside the compound, I saw that large portions of the roof and walls had been blown off by the Khmer Rouge's artillery shells.

One day, I picked up a cartridge and threw it on the ground and the bullet fired and almost hit one of the boys. A Khmer Rouge soldier yelled at me saying, *mit eng brayat but khluon* (be careful comrade or you will disappear). Disappear in Khmer Rouge terminology meant you would be taken away to be executed in an unknown location. I was scared and promised him that I would not do anything like that again.

There were thousands of bullet holes in the compound's walls which struck them during the fighting between the Khmer Rouge and Khmer National Armed Forces. I could smell the burned bullet propellant powder. There were hundreds of thousands of bullet cartridges, thousands of ammunition cases, artillery shells, and rockets lying everywhere inside the compound. The smell of dead soldiers' bodies still hung in the air. We were warned not to roam the area because there were still many unexploded bombs and rockets lying on the ground outside of the barracks. The military compound of Kampong Seila had been the last to fall to the Khmer Rouge. When the government soldiers of the Khmer Republic of Lon Nol surrendered, they dropped their weapons came out from their compound, and greeted the Khmer Rouge fighters. They hoped that after years of civil war, some sort of normality might return. At first, the Khmer Rouge welcomed them warmly but shortly after their surrender, most of the Khmer Republic soldiers had been blindfolded and executed in cold blood.

That first night, we were given a small portion of plain rice porridge to eat and slept on the floor of the compound with no blankets. I could hardly sleep because I was still so hungry. Making things worse, many mosquitos were buzzing around us all night long. In the morning, I felt exhausted. I felt like I had no more blood left inside of me. Each of us had to find a corner inside the compound to pee and poop at night.

Under the Khmer Rouge, males and females lived separately. Although they were allowed to work together, falling in love was prohibited. The Khmer Rouge leaders decided whom a person could marry. The ceremony would involve from three to one hundred couples at the same time. Shortly before the ceremony, persons would be approached and informed that they were to be married. Most had no choice in choosing who their partners were. Many had never met their future spouses before. Refusal often resulted in imprisonment, torture, or death.

Kampong Seila was a sub-province of Koh Kong located on the National Highway 4. It was rural, with rice growing and forestry. Outside the barracks, there were artillery shells, unexploded bombs, and rockets everywhere. I saw many big holes caused by the U.S. B-52 bombers. I saw many Khmer Rouge soldiers get wounded and die from unexploded bombs and rockets when they cleared the area for farming. During the first few weeks at the compound, I cut and collected *kantreang khet* and chopped them for fertilizer.

When the brush was finally cleared away, the Khmer Rouge started to build small wooden and bamboo huts on stilts away from the highway near the mountains and rice fields. They used rattan vines to tie wood and bamboo together. All the huts had straw walls and roofs and all of them were in rows. They all looked the same. When the huts were completed, they moved us from the former army compound to the huts. There were about ten boys, between the ages of seven and ten in each hut. No adults, just young children like myself. No blankets or pillows were provided only a couple of straw mats for us to sleep on. After moving into our huts, the Khmer Rouge provided each of us with a suit of black clothes that looked like pajamas. No shoes, scarves, or hats were provided. We ate as a group in a communal open kitchen hall. We were each given a half bowl of soft rice. In the middle of the long table, three bowls of vegetable soup were set up and each of us had to fight for some of it. Usually, the soup was made of water lily stalks with some sea salt for flavor. The fastest ones got the soup. Most of the time I ate plain rice because I was too slow and tired to fight for the soup.

While in Kampong Seila, I felt far away from my family and missed them terribly. Every night, I heard other children cry for their mothers. I cried quietly for my whole family. I constantly worried about my little sister and brothers. At nighttime, while it was always dark in our huts, the Khmer Rouge leader's house had an oil lamp, the only light visible. He decorated the lamp with 24K gold necklaces and diamonds. During Pol Pot's time, valuable items such as money, gold, diamonds, and gemstones were worthless. The Khmer Rouge banned money currency and trading. They aimed to implement total collectivization of agriculture and complete nationalization of all sectors of the economy, believing that Cambodia had to turn away from all aspects of capitalism. It was decreed that private property should be confiscated and all people return to work on the land. They envisioned that to achieve economic and industrial development, the country had to increase and expand agricultural production.

It seemed that every night some children in my group died from malnutrition, diarrhea, or brutal treatment. I slept next to friends and we did not know until the next morning when someone had died. Very often, I saw the bodies of children and adults wrapped in straw sleeping mats being pulled from their huts and taken and thrown in the ditches on the other side of the bushes. I was constantly hungry and I worried whether I would live through the night to the next morning. I ate whatever I got my hands on to keep up my strength. The Khmer Rouge warned us at our nightly meetings that they would either reduce our rations of rice or not allow us to eat if we could not work. We got up at dawn and walked in line for half an hour to work cutting *kantreang khet* at the foot of mountains, pulling weeds in the swamps, and planting rice plants in the paddies. We were only allowed to take a short break for lunch. We worked nonstop under the sun or in the rain, then walked back to our huts before dark for dinner.

At night before falling asleep, we had to listen to the Khmer Rouge leader lecturing us about the revolution. Yet, no one had enough to eat, children and adults alike. It seemed that the more we farmed, the more starvation we faced. Gradually, our rice porridge was mixed with corn or cassava roots. Eventually, our meals were reduced to one a day.

I saw a man drop dead while working. All he had wanted to do was fill his stomach once and he would die happily. I did not know exactly what arrangement he had made with the Khmer Rouge leader, but it seems he was allowed to have a good meal, whereupon he would work himself to death. A Khmer Rouge lady cooked a big pot of rice which he ate with sea salt. My mouth watered from looking at the steamy white rice in the pot. I had not seen such a thing for many months. The man gobbled up the rice and chewed the salt like roasted peanuts. After eating this meal, which was his last, the man grabbed a hoe and started digging a ditch. He collapsed and died instantly. He was buried in the same ditch he had been digging. Although it was sad to see what the man had gone through, at least he knew that he died with a full stomach.

One evening at our nightly meeting, the leader told us
that he needed fifteen healthy kids to serve the new government organization in Cheung Ko, south of Kampong Seila
on National Highway 4 in the province of Sihanoukville. He
asked for volunteers. I saw Bith and Sith raise their hands. I,
too, raised mine without knowing what would happen to me.
The leader hugged us and thanked us for our willingness to
serve the new government. "Our *Angka* needs brave and dedicated children like you," he said. I was nervous about my decision, but I made the choice hoping that I would have better
working conditions and food. In Kampong Seila people died
almost every night. I felt unsafe and scared. "Nowhere could be
worse than being here," I told myself. I felt no regret with my
decision after thinking of all the negatives if I stayed.

The leader in charge in Kampong Seila was a big man
with dark skin in his forties. He smoked constantly. He rolled
dry tobacco with tree leaves of *(sleuk sangke)* to make his cigarettes. He had gold teeth and talked fast and loud. That night,
I did not spend too much time thinking about my decision.
All I did was pray to my ancestors and mother to guide me
and ask for their blessings. The next morning, fifteen of us
children were loaded into a truck traveling south on National
Highway 4 back the way we had come a few months earlier.
About one hour later, we got to Cheung Ko and were dropped
off in front of a brand-new wooden building with a flagpole.
This building was used as the Khmer Rouge headquarters. We
were led to one of the newly built wooden huts in a row of ten
to fifteen homes, *phteah komrou,* by the bushes away from an

empty highway across from the headquarters. We were each given a small straw mat and a suit of black clothes. No time was wasted, as they put us to work right away.

Our first assignment was to clear the forests with some other children who were there before us. They gave us each a sharp machete telling us that we must not lose it. "If you lose your machete, your life will be lost as well," declared one of the working group leaders. After that first meeting, we were assigned to meet other group leaders. Mine was a Cambodian-Chinese young man named San. He seemed very nice. He welcomed me warmly. Other children in his group of fifteen seemed to welcome me as well.

After hearing a whistle blow, everyone scattered and went to work. I began working, as I had been told. We cleared bushes and cut down trees. It was kind of fun to see trees fall and we would scream a warning to each other about the falling trees, and run away. "Hong, run quickly!" a boy called out while his cut tree was falling above me. He seemed to be the oldest among us and strong. That day he told me that his name was USA, pronounced in French. He showed me a U.S. military belt he wore and said jokingly that President Gerald Ford had given it to him. That was the first and only time I heard an American president's name. Later, USA was promoted to a teenage Khmer Rouge spy *(korng chlop)* carrying an AK-47 and wearing rubber-tire sandals. In fear of losing my machete, I hugged it close to me every night.

For the first few months, we were treated better by the Khmer Rouge leader than we had been in Kampong Seila.

We awoke before dawn to do exercises and then stood by the flagpole singing a revolutionary song and saluting the communist red flag. The song went like this: *Cheam kraham cha'aw srach srong sophea Kampuchea meat taphum...,* "Glittering red blood gives up to liberate the beautiful land of Kampuchea...," and so on. The song was long and the rhythm was slow and boring. We were reminded to call our supreme leader of the Democratic Kampuchea, Pol Pot *Oum* (an uncle or an aunt, older than a father or mother).

As time went on, they started to treat us differently. After we saluted the red flag, the Khmer Rouge made us line up and march into the woods to clear timber and cultivate crops of cassavas and pineapples. We were not allowed to talk to each other anymore. Our working group leader made us chant while we walked in line. The chant went like this: *Kab chamkar kab chamkar bangkat phala june pakdavat yeung...,* "Chop the forests, chop the forests making products for our revolution...," and so on. They pointed to pineapples telling us that, *"Angka* has eyes like these pineapples and *Angka* can see everything." Those words scared the hell out of me. I believed everything they said. I began to think that *Angka* was not only powerful but magical and could see through people. So I made a promise to myself that I must be loyal and faithful to *Angka* at all times.

One evening, the Khmer Rouge had us watch a documentary film of the new Democratic Kampuchea they claimed to be building. The film showed the happy faces of people working in groups. Revolutionary music and songs cursing the Americans, the French, and Japanese imperialists blasted from loudspeakers, while people competed with each other carrying dirt to build dams and to dig irrigation canals. People appeared to be having fun. Everything seemed pure and everyone seemed equal. Everyone wore the same kind of black clothes and scarves around their necks. Children happily collected leaves and pulled weeds. The soldiers worked alongside the people. Everyone seemed to be well-fed and loved by the new government.

When the film ended, Pol Pot appeared on the screen walking on a dike while he touched the shiny green and gold of rice plants. He smiled sincerely. He was in a Chinese communist Mao suit, with no hat. Everyone applauded and cheered loudly. I applauded along with the rest of the audience. It was my first time seeing Pol Pot. He appeared to be so friendly and humble man. The film was brief. I did not hear him talk. He earned my respect, and I thought I would be proud to address him as *Oum* Pol Pot. However, I began to wonder why the local leaders acted so cruelly. I asked myself many questions: why isn't the supreme leader ordering his subordinates to behave like him? Why do they kill innocent men and women? Why do they force us to do hard labor and not give us enough to eat? What happens to all the rice that we produce? There were so many things I did not understand.

Each night in Cheung Ko, we were forced to dig ditches and build brick ovens. One evening, when I was moving too slowly, the Khmer Rouge guard who oversaw our work hit my head with the back of a hoe and pushed me into the ditch that I was digging. He left me there the whole night. His name was Ching, a tall skinny teenager. I assumed that my friends at work were frightened and had pity on me, but they did not want to help for fear that they would end up like me. Perhaps, they thought that I was dead and did not want to make any trouble for themselves. But I was not dead. Thank the Lord Buddha! In the morning, I was able to climb up from the ditch and walk to join the group at the flagpole with a bloodstain on my head. No one seemed to notice or care. I saluted the red flag with them and marched to work in the forests as usual. My eyes met Sith's eyes looking at me from a distance, but he could not do anything. Bith was assigned to work in a different group so we did not see each other often.

The time for public executions was usually in the late afternoon. The Khmer Rouge soldiers forced us children to watch them execute people whom they claimed to be enemies of a new Khmer Rouge society under Pol Pot. They warned us not to show any emotion or fear of the violent acts. I saw them make the victims dig their graves and then tie their hands behind their backs above the elbows. The poor victims were forced at gunpoint to kneel on the edge of their graves. The murderers would hit them on the back of their necks with a hoe just like Ching did to me. The victims fell into the graves and were left there to die. I sometimes saw the Khmer Rouge soldiers cut the victims' bellies open to remove their gallbladders, letting them bleed out. I was frightened but tried not to show any emotion.

Every time they made us watch the killing, my mind was thinking of my father, my grandparents, and my aunt. I worried about them constantly because I knew that the Khmer

Rouge considered people of Chinese descent, my family's lineage, as their enemies. My family could easily be on their death list. I also knew that the Khmer Rouge hated the landlord class. Although we were somewhat poor, my family owned land and everybody in the village knew that. There were no secrets about my family's background.

The leader in charge of Cheung Ko was named Leak. He was in his late thirties with brown skin, tall, and good-looking. I never saw him smile. He lived in a nice wooden house on stilts with windows and a tin roof near a stream by the woods. He had a young male bodyguard who carried a brand new Chinese-made AK rifle. I never saw Leak carry a rifle, but he always had a black pistol on his hip. A Khmer Rouge soldier who had a pistol and a bodyguard was someone in a high-ranking position. I never saw him kill anyone by his own hands, but I saw barbaric conduct. He placed human gallbladders in a basket tray in front of his house under the sun, and dried them on a clothesline, sometimes mixing them with wine. There were always soldiers, young and old who came to his house to eat and drink. Their eyes were bloodshot red. Many of them were mean. They yelled all the time. I was scared of them, and always tried to avoid making eye contact with them.

During the rainy season of 1977, the Khmer Rouge sent a small group of us in an oxcart to Keo Phos to work in rice paddies there. We sowed rice grains on a muddy field to let them sprout. We pulled rice plants shaking the mud off by hitting them against our feet and replanted them in the paddies so they could grow tall and strong with flowers and produce grains. The rice plants took between four to five months to be ready to harvest. Sometimes, we were forced to collect animal manure to mix with vegetation for fertilizer. One day, I was forced to taste the fertilizer, and I did. I told my group leader that it had no taste. I told him that my grandfather was a good gardener and he mixed human urine with rain water and his plants grew very tall and healthy. He took my advice and asked everyone to pee in a barrel for this purpose.

Keo Phos was on farmland located by the Gulf of Thailand west of Cheung Ko in the province of Sihanoukville. Thai fishermen very often piloted their boats into Cambodian waters. The Khmer Rouge sometimes shot the fishermen and then took them into captivity. Frequently, the Khmer Rouge who patrolled the water and Thai soldiers clashed in the gulf. At our nightly meeting, our leaders would tell us that they had captured Thais and killed them. They said that sailors in the Thai navy were afraid of them. They bragged that one of them could destroy ten enemy men. Their claims were somewhat correct. Thai soldiers were afraid of them and they believed that the Khmer Rouge soldiers were barbarians. The Khmer Rouge soldiers vowed to kill any encroachers that attempted to cross into their territory.

One day, I saw some Khmer Rouge confiscate a Thai fishing boat and take captive two fishermen. The fishermen were put in a warehouse-like cell. Their ankles were locked to two heavy pieces of lumber and their arms were tied behind their backs. One of them died in the cell a few days after his capture. The man who survived was severely traumatized. He talked to himself every day. One day, when I was on my way to work I passed by his cell. He grinned at me when our eyes met. I was terrified and ran off. When I came back from work late that afternoon, I saw him laughing and talking to himself. I felt sad and pained to see him go through this, although I had seen worse. I wanted to help him, but could not do anything about it. I was thinking of his family back home in Thailand. How devastated they must feel about their missing loved one! When I was sent back to Cheung Ko, he was still in captivity. I do not know what happened to him. No one talked about it. After that incident, I tried not to make any attempt to look at a prisoner or his eyes because I was afraid of showing my emotions to my not-so-friendly group leader.

In Keo, Phos it rained nonstop, and I was always cold. Although a thin plastic sheet had been provided to substitute for a raincoat to cover my body, it did not help much. The rain and wind would sweep it away and very often left me soaked in wet clothes. We worked in the paddies in the rain pulling and replanting rice plants every day. Sometimes, the water came up to my waist; leeches would suck blood from my skinny body. At night, we slept in our wet black clothes. Rain would pour in on us through the leaky roof. Besides leeches, there were a lot of body lice in my pants waiting to suck the last drop of my blood.

When we were done with farming in the wetland, we were sent back to Cheung Ko to cultivate land in the forests. By this time, I began to see my working friends die off one by one. Some died from overwork and some suffered from cholera and infection. Some died quickly and some died slowly. I reminded myself that I must live. The rice porridge that the Khmer Rouge provided us did not fill me up so I ate *chrach* (a type of weed that has a crunchy stem and tender leaves that grow in the fields) to keep some of my strength.

One night at our nightly meeting, the leader announced that some of us would be relocated. I was happy about the news. I wanted to leave this place at once. I was so sick of seeing the inhumane acts of the Khmer Rouge soldiers based in Cheung Ko. I wished they had picked me, but I was a little cautious about my wishes because I did not know what to expect about the next working camp. I decided to let fate decide. One day in February 1978 during the harvest season, the leader called a meeting. He did not tell us what it was about, but I was hoping that he would send me to harvest the rice that I had helped plant in the swamps of Keo Phos. I hoped that I could collect some grains left on the ground. Also, that would be a good opportunity for me to catch *kdam sre* because the ground would be soft and the rice field crabs would come out of their holes.

When I was working in Kampong Seila, I hid some rice grains in my shirt pocket while I helped harvest the crop. I ate them in the dark at night in my hut. I would suck the rice grains making them soft; then, I swallowed them without chewing to avoid making a noise. They were sweet and delicious, especially so freshly picked. I did not let the other children, who slept in my hut know that I stole the *Angka's* rice, as they could report me to the leaders at our nightly meeting. The punishment for stealing things from the new government of Democratic Kampuchea would most likely be a death sentence.

The Khmer Rouge had been repeatedly reminding us that everything belonged to the government organization. They announced, "Anything that lies under the sky and on earth, belongs to *Angka*. Nothing belongs to you. If you get caught stealing, you will be sent to be re-educated, an example for others to see." The words "re-educated" and "example for others to see" meant an execution in public. This is what we heard over and over again at every meeting.

At the next meeting, my name was called along with a few other children. We were told that we would be leaving in two days for a new location, Veal Renh. The name of Veal Renh rang a bell. I had been there seven years earlier. Sweet memories started pouring into my head. I remembered everything. I smiled with high hope, imagining the wonderful things that would happen when I got to Veal Renh in two days: "Comrade Hong is happy, he will make our *Angka* proud. He is a true comrade. Give him a big round of applause," the leader proudly announced aloud. I was woken from my reverie by the sound of applause. I also applauded my colleagues with a fake smile. When all the names were called, I had not heard Bith's or Sith's names called. After my eyes scanned the room, I felt sad because they were not at the meeting. I began to feel nervous and scared. That night, I could not sleep. I was thinking of them.

I whispered to one of the boys who slept next to me, asking if he had seen Bith and Sith, but he said he had not seen

them. The next day came but still did not see them. I started
to worry even more. I just hoped that they were all right. My
hands were shaking all day from fear for their safety. We had
come a long way together. I had followed them here because
I considered them as older brothers. When I missed my sister
and brothers, Bith and Sith were the ones who would make
me feel better because we had come from the same village and
spent our whole early childhood together. But I tried to convince myself that they were sick at home or had been assigned
to work somewhere else for a few days and would return. I
was hoping that they would return on time to send me off. I
wanted to see them one last time and say goodbye. To me, they
were my only family in this cruel environment.

That last night at Cheung Ko, I went to sleep thinking
of all the good times we had together in our home village. I
thought about the ghost stories they had told me to scare me.
I would cover myself in a blanket to avoid seeing ghosts until
I sweated like I was in a sauna. I also thought about the days
we chased after a logging truck, climbed up the trees, jumped
in the mud, and chased each other after school. My feelings
were mixed with sadness and happy memories of our peaceful
village. When everyone was asleep, I closed my eyes and tried
to put all my feelings aside. Finally, I fell asleep.

The next morning I overslept. All the children in my
wooden row house had gone to work. When the morning sun
shined into my eyes, I jumped up. There was my group leader,
San, standing on top of me blowing a whistle repeatedly to
wake me up. "I'm so sorry *mit bong* (big brother comrade),"

I begged for his forgiveness. Before he even had a chance to open his mouth, I ran to wash my face and then grabbed my machete, then took off fast. "Where are you going?" San shouted. "I'm so sorry for being late to work *mit bong,*" I replied. He yelled, "You are supposed to go to serve *Angka* in a new place." I stopped and asked, "When?" He motioned for me to return. "Everyone is waiting for you, go now," San ordered. "Where should I go *mit bong?*" I asked him calmly. He started to walk without saying anything. I ran after him. San was in his early twenties, of medium build with a fair complexion. He was not mean but followed a strict rule. He never carried a gun, only a machete and a whistle. He supervised our working group and worked alongside us.

After a short walk, we reached the headquarters. An army truck was parked in front of the headquarters waiting for us to get on. I thought that I would be punished for being late, but I was not. Everyone seemed to be relieved when I arrived. There was no yelling or screaming from the leaders. In the front of the truck was a driver and one other soldier with an AK-47 rifle and RPG launcher between them. They both were in olive-green uniforms with Mao hats. Again, I tried to look for Bith and Sith; but they were nowhere. "If our mothers' milk is dear, we will be all right and reunite in our village someday soon," I kept murmuring. With a heavy heart, I climbed into the back of the truck. I did not realize that tears rolled down my cheeks until one of the boys asked me if I was crying. I told him the truth that I had not seen my friends for two days and was worried about their safety. About a half hour later, we reached Veal Renh and were dropped off in front of one of the former school buildings.

I remembered the town well because seven years earlier I had been here with my parents and sister changing onto a bus for Kampot. Everything was completely different. The town was now like a ghost town. I saw silent people in black clothes working in the fields, Khmer Rouge soldiers, abandoned vehicles and motorcycles, and Khmer Rouge checkpoints. The crowded town I remembered was deserted. The National Highways 3 and 4 were partly destroyed. The outdoor marketplace had been turned into a Khmer Rouge warehouse. The bus station was being used for storing Khmer Rouge military trucks. The school buildings were used as Khmer Rouge soldiers' barracks. There was a big Khmer Rouge checkpoint where the National Highways 3 and 4 and a railroad merged.

As soon as we stepped off the truck, they led us to join the workforce digging an irrigation canal near National Highway 3. Seven years earlier, I had ridden on a bus and stuck my head out of the window to enjoy the scenery along the beautiful newly paved highway. I remembered an affectionate smile on my mother's face when I pointed out of the window with excitement when I saw a long train traveling parallel to the bus. "Look *Maek,* the train is beating us," I told my mother. I also remembered the sweet juicy sugarcane on sticks. "Is it sweet *kon?*" asked my father with his soft voice.

While I was having my moment of fantasy of a trip with my family, I heard a voice calling out, *nae mit!* (hey comrade). I turned around and saw a man in black clothes with a scarf around his neck holding an AK-47 rifle in his hand. He screamed at me. "Go get your basket and work," he yelled in a demanding voice. I quickly grabbed my basket and ran to join the group. All day, they forced us to dig and carry the soil from the ditch to make a dike in the rice field. Before sunset, the man with the AK-47 and one of his comrades herded us into line. We walked for about twenty minutes, crossed the highway, went through a barrier at a checkpoint, and entered a broken-down stucco building at the foot of the mountains.

A Khmer Rouge woman with short hair in black pajamas, buttoned from her neck down, told us to pick up a metal plate and a spoon from the table in the kitchen. "When you finish eating, give the plate back to *Angka,* but the spoon is for you to keep. Don't lose it, otherwise, you must eat porridge with your fingers," she shouted in an angry voice. I did not understand why she was so upset. I leaned toward to whisper to the boy in front of me. "What did we do wrong?" I asked. "Nothing, that is how they talk," the boy responded. "She is our cook," he added. "I understand," I told him. With her job as a cook, she was in a good position because she would not go hungry.

We were told to line up to get our dinner. The mean lady gave each of us the same amount of rice porridge, one ladle-full. It was plain rice porridge. Cambodians and other Southeast-Asian people usually eat rice porridge with something else, such as dried fish, steamed fish mixed with vegetables, salted eggs, soy sauce, or pickled cabbage to give it some extra flavor, but there was nothing like that in Veal Renh. While we sat on the ground eating our dinner that evening no one spoke. The porridge had more water than rice grains, but at least it was hot. *Don't lose it, otherwise, you must eat porridge with your fingers.* The cook lady's words echoed in my ears as I examined my spoon. It reminded me that I must find a way to avoid losing it. All of a sudden, the spoon became a precious possession to me. All I had were the pair of black pajamas I was wearing and the metal spoon given to me by the new government. I knew that they had every right to take both back at any time.

Besides the clothes on me and the spoon in my hand, I had no other possessions. To prevent the spoon from being misplaced or stolen, I made a hole in the soft metal at the end of its handle and wore it around my neck at all times, like a necklace or cowbell. I wore it every day, to work and sleep. At first, many children thought that I was crazy, but soon enough, it had become quite common as other children copied me.

After dinner, they let us wash ourselves at the well across the highway, behind the Khmer Rouge barracks. We scooped water out of the well and poured it on our heads. It was fun, and the water was nice and cold. Life in Veal Renh was harsh, but we were not forced to watch executions. We did everything: worked in the rice fields, cleared forests, cut weeds, dug irrigation canals and ditches, and built dams. We worked twelve to sixteen hours a day. At night before going to sleep, we had to listen to the Khmer Rouge leaders lecturing us about the purification of society.

I ate all kinds of exotic animals and insects such as rats, tadpoles, lizards, grasshoppers, crickets, tarantulas, snails, crabs, and anything that I could lay my hands on. I worked hard day and night, seven days a week, with no days off. I was given a pair of rattan baskets. Like everybody else, I realized that I had become a slave to a new society of Pol Pot's Khmer Rouge. I lived with about thirty to forty children in my age range in a one-floor run-down stucco building with multiple windows, and no doors. It was located at the foot of the Veal Renh Mountains off the National Highway 4 and railroad track. The Khmer Rouge soldiers lived in former school buildings across the highway. Our group leader and his comrades lived in a much nicer building in front of ours. Their house had electricity running from a car battery, while our house was lighted with an oil lamp.

Run, a light-skinned man, was our group leader. He lived in a house with electricity and ten to fifteen other Khmer Rouge soldiers. They always had plenty to eat and looked healthy. Every time we felt sick, we would go to Run and plead for medicine who would accuse us of being lazy. When my feet got swollen, he did give me some medicine but warned me not to be lazy or fake sick. I never stayed in my bed, even when I was not feeling well. I always went to work because I wanted to eat. At our nightly meeting, the leaders had warned us that if we did not go to work, we would not be fed.

No Western medicines were used. The Khmer Rouge did their research and invented their own medicine. Although it never worked, I loved the taste of their medicine. It tasted like grain, but a little bitter. The medicine was made out of fine rice husks mixed with honey and bitter herbs *(bandol pech)* and rolled into small balls, the size of a pinkie finger. We called it *thanam ach tonsay* (a rabbit drop) because it looked like a rabbit turd. It was the only medicine and it was used for all types of sickness.

Every day we had to get up before dawn and get ready to be in line. We marched as a group to the fields across National Highway 4. It took about twenty minutes each way, to work and back. When we were required to cut weeds in deep water, we traveled by canoes along the canal. The canal water was always filthy. I often saw plastic bags and human corpses, and it was a lot worse near the sides of the canal. The Khmer Rouge used plastic bags to suffocate people by covering their faces. After people died, the Khmer Rouge would push their bodies into the water or would just leave them in the fields to rot. The smell was unbearable, but we pretended nothing was amiss.

At lunch, Run always forced us to eat fast and to hurry back to work. Every day, he reminded us; "If you work hard, *Angka Leu* will let you eat three meals a day." Like San, Run never carried a gun, only a stick and a machete. He would threaten to strike us with his stick and cut off our fingers if we were to slack off. Unlike my previous group leader San in Cheung Ko, Run never did menial work himself. He only supervised us and helped the cook. He would give us sharp machetes and sickles to cut the long weeds in the deep water so adults could plow the fields for farming. No one was allowed to use machines to plow. They used either cows or water buffaloes, and sometimes humans to pull the plows to break up the earth in the wetlands.

Most of the time, I volunteered to carry the cut weeds to piles on the edges of the rice fields or throw the weeds into the ditches to compost for fertilizing. We worked until sunset and then we marched back home for dinner. But the work was not done yet, we still had to help *Korng Chalat* (a mobile youth group) to dig irrigation canals and build dams. They were a team of youth that kept moving from place to place building dams and reservoirs throughout the region. The Khmer Rouge leaders believed they were the future of Democratic Kampuchea, just what was needed to build a strong economy for the country.

Their policy was inspired by China's radical *"Great Leap Forward"*—the collectivization of the countryside—but their practice was far more radical than what the Chinese communists had done. They established the idea of state-owned farms. The national currency was abolished and domestic trade or commerce was conducted only through barter in some parts of the country. Rice became the most important medium of exchange. From the Khmer Rouge perspective, Cambodia was free of foreign economic domination for the first time in its history. By mobilizing the people into work groups organized militarily, the Khmer Rouge hoped to unleash the masses' productive forces. They took the model of Angkor's economic system—the ancient Cambodian kingdom that grew rich and powerful because it controlled extensive irrigation systems to produce surpluses of rice. The Khmer Rouge also believed that by building a nationwide system of dams, irrigation canals, and reservoirs it would be possible to produce rice on a year-round basis for the whole country.

Every night after dinner, we were forced to build dams and dig irrigation canals with electricity operated by generators. The adults would dig the ground with hoes and fill our baskets with dirt for us to bring to the top of a dam, and then we would come back for more. It was very hard and heavy work for children my age. We worked like a colony of ants and marched in military style to work and back to the camp. We worked every day nonstop, doing hard physical labor. On top of that, we were reminded to spy on each other and were encouraged to tell our leaders about the mistakes that others made during the day. They never praised our efforts or told us to bring up good things about others. They did not want to hear anything good about us. They seemed to be only interested in finding faults so they could punish us.

I was often criticized for my weakness in crying. I was not crying. I rubbed my eyes a lot because I had poor eyesight, especially at night. I never made any attempt to defend myself because I knew that it would not do me any good. I swallowed all the criticisms just to avoid making enemies. Besides, I felt that I had no energy to fight back. I just put my head down and accepted everything in hoping that I would win some sympathy from the leadership. It worked. They did not bother asking me about my family's background like they did to other children. I never had enough sleep and was always hungry. Sometimes I had a hard time walking because my feet and my whole body swelled up; sometimes I looked bony. It was very painful not being able to be in touch with my family back home, and I constantly worried about their safety.

One morning, our *mekorng thom* (high-ranking leader), dressed in brand new black clothes with a red and white checkered *krama* neatly wrapped around his neck, wearing rubber-tire sandals and a Mao hat called out into a megaphone for us to gather in the common in front of the former school buildings. First, I was confused because I did not hear him. When I saw other children running there, I went along with them. When I got there, I did not see Run. I thought it was strange and began to worry. Every morning, Run always announced his presence put us in line, and then would herd us off. But this time, he was nowhere to be found. "What's going on?" I murmured.

The *mekorng thom* asked us to line up. We quickly did as he ordered. "Listen up everyone, today *Angka Leu* is very happy and has gifts for you," he spoke calmly through his megaphone with a big smile. He was a short man with big eyes. He had a pistol on his hip and a bodyguard with an AK-47 rifle standing behind him. The bodyguard, a skinny young boy, seemed like he was ready to shoot if anyone made a move to attack his boss. I immediately flashed back to Leak, my former *mekorng thom* in Cheung Ko. "Oh! Lord Buddha, please don't let us observe any more executions," I prayed and began to shake with trauma. I had been traumatized by inhumane, cruel, and violent acts committed by the Khmer Rouge. After leaving Sre Ambel, I had many nights of troubled sleep filled with nightmares.

The leader kept praising the generosity of the new government and told us to love and be loyal back to the organization. "Our *Angka* never abandons us. We are the children

of *Angka* and *Angka* always nurtures us and loves us unconditionally." He went on and on. We kept applauding throughout the whole speech. Unlike Leak, this guy could talk. It
seemed like he talked for almost three hours without taking a
breath. He added, "We're very fortunate to live under *Angka*.
The old society was so corrupt, materialistic, and divided between the rich and the poor. The rich exploited us for generations. Now, look around us, we all look the same. We work,
sleep, and eat together as one big family. And *Angka Leu* is
our father and mother. From now forward, we don't need
to worry about anything. Our *Angka* has fought very hard to
eliminate all classism and imperialism. Our *Angka* needs us
to fight and free ourselves from our enemies, the exploiters."
There was a lot more. It was a very long speech. I thought
our usual nightly meeting was long and boring, but this one
made me almost die standing up. I was tired of standing in
the sun. The speech was boring as hell. I had heard it all before, too many times.

When the speech ended, we applauded again. Then, we
shouted glory to the government organization three times
punching our fists in the air and saying, *"Chey yo! Chey yo! Chey
yo!"* Then, I saw an army jeep speed into the common. Two
Khmer Rouge soldiers in olive-green uniforms jumped out
and dropped four or five boxes on the ground. Then, they sped
away. This stocky-looking man with big eyes did not lie. *Angka
Leu* did bring us gifts. It was the first and only time that *Angka
Leu* had ever brought gifts to me. I was excited and felt it was
worth it, standing in the sun for three hours listening to the

lecture. One of the men opened the boxes and then ordered us to come forward and receive our gifts. I extended my neck and saw brand-new black fabrics and new rubber sandals neatly organized in the boxes. All the boxes were labeled in Chinese. I immediately knew that the new clothes and shoes sent from China were gifts for us. My excitement subsided because nothing was really special. But at least, I would have new clothes to wear and shoes to protect my feet.

That was a very exciting day for us. We were told that we did not have to help the adults with building the dam in the evening. After our belongings were distributed, we were allowed to wash ourselves. I washed my old working clothes and spread them out to dry. I put on my new clothes, but they were very loose. It probably had not occurred to the bosses that the children in the workforce labor camp would be very thin because we had so little to eat. The Chinese probably did not know that the new government of their friend, Pol Pot, had starved his people, and was exporting all the rice that we produced in exchange for guns, military trucks, and these clothes. Next, I tried my first and only rubber-tire sandals, but they were too tight in the front because my feet were wide from walking barefoot for so long. But, they did not hurt because the rubber stretched with wear. Overall, I was happy with my new possessions. At the same time, I felt proud and thought that I might be promoted *yothia* (a teenage Khmer Rouge soldier) so that I would not go hungry and be scared anymore. I was waiting for two more items, a hat, and scarf. But, they were never provided. I was so disappointed.

Before sunset, they asked us to get in a few oxcarts and we headed south on National Highway 4. A barrier at the checkpoint where National Highways 3 and 4 and a railroad merged, opened up to allow our oxcarts to go through. I felt powerful because the mean-looking Khmer Rouge guards that were stationed at the checkpoint did not bother to search us. I was excited and my heart beat fast. I felt like a bird out of its cage. The highway was nice and quiet. The late afternoon was pleasant and the air was clean. There was no bad smell like the building where I lived and the swamp where I worked. At the building where I lived, there was human waste everywhere, and at the swamp, there were rotten human corpses and animal dung.

Green banana fields and coconut, peach, and palm trees were on both sides of the route. The lush vegetation was pleasant to look at. I wondered why *Angka*, which had so many delicious fruits so close had never shared them with us. There were many small wooden houses along the highway occupied by Khmer Rouge soldiers. I saw a beautiful Muslim mosque with a blue and white stucco dome-like building on the left and a Buddhist temple in a bright gold color with a shiny roof peeking out above coconut treetops on the right. I started to realize that before the war, both Buddhists and Muslims had lived side by side peacefully, at least around here. But now Khmer Rouge soldiers were occupying these sacred places.

About one and a half hours later, we went through another checkpoint and turned toward a gate that read in Khmer, *Sala Rean Prey Nob* (school building of Prey Nob). We were told to get off in the schoolyard. The sun was about to set, but it was still light outside. It was a beautiful afternoon. The air was cool in the schoolyard of Prey Nob. My new clothes and sandals made me proud. I looked fresh and smelled good, too. I could not wait for what would happen. We were led to a barn behind one of the school buildings and told to wait. Many children sat on a long dusty bench in the barn, but I preferred to stand because I did not want to make my pants dirty. I had been dirty enough, working in the swamp and mud. "This is my first time in a long while to stay clean and fresh. I am not going to ruin it," I reminded myself.

One of the leaders briefed us. "Tonight, we have to be on our best behavior because our *Angka Leu* and our great friends of the People's Republic of China will be here. *"Chey yo Democratic Kampuchea! Chey yo the People's Republic of China!"* he shouted. And we all shouted in unison after he punched the air.

By sunset, I started to see many children from different camps come and join us. Boys, girls, teenagers, and young adults were in attendance. Among the girls I saw Jik, the one who had been arranged for me to marry. Although we did not talk, our eyes met. She looked the same as before I left the village. She wore a black long-sleeved shirt and a long-folded skirt *(sampot)*. Her hair was shoulder-length. She was slender and pretty with fair skin in a black outfit. As soon as I saw her, I started to miss my family and everyone else in the village. While my mind was floating around in the beautiful evening and the excitement about the gathering, I heard a sharp sound of a whistle. We were told to stand in line, in two long rows.

Boys and girls stood in separate lines. We stood patiently, waiting for the next order from the man with a whistle. Nobody talked. I could not wait for this to be over, so I could ask Jik for news from home. Also, I wanted to see who *Angka Leu* was.

About fifteen or twenty minutes later, I heard the same man blow his whistle and he instructed us to clap our hands. My group was in the middle and Jik's group was at the front, on the opposite side from mine. I noticed that there were two black sedans and a green Chinese-made military convoy truck that had pulled in and stopped at the gate. Jik's group and others that were close to the gate started to clap and cheer. All of a sudden, everyone, including me, clapped our hands and cheered with excitement. I was kind of nervous and anxious at the same time. I started to have butterflies in my stomach. The light bulbs and fluorescent bulbs were everywhere, brightening up the whole area. It was clear as daytime. I could even see insects crawling on the ground. I could see vehicles coming clearly from the distance.

I saw the doors of the first car swing open. Five Chinese officials got out and stood by the car looking at us. Seeing their healthy-looking bodies in Mao suits with smiling faces, made the crowd cheer even louder. A moment later, a few Khmer Rouge leaders opened their car doors and came out of their vehicles clapping. They led the Chinese between the lines. We continued to clap, cheer, and chant, *"Chey yo pakdavat Kampuchea!* (glory to the revolutionary of Kampuchea) *Chey yo pakdavat Brachea Menit Chen!"* (glory to the revolutionary of the People's Republic of China). We punched the air while we chanted. The noise of clapping and chanting continued while the Chinese and Khmer Rouge leaders walked slowly past us on their way to the platform. The Chinese and Khmer Rouge leaders walked side by side. There were no greetings of *sampeah* or handshakes with us. They walked and clapped their hands in unison. I also noticed that the Khmer Rouge soldiers, who were in their olive-green uniforms, jumped off their trucks and spread around the schoolyard. They were heavily armed with brand-new Chinese-made AK-47s and RPG launchers. They seemed ready to engage in a war against us.

On my side, there were the Chinese and on the other side, there were the Khmer Rouge leaders. Among them, I paid special attention to an older man in his fifties, tall and skinny in black clothes with a folded red scarf on his left shoulder. He led the group. He applauded, smiled, and kept nodding his head with great satisfaction. In my head, I thought that he must be the *Angka Leu,* but he looked nothing like the man I had seen in the documentary film at the Cheung Ko's labor camp. When they reached the platform in front of one of the buildings, this particular man motioned to his Chinese guests to line up beside him and to his comrades to line up behind him and the Chinese.

When he extended his hands to reach the microphone, the crowd became silent. A giant megaphone that was hanging on the building started to echo. He began with *"Chey yo pakda-vat Kampuchea dor rong roeung!"* Glory to the advancement of Kampuchea, and continued: Glory to our great friendship with the superpower of the People's Republic of China! Glory to the bravery of our national army of Democratic Kampuchea! Glory to the greatness of our revolutionary pioneer youths! Then he pointed at us. After hearing these words of *Korng Koma Chean Mouk,* I knew immediately that I was part of the new government organization's future youth group and that we were all being brainwashed by the Khmer Rouge.

The man talked about the friendship between the two communist countries of Democratic Kampuchea and the People's Republic of China and the Khmer Rouge's *"Great Leap Forward."* He forcefully reminded us to commit to serving the new government and fighting against all social and economic inequalities, and proudly talked about the organization's massive purges that he had personally directed. He vowed to destroy all enemies of the Democratic Kampuchea and praised the bravery and commitment of the armed forces of Kampuchea. He added, "One Kampuchean soldier is capable of destroying between ten to one hundred Vietnamese and Thai soldiers. We must take back our lands that were lost to the enemies." He referred to the massive losses of Cambodian territory to both Thailand and Vietnam. He continued, "Our patriotism helped them behind the line, by producing rice three times in one year."

Thailand took a big chunk of Cambodia to the northwest, while Vietnam annexed the last piece of Cambodian territory which would become the southwest region of Vietnam, including modern-day Ho Chi Minh City. Although Thais took more land from Cambodia, the Vietnamese took strategic land. Therefore, both countries had directly weakened the Khmer State, which was once known as the Khmer Empire.

During the speech, I heard the word "purge." My mind flashed back to the public executions that had taken place in Kampong Seila, Cheung Ko, and Veal Renh. In those places, the Khmer Rouge executed mostly men. They were transported blindfolded in army trucks and then killed. Among the victims were some who wore the Khmer Rouge soldier's uniform. I wondered why they killed their comrades. In the beginning, the victims were accused of the crime of being educated, wealthy, and bourgeois. They also started to kill whoever they suspected of being American CIA, Soviet KGB, Lon Nol government officials, teachers, doctors, lawyers, engineers, and even people who wore glasses. As time went on, I saw the Khmer Rouge kill their comrades accusing them of treason or being traitors. I heard them cursed for being "Vietnamese and Thai spies."

When the speech ended, everyone on the platform in front marched back to their vehicles and disappeared into the darkness. The soldiers, in olive-green uniforms, hopped onto their convoy truck and followed them. I looked for Jik, but her group was gone. We rode in oxcarts back to the camp under a clear night sky that shined with moonlight. It was a fun evening and for the moment I felt safe.

On the way back to our smelly stucco building in Veal Renh, we were told that the Chinese and Khmer Rouge leaders had gone to see the adults and another mobile group of *Korng Chalat* working at the nearby dam. A dam and reservoir at Prey Nob was a major source of water for farming in that region at the time. Later on, my working group of *Korng Koma Chean Mouk* was sent to help them complete their ambitious project.

Later that evening, I learned that the tall and skinny man who led the delegations was our regional leader Ta Mok. After assuming power, the Khmer Rouge abolished the old provinces *(khet)* and replaced them with seven zones, northern, northeastern, northwestern, central, eastern, western, and southwestern. The zones were divided into regions *(damban)*. I worked in the southwestern zone headed by Ta Mok. This area was infamous for executions, torture, and slave labor in the rural communes.

After I resettled in Veal Renh, I saw Khmer Rouge soldiers in olive-green uniforms riding in Chinese six-wheeled vehicles. They all had new AK rifles, machine guns, rocket-propelled grenade launchers, and hand grenades. The six-wheelers also pulled massive rocket launch artilleries behind them. They were traveling from north and south on National Highway 4, heading toward National Highway 3 to the eastern border. There were at least three or four truckloads of soldiers every day. There was no cheering when the troops left. Nobody knew where they were going and what for. Everything seemed to be so secret. I never saw them return. By the end of the year, there were no more olive-green uniformed soldiers left. Only Khmer Rouge *yothia* and some *korng thop* (soldiers) in black uniforms stayed behind to watch workers like us. I also noticed that all the Khmer Rouge *korng thop* in olive-green uniforms were adults. Months later, I learned that they had been sent to fight the Vietnamese along the southern border, and were all killed in ambushes by the Vietnamese army.

For the last few months of 1978, the Khmer Rouge went around with portable megaphones asking if anyone wished to leave Cambodia. Supposedly, the government would arrange transportation for them to leave the country. They also offered that anyone who had bloodlines of Chinese, Vietnamese, Thais, Cham Muslims, or any other national origin would be free to leave Cambodia. The news made people happy and hopeful. Many people thought that it was an opportunity for them to be free and safe. Many people, young and old revealed their identities. Some children from my working group also revealed their identities to the Khmer Rouge leaders, and they were welcomed for their honesty. They continued to press us to come out telling them our true identities. Unlike those who volunteered their ethnicity, I declined to do the same because my family had been living in Cambodia all our lives. All I wanted was to go home to reunite with them. I saw skeletal people walk out of their work sites and huts and climb into the back of Khmer Rouge trucks. Almost every day, I saw truckloads of innocent people with smiling faces going north on National Highway 4. Later on, I learned that those people who were taken by the Khmer Rouge trucks were massacred. They were dumped and pushed over the cliffs of Pich Nil Mountain, burned alive in brick ovens, and shot to death in the ditches of Cheung Ko.

By the end of that year, Veal Renh and Prey Nop were almost turned into ghost towns. There was a shortage of labor, and the burden of work fell on my group. We were forced to do everything. The work grew harder and took even longer. Many children in my group began to die from overwork and malnutrition. My body swelled badly, my skin turned yellow and my eyes started to blur. I was scared of dying like many of my friends at the working camp, but I kept working and never even thought of taking a day off, lest it draw punishment on me, or execution.

CHAPTER 5

The Invasion

*O*ne night, I went to sleep later than usual, as I had an awful feeling in my mind. I wondered why the soldiers in green uniforms had not returned. I did not understand why the organization would let people out of the country, and why *Angka Leu* allowed his soldiers to kill people without reason. Why did they force people to work hard, and sometimes starve them to death? Who did we work for anyway, and my biggest question of all: who was *Angka Leu*? I had so many questions, but no answers.

Exhausted from work, I finally fell asleep on the cement floor of the building half destroyed by bombs and bullets during the country's civil war. I used any extra clothes I had as a pillow. Suddenly, I woke to the sound of a loud explosion which shook the earth. A few seconds later, I heard more explosions. It was about midnight. I saw bright lights like fireworks lighting up the sky and brightening the ground where I could see small creatures moving. At the same time, I heard loud sounds of machine guns mixed with rockets.

I ran out of the building and saw many tanks speeding from the rice fields along National Highway 3 toward downtown Veal Renh. Behind the tanks, there were hundreds of Vietnamese soldiers fanning out to conquer the area. The Khmer Rouge barracks at the former school buildings were quickly overrun. The Khmer Rouge soldiers scattered everywhere. Many were captured, killed, and wounded. Within minutes, all their posts were abandoned. Some fled to the nearby mountains and some to the bushes and woods along the railroad track. A few fired back. All of a sudden, we children were caught in the crossfire. I did not run, instead, I stayed flat on my stomach and prayed, asking for Buddha's protection. Suddenly, I remembered what my mother had done to protect us when the government of Lon Nol's fighter jets were bombarding our farm. I grabbed a handful of dirt to put on my head asking Mother Earth to protect me from being seen by my enemies.

I lifted my head and saw soldiers in green with Hanoi hats on the other side of the highway and around the Khmer Rouge barracks. At first, I thought that the green-uniform Khmer Rouge soldiers had come back to attack the black-uniform soldiers. But when they came closer, I saw red stars on their hats and tanks and realized these were Vietnamese armed forces. Many tanks were speeding along National Highway 4 to the south. I heard the sound of explosions and machine guns where the tanks were heading. However, many of them were still shooting in our direction. The sound of gunshots and rockets was intense. Rockets fired from tanks mixed with the sounds of machine guns made a deafening gun battle.

Many of my friends at the labor camp, along with the remaining Khmer Rouge soldiers, ran to the mountains behind our shelter. Mortar shells and rockets fell very close to me, killing and wounding Khmer Rouge fighters and children all

around me. The terrifying noise left me unable to hear anything as the buildings and houses were burning. The smoke
made me choke and my eyes burned, making it hard to see.
About fifteen or twenty minutes later, Khmer Rouge artillery shells were launched from Prey Nob toward Veal Renh.
By six o'clock in the morning, the Vietnamese military trucks
and tanks had reached Kampong Som. By this time, all the
Khmer Rouge had disappeared into the nearby mountains or
the woods by the railroad track. Then, I too decided to run to
the mountains behind our shelter.

The Vietnamese continued to shoot and launch rockets
toward the mountains, setting small trees and shrubs on fire. I
took what little shelter I could find behind a termite hill. I did
not look, I just sat there covering my ears and crying. However, I was surprised that the Vietnamese did not follow us into
the mountains. If they had, we would all have been either dead
or captured. Instead, they kept attacking from a distance. Perhaps, they were afraid of being ambushed by the Khmer Rouge
at the foot of the mountains. By this time, the casualties on our
side were immense. The fighting continued for several more
hours, mostly attacks by the Vietnamese.

By sunrise, the fighting had ended. In midmorning, I came
down from the woods with the other survivors, our hands in
the air or on our heads. I put mine behind my head and walked
toward the highway. I saw the Vietnamese take their enemies
captive with their hands tied behind their backs and loaded
them into trucks heading east on National Highway 3. There
were bags of military meals ready to eat (MRE) lying along

National Highway 4 and by the railroad tracks at the main Khmer Rouge checkpoint. I also saw two tanks burning on National Highway 4 and one at the checkpoint, all shot up by Khmer Rouge RGPs. I hurried, collected some bags of MREs, followed other people running along the railroad tracks back to the woods, and hid there for two days. I ate the MREs and for the first time in a long while felt my stomach was full. As far as I can remember, the date of the Vietnamese invasion was December 28, 1978.

After the surprise attack on Veal Renh, I saw that the Vietnamese forces had occupied all the buildings, but I did not care. I was happy because I felt free. I did not have to be watched and marched to work in the swamps and to the dam anymore. I was just happy to be hiding in the woods eating the delicious Vietnamese MREs. The taste of dried rice in those bags built up my strength. When I put the rice in my mouth, the grains turned soft and sweet. The little taste of salt and sweetness, which I badly needed after such poor nutrition for so long helped to boost my energy. It was ideal food, though I knew I should not eat too much all at once because the rice grains could expand and give me a bad stomach ache or even kill me. After a couple of days, my energy resumed even more. After the Khmer Rouge disappeared into the woods and mountains, the Vietnamese soldiers took the opportunity to rape former Khmer Rouge women. Underestimating the commitment and strength of the remaining Khmer Rouge soldiers, the Vietnamese transferred their forces from Veal Renh to Prey Nob, Ream, and Kampong Som. It was a golden opportunity for the

Khmer Rouge to regroup which they did very quickly. Within a brief period, they were able to retaliate against the Vietnamese in Veal Renh.

At dawn, on the third day I was hiding, the Khmer Rouge came down from the mountains and launched a surprise attack. They killed many Vietnamese soldiers and confiscated most of the Vietnamese weapons, ammunition, food supplies, and vehicles. They stole two trucks and sabotaged the rest. They also forced the people including my working group to go with them. They demanded we get into the trucks and handed us guns, grenade launchers, and other supplies to carry for them. I thought that they took a very risky chance to allow us children to carry weapons. We could have attacked them, but we did not because we did not trust the Vietnamese, either. We had heard stories of *Bramat Bramong* and the genocide of *Tae Ong* (master's tea).

The story of Master's Tea took place in Kampuchea Krom, the lower land of Cambodia when Khmers faced the brutal massacre between 1800 and 1845. When the massacre took place, the governor of Kampuchea Krom, Son Kuy, was beheaded and many of his people were slaughtered and others were buried alive using their heads as tripods for the Vietnamese to boil tea for their master. They shouted at the victims not to move to avoid spilling the tea. This story had been told to us over and over again by the Khmer Rouge so that we would hate the Vietnamese. And yet we were also afraid of the Khmer Rouge soldiers who were among us. The tortures and executions they had committed traumatized us severely.

Fear of them had been built in our minds and souls for so long, that we would not make any attempt to challenge them even though we had occasional opportunities. Perhaps, the Khmer Rouge had not even thought of the possible consequences before handing us those deadly weapons.

We were loaded on top of each other into a convoy of two huge military trucks. We rode in the backs of trucks holding AK-47s, M79 grenade launchers, RPG launchers, pistols, hand grenades, and food supplies. The vehicles sped fast along National Highway 4, heading north.

I was not so scared this time because I knew that the Khmer Rouge was on the run and they would not kill their captives. They needed us. Plus, we also had guns in our hands just like they did. However, they had more experience in combat and outnumbered us. National Highway 4 was so quiet. There were no Khmer Rouge at any of the usual checkpoints.

When we reached Cheung Ko, I saw smoke coming out from the brick ovens that I had helped build and the smell was horrible. However, there was no Khmer Rouge to be seen there. Sad memories came back to me right away. I started to see the sorrowful eyes of victims, hearing them beg for mercy, screaming to heaven for justice, and crying goodbyes to their loved ones. All this had been caused by the murderous Khmer Rouge. Also, I was reminded of the sinful act of the *korng chlop,* named USA, the boy who had been brainwashed and turned his father over to the monstrous Khmer Rouge dictator Pol Pot. USA's father had served in the Khmer Republic of Lon Nol as an army captain. We all knew exactly what they would do to the poor and heartbroken captain. As we were passing the labor camp in Kampong Seila, I remembered the many children who had died from starvation, diseases, and executions. Again, I could hear in my head the other children sleeping next to me crying out for their parents at nighttime. I remembered their bodies being dragged down, wrapped in straw mats, and thrown into the nearby ditches. I had goosebumps and felt a chill run down the back of my spine. We went through the Pich Nil Mountain, which was one of two places where the Khmer Rouge took many families of Chinese, Vietnamese, and Cham from Veal Renh and Prey Nob to dump or to push off the cliffs of this mountain, just weeks and months before our arrival there. I remember some of them were smiling from happiness in hoping that they would be reunited with their families. Sadly, they had no clue that they were being tricked by the bloodthirsty Pol Pot and were going to be dumped alive off the mountain by the Khmer Rouge. I closed my eyes and prayed for their souls to rest in peace.

Among us, there was Run, our working group leader. By midday, the trucks turned left onto a dusty red road. It was a hot afternoon, and hard to see anything around us because the truck in front of us was throwing off dust in every direction. Along this sleepy dirt road, there were parched farmlands, small houses, and tamarind trees covered with dust. By late afternoon, we reached the village of Amleang in Kampong Speu province. We stopped there and occupied a few small houses in that village. At the time, the village was still under Khmer Rouge control. A few days later, we moved again. This time we were moved around Aural Mountain, the tallest mountain in Cambodia. We camped at the edge of a forest between a channel of water and some abandoned rice fields, joining up with other groups of Khmer Rouge there. Fortunately, there was plenty of rice from the fields and fresh water from the mountain. We hunted animals and caught fish for our daily meals. Our abductors, the Khmer Rouge, allowed us to live with them as their comrades. After so much we had been through, life was good for a while.

Run took an interest in me and warned me to be alert at all times. Besides carrying a weapon and ammunition, I also had been assigned to carry a cooking pot and a rice sack that was made out of fabric. It was long and snake-like, tied at each end and I wore it around my neck. By this time, I had heard the Khmer Rouge's radio announce that the Vietnamese had invaded Cambodia in full force and captured the capital city of Phnom Penh. It was January 7, 1979. It had been a week that my working group and I had been traveling with the Khmer Rouge forces.

One day in mid-afternoon, a few weeks following the capture of Phnom Penh, I heard news on the radio that the Vietnamese had advanced their attacks and captured the Khmer Rouge base in the village of Amleang. I started to panic because it was so close to our camp. On the radio, I could hear the Vietnamese and Khmer Rouge cursing each other and the sound of gun battles in the background. I tried to get a clear sound of the broadcast while making a fire to cook rice. Suddenly, I heard gunshots erupt nearby, and the Khmer Rouge

soldiers began to take their positions. "What is going on?" I
murmured. "Run for shelter now," a loud voice shouted. I
stopped everything and prepared for the worst to happen. My
heart beat fast because I was so scared.

Out of nowhere, the Vietnamese tanks came from the
fields and dusty roads and shot at us. "Oh! Lord Buddha, I'm going to die this time," I screamed. Many mortar shells and rockets landed in the middle of our camp, destroying all the vehicles.
The Khmer Rouge was quick to respond. I saw them blow up a
few Vietnamese tanks with RPGs. Three were destroyed in the
fields and more on the dusty road. Like the Khmer Rouge, the
Vietnamese soldiers had suffered heavy casualties. I saw many
of my friends from Veal Renh die. Body parts were scattered everywhere. The innocent blood of my friends spilling out from
their mouths and ears made me vomit. My heart sank from so
many sorrows. My friends had survived the darkest days and in
the end, they were murdered by the Vietnamese armed forces.
All those years, they were dreaming of being freed and well-fed.
Some of them died with their eyes open. We all were about the
same age, between ten and fifteen.

While I was standing and panicking, I felt something
like a great wind knock me down. Bullets sprayed above me
like rain causing tree branches to fall on me. I hid behind a
big tree and started to pray. I was terrified. Bullets were still
flying above my head like rain and swept leaves and branches
off tree trunks like hurricane winds. Debris was everywhere.
RPGs and mortar shells landed close by and far away, causing
rice plants and shrubs to burn all around. The Vietnamese

troops outnumbered the Khmer Rouge fighters. I saw they were gaining ground and getting closer to the Khmer Rouge base. The fighting must have lasted at least one hour. I stayed in one place looking left and right just to make sure the Khmer Rouge would not abandon me.

After seeing the strength of their enemy was far superior to their own, the Khmer Rouge forces began to retreat. My protector Run motioned for me to come out from my hiding spot and follow him. I did not stand up straight or run. Instead, I crawled quickly and grabbed my rice sack and cooking pot and then started to run as fast as I could into a deep jungle with Run and the rest of my group. Everyone went separate ways, but I kept following Run. We could hear the fighting continuing but to a lesser extent. After running for a while, the sound of machine guns and rockets began to fade away little by little as we moved further from the battlefield. A group of fifty to sixty people ran for at least an hour before stopping.

It was getting dark in the woods because the big trees and leaves blocked the sunlight. Run and his men instructed us to camp there for the night. We were reminded to stay with the group. They also told us to look out for booby traps. Hunters would set up their traps by digging a hole in the ground planting sharp bamboo spikes and covering them up with dry leaves. When animals fell into the hole, the bamboo strikes would poke through their hearts. "It could happen to us, if we fall into one of those holes," one of them warned us. "I must stay vigilant," I said to myself. That night, we went to bed without dinner, and got up early the next morning, moving out from our makeshift camp as quietly as possible. We walked almost the whole day in the forests and finally ran into a small stream. Thank you, Lord Buddha! I was thirsty, hungry, and exhausted. We camped by the stream and cooked our dinner that night. We bathed in the stream's crystal-clear cold water. I loved it, remembering happy days when I had bathed in a river with my friends and my uncle after herding our water buffaloes in our village.

I slept well that night. I felt clean and my stomach was full. A military-style hammock had been given to me by one of Run's men. It became my friend and savior. When I slept on the ground I felt like the earth absorbed the energy out of my body, and left me tired the next day. As we walked during the day, we ran into Vietnamese forces that were patrolling with whom we had brief exchanges of gunfire. We always ran before the enemy had a chance to call for any backups. At first, I ran slowly but I grew faster and smarter about staying alive. I ran with my body bent low and always tried to stay ahead of others to avoid being hit on the back by the enemy's bullets or rockets. A lot of people who were on the run like me were shot in the back as they retreated from the enemy. Some died at the scene and some were wounded and left behind to be captured or die. After we cooked our meals, we had to put out the fires to avoid being seen by the Vietnamese. We all became paranoid and felt that we were being hunted down at all times.

A few days later, we reached a vast checkerboard of rice fields lying between mountains and jungle. I was very happy to finally be out of the woods. No one knew the name of the

area, but we called it *Veal Veng* (a long field). It was very remote but secure. I began to feel that the danger had passed.
In the surrounding fields and at the edge of the jungle, I saw
many different groups of Khmer Rouge camped out. At first,
they threatened to shoot us, but after we convinced them that
we were friends they allowed us to enter their territory. My
eyes scanned the camp; I saw anti-aircraft guns, artillery, tanks,
trucks, weapons, and stockpiles of ammunition. After earning
their trust, they started to welcome us as their comrades. They
even provided weapons and ammunition to us. I began to feel
safe there. The Vietnamese troops had launched attacks on the
camp multiple times before our arrival, but the Khmer Rouge
held on to their base.

There was a small lake in the field and a deep river in
the jungle behind the camp that provided us with plenty of
fish, crabs, and snails, giving us enough to eat. I began to gain
strength and my body, swollen from malnourishment, was becoming normal again. The Khmer Rouge shot monkeys and
other animals for meals. I also saw them throw Chinese-made
hand grenades into the water; fish would float to the surface
after the grenades exploded at the bottom of the river. I ate
anything that the Khmer Rouge ate. I felt comfortable and got
used to the lifestyle they lived. They were not mean to us anymore. Perhaps they realized they needed us to fight alongside
them against the Vietnamese. In the base camp, Khmer Rouge
troops were constantly on the lookout; they were capable of
communicating with their comrades throughout the country.
I noticed that they followed nonstop the news through their

radios. The Khmer Rouge base seemed secure and strong and the Vietnamese troops seemed afraid to attack. I heard on the Khmer Rouge radio that the Vietnamese of Van Tien Dung and their puppet, Cambodian General Heng Samrin were losing and running back to Phnom Penh. I was happy to hear such news.

Van Tien Dung, along with Le Duc Anh and Tran Van Tra, helped Heng Samrin and Hun Sen raise a rebel army against Pol Pot in 1978. Also, he and the other two generals planned and launched the Vietnamese attacks on the Khmer Rouge from 1978 to 1979. Heng Samrin, on the other hand, had served as a commander of the Khmer Rouge's fourth infantry division from 1976 to 1978. He led a failed coup against Pol Pot and then defected to Vietnam in 1978 after he was marked for death by Pol Pot's troops. In 1979, Heng Samrin was installed by the Vietnamese authorities as leader of the People's Republic of Kampuchea and People's Revolutionary Council, following his occupation of Cambodia. Along with the late Chea Sim, former president of the Cambodian People's Party (CPP) and Cambodian Senate, Heng Samrin was an early mentor of Hun Sen, who would later become ruler of Cambodia after the Khmer Rouge period. As of 2021, Heng Samrin still serves as president of the Cambodian National Assembly.

At first, I was frightened when fighting broke out. My job was to stay behind and reload the soldiers's weapons, while they were engaged in battles against the Vietnamese troops. I saw Khmer Rouge soldiers get shot and drop dead next to me. I sometimes saw their bodies blown into pieces by Vietnamese rockets. Up until then, I had never fired one shot and had no intention of doing so. Sometimes, the battles lasted for days and the casualties on both sides were heavy. However, during the farming season in mid-June of 1979, the Vietnamese began a full-force attack on the *Veal Veng* base. The fighting lasted for several days. Vietnamese fighter jets, tanks, artilleries, and ground forces attacked the Khmer Rouge armed forces with all their mighty war equipment.

One quiet night, Run gathered some of us and we left the base camp in the middle of the night. We walked nonstop only cooking and sleeping. We walked at night on the roads and during the day in the woods or trails. For about one week, we walked every day, with no breaks, and then reached a river by National Route 48. There were only about twenty-five of us left from Run's men. More than half of us had died and been wounded from fighting along the way. We gathered tree branches and made some rafts to cross the river. We camped by Route 48. We could hear the sounds of big guns in the distance on the other side of the river, but I felt safe. I dropped everything on the ground and rested my head against a thick bush. It felt good to be able to relax.

Our clothes were ripped and some of us had been walking barefoot. My pants were ripped. But, it was a blessing to still have sandals that protected my feet from being pricked and scraped by sharp thorns. We children were allowed to address all the Khmer Rouge soldiers as big brothers. Although I was proud to be treated equally to the Khmer Rouge, I had no intention of fighting the Vietnamese forces with them. I still felt very traumatized after seeing so many deaths. I saw with my own eyes that the Vietnamese courage and weapons were way superior to ours. I was an expert in reloading ammunition, though I had never fired a weapon. "What good is it, if I can only reload ammunition?" I asked myself. I did not have any experience in engaging in battle. I asked them if I could practice shooting, but they denied my request fearing that this would give away our location to the Vietnamese. I realized then that I was with a small group of fighters with little experience in fighting a battle. The Vietnamese armed forces were full of experience in fighting and far more advanced. They hunted us like villagers chasing after a small rabbit in the field, so I had a new idea: I wanted to run away.

I was not interested in fighting. All I wanted was to look for my family. Knowing that I was close to my village, I was nervous and anxious at the same time. I wanted to run away immediately. I could sense freedom and reunification with my family. All of a sudden, I started to miss all my family members terribly. I made up my mind that I would run away and was prepared for it, but I had to wait for the right time. While helping my group to cook rice, I told them that I would go to look for edible vegetables to make soup. I took my rifle with me and was ready to take off. I made my plan: If I ran on the road, I would meet Vietnamese or other Khmer Rouge and would surely be shot. If I ran in the fields, I might be seen by others. But if I ran in the woods, it would be very dark and I would get lost. "What should I do?" I asked myself. While having all these crazy plans of mine about escaping, the sound of rockets erupted. After hearing rockets fall on the other side of the river, I ran back to join my group with empty hands. Everyone grabbed their belongings, put out the fire, and started to run west. I went along with them without having a chance to eat dinner. At this point, I was not hungry only focused on getting away from here before the Vietnamese soldiers caught up with us. But they never did. Once again, we ran with empty stomachs all night.

I remembered the road well, but it was cut up in many places and wreckage was everywhere. It was heartbreaking to see a beautiful red gravel road turned into something like a trail. All the bridges had been blown up by bombs. It seemed as though no logging trucks or *remauk* had been on this road for years. I had so many wonderful memories of my family traveling on this road to the market in Sre Ambel and also, on our memorable vacation in Kampot. I did not see any beautiful water lilies or lotus flowers along the road, only rice plants. It must have been farming season because all I saw was a green canopy of rice plants in the fields.

I did not miss it. I had seen and worked hard enough pulling and replanting these green shoots. It reminded me of the labor camps in Kampong Seila, Veal Renh, and Keo Phos. We just kept on moving the whole cloudy night. I could spot a few stars, but they seemed far away from Earth. We children walked between Run and his men. It was midnight when we came to an abandoned home on stilts with a roof of straw in a rice field. We rested there. I quietly asked permission from the owner and the spirit that took care of the house to keep us safe. I remember my parents had always asked this of the spirits that take care of a place, even in the forests. They said that everything belonged to someone else, therefore we must ask permission first. Some of us slept on the floor and some on the ground. I chose to sleep on the ground and let the adults sleep on the floor.

At dawn, we all got up and started to cook porridge for our breakfast. We fetched water from the rice field to cook our porridge and drink. It was clean. At sunrise, I saw some people coming to work on the farms and saw some families start to move out of their homes and walk along the road west, just like us. I did not see any Khmer Rouge or Vietnamese soldiers, only ordinary people walking on the road and working in the fields. Our group did not waste any time. After breakfast, we continued walking in line along the road with weapons in our hands and on our shoulders. I strapped my gun around my shoulder pointing to the ground. Sometimes the muzzle touched the ground, as I was still just a teenager and not very tall. My Russian-made AK-47 was almost as long as I was and heavy.

By afternoon, we reached my village, Chi Kha. I felt butterflies of anxiety in my stomach. I tried to calm myself. Nobody knew that I came from there. No one asked, so I had no intention of revealing my background. I could not believe it. I was finally home. "Soon, I will see my house." What should I do? Run away from my group to join my family or stick with the group?" I asked myself. But there was no clear answer. I told myself that if I were to run away, I could be shot. But if I stayed with my group, I might never see my family again.

My eyes were scanning everywhere. I was excited and nervous at the same time. Nothing much had changed, only more coconut trees that had been planted along the road by the Khmer Rouge. I saw that the communal dining hall was still standing and that the wooden houses all in a row were intact but empty. I tried to look for my house, but it was not there. I saw only a green rice field and some small bushes on the dikes. Also, I saw bushes and vineries spiraling on an old hut where my grandparents' house once stood. The mango tree was still standing but looked much smaller and shorter than I had remembered.

I saw the school buildings were emptied and left to deteriorate. The dam and irrigation canals were completed. I proudly walked on top of the dam I had once built under a scorching sun when Kou punished me. I saw canals full of water flowing to the rice fields away from the dam. They looked so straight and organized. They were beautifully done. From the top of the dam, I tried to look for the tiny stucco home I once occupied with sixty or more children before I had left for a long journey. But the stucco home was crumbled and only a frame of it was still standing. It was quite emotional for me. All of a sudden, my tears started to roll down my cheeks. I tried hard to hold back my emotions, but I could not. I could not talk. I felt my throat dry up. I tasted bitterness in my mouth. It was strange, but I did not make any attempt to tell anyone what I was thinking of. All of a sudden, I felt tired and everything on me seemed to be so heavy. Besides, I was hungry and thirsty. I wanted to drop off my weapon and plunge into the water drinking it as much as I could to satisfy my thirst. At that moment, we reached the stucco home. I imagined that I would see my uncle, my friends Man, Seak, Bith, and Sith waiting for me there. I was hoping to see my father, sister, and brothers welcoming me to our house. I started to miss my grandparents and my aunt terribly. All at once, everything and everyone that I had been associated with came back to me. The village had been full of happy people and now was just an abandoned, sleepy place. I had no hope of being reunited with anybody. I walked like a zombie with no brain. I could not think or hear anything anymore. I was completely numb.

Continuing, we reached Chouk village, west of Chi Kha. We decided to camp by the road, behind the bushes. I saw many families traveling west like our group. We made a fire, cooked our dinner, and slept on the ground close to each other. Many families made fires and cooked their dinners for their families and some sat in circles talking about their journeys. I noticed that many of Run's men stood guard. I did not care. I was tired and quite emotional about everything. I was disappointed and saddened for not being able to look for my family as I had planned. On the other hand, I sort of expected they had been transferred to live in some other part of the country just like what had happened to me. While thinking of all the worse scenarios about my family, I fell fast asleep hugging my automatic rifle close to my chest.

The next morning, we decided to stay late. We did not hear an order from either Run or his men to continue our journey. I did not complain. I did not want to go further at all. I wanted to get the news about my family. The sun rose above the treetops, I would say it was around nine or ten o'clock. As I was roaming among the refugees, I heard a voice calling my name, "Hong! Hong!" I walked toward the family and a middle-aged woman asked, "Are you Hong, *Gu* Uok, and *Je* Muoy's son?" I enthusiastically responded to her, "Yes, indeed! It's me, Hong. Yes, *Gu* Uok and *Je* Muoy are my parents." She asked me if I knew that my father and younger siblings were still alive. I told her that I was hoping to reunite with them and missed them terribly. She said that she knew my family well, but did not tell me what her relationship was to us. She also told me that she heard my father and the rest of my family were living in a new village, Chouk, in one of the wooden houses across the road. I thanked her and quickly ran back to my group. My heart was racing with excitement and anxiousness.

At the same time, I was worried that the woman had given me the wrong information. I prepared for bad news, just in case some of my family members were missing. I wondered how everyone would look and if they would recognize me. I started to feel sad that I would not see my beloved mother and brother Mouch. Also, I was scared my family might reject me or that the group would prevent me from seeing my family. What would Run and his men think? I wondered about all these things. I had been keeping my family's whereabouts to myself all this time. They probably would be shocked and angry. I might be punished because the danger was not yet over. After all, I was still under their control. All of these negative thoughts once again came to me. But, I had to take a chance. I took a deep breath and tried to find the right words to tell Run.

I walked slowly toward him and asked if we were going to leave soon. *"Mit bong,* when are we leaving?" I asked Run. "We plan to leave around noon," he responded while cleaning his rifle. "Go and make a fire to prepare our meal before we leave," he continued while still focusing on cleaning his gun. *"Mit bong,* I have a request to make," I told him with a shaky voice. He stopped rubbing his gun looked up and said, "What is it *mit* Hong?" I told him the truth that I wanted to look for my family in the village. I told him exactly what I had learned from the nice lady. I promised him that I would come back soon.

After getting an assurance from him that I would not be punished, I dropped the gun on the ground and ran to the wooden houses in a row across the road; this was about a ten-minute walk from where we were camped. I ran to the village and searched from house to house. At the second house toward the end of the row, I spotted a skinny girl with a light complexion standing by the steps of the house on stilts. She looked familiar and about my sister's age. I walked slowly toward her. When I got closer to her, I heard her yell out in excitement. *"Pak! Pak!* Hong is here!"

"Suon, is that you?" I asked. "Yes, it's me, Suon," my sister responded quickly. When I got to the front steps, my sister ran up into the house to get my father. I did not move, I stood still on the front steps of the house waiting for what would happen. Soon I saw a skinny middle-aged man and a younger woman slowly emerge from inside the tiny wooden house walking to the doorsteps. *"Pak!"* I cried. He ran down quickly but missed a step which almost made him fall. He lost his balance, but

I quickly grabbed him and held him in a standing position. "Hong, *Pak neuk kon nas!*" my father cried in excitement and said that he missed me so much. He also said that he prayed to Lord Buddha every day for my safety and our reunion. He sniffed my forehead very gently. That was the first time I remembered that my father ever kissed me. Cambodians, during that time, used a nose to sniff, instead of using lips for kissing. I had never seen lovers kiss each other on the lips. Only men kissed their lovers on the cheeks with their noses. Parents did the same thing, they would kiss their children with a nose, at least in my village.

My father turned around and then a young lady came down and said, "Hong! I'm your auntie, Yong!" I hugged her and cried. My aunt told me that she thought she had seen me walking in line with the Khmer Rouge. She also told me that the Khmer Rouge had married her to my father two years after my mother passed away. I nodded in approval. My aunt asked me to stay, but I told her that I had to leave and go west with my group, but did not know exactly where. I told my family that I had been with the Khmer Rouge since the invasion of Vietnam. All of us went inside the house. I saw my brothers Kun, Hing, and my cousin Hech all sleeping. They woke up from the sound of joyous cries. They were confused. I told them who I was. But, they were too shy to introduce themselves to me. After about twenty minutes of joy, I told them that I must go back to my group as I promised Run. My aunt tried to get me to stay, but I insisted that I must go because I did not want Run's men to come after me and bring trouble to the whole family. My father gave me a handful of dried tobacco, which he wrapped in one of his scarves. But I told him that I did not smoke. My aunt jokingly reminded me that she had tricked me when I was younger to inhale a cigar. We had a nice laugh at that memory.

All of them were skinny and looked much older than their ages. Although my father was only 37 years old, he looked like an old man. I asked about everyone else. My father told me that all my grandparents had died from sickness and starvation. I was told that my grandmother Kuoy asked for me the whole time and had waited for me until her last breath. Also, my grandparents Cheng and Khan had asked for me and their son Hai every day before they passed. My aunt also told me that her brother had been transferred out of the tiny stucco home shortly after me. He was stationed in a Khmer Rouge camp in Sre Ambel and was training to be a child soldier. She had not seen him since he left the village.

I left my family after a brief visit and was so relieved knowing that they were alive. Run was very happy to see me return as I had promised. I certainly made a smile on his face when I gave him the dried tobacco. He was kind and shared it with his men. As soon as we had our late breakfast, our group continued with our journey. Some families were ahead of us and some were still feeding their young ones.

CHAPTER 6

My Escape

Word had spread that we were going west to Thailand out of Cambodia to avoid the war and living under Vietnamese occupation. People said there was no war and we would be safe in Thailand. The news encouraged everyone to head west and to escape into jungles in the hope of finding a haven. I overheard that if we reached Thailand, we would eventually be resettled in countries like America, Canada, Australia, France, Switzerland, New Zealand, Finland, Denmark, and West Germany. I did not pay much attention to the rumor because of those countries I had only ever heard of America and France.

My journey to Thailand took over a month, walking through the rainforests of the mountain range in the province of Koh Kong. I spent many weeks in July and August, wandering around eating wild leaves and vegetation or anything I could find in the deep jungles. We called the journey *rout yuon* (escape the Vietnamese). In the mountains, I witnessed depressing scenes. People died along the trail that seemed to lead nowhere. They died of exhaustion and from the detonation of land mines that soldiers had planted in the ground. Along the trails in the forests, I saw babies abandoned by their families because they feared being found by the Vietnamese.

I saw babies crawling over their dead mothers searching for breast milk. I also witnessed toddlers crying next to their sick or dead mothers.

I remember a little boy who was traveling with his parents and siblings. He was about two or three years old. He cried nonstop and sometimes had temper tantrums which led his mother to carry him. Other refugees complained and demanded that the family had to go back or stay behind. His parents tried every possible way to calm him down, but the tantrums continued. He must have been either hungry or tired from traveling under the sun and in the rain. Out of the blue, the father snatched the little boy from his mother's arms, smashed his head on a tree trunk, and tossed him to the side of the trail. The boy's crying stopped. I saw his body shake and his eyes turn white. The mother started to cry and ran to pick up her son and refused to leave him. She threw herself around the poor little boy and kicked at the wet ground while cursing her husband. I was scared and shocked and did not know what to do. I held my breath and continued walking past the family.

It was the wet season and it rained a lot in the mountains. Everyone had to walk quietly. All I heard was the noise of monkeys and gibbons during the day and the sounds of owls and other birds at night. The sick and crippled were often abandoned on the trail in the rainforests. By this time our rice had run out, but I still carried the rice pot on my back. Within a couple of weeks, we reached a small village in the middle of the deep jungle. There were no more than five or six tiny thatched huts on stilts. Also, there were a few small plots of rice and a big cassava plantation on each side of the abandoned village. It looked like the villagers had just left, so we took shelter there. I relaxed a little bit and then I started to walk from one hut to the next looking for rice grains, but there were none. I saw 24K gold chains, silver coins, and gemstones in coconut shells and tin cans on altars high up on the huts' beams. I also saw Thai paper currency in rice sacks leaning against the walls of straw. I had witnessed people desperately fighting each other for jewelry and money. I did not care about those things so I decided to pull up some cassava plants. I searched only for young roots and these I ate raw. I felt great. My stomach started to feel full again.

I also dug into the ground with my fingers looking for young, sweet, and tender roots. They tasted like young coconut meat and were so delicious. It was not strange for me to eat these because my grandfather planted many of them in our village. I used to volunteer to help him pull out the roots because I wanted the opportunity to select the youngest roots for myself. While I was busy pulling the cassava plants, gunshots erupted suddenly. I kept my head down and tried to see where the shots were coming from. There were only gunshots; no rockets were fired. I grabbed two cassava roots and ran as fast as I could further into the plantation. I was alone this time. I stood there searching for other people, but no one came. I looked for a way to go west but got lost. I tried to think. Finally, I spotted a tall tree that I had just passed. I immediately knew that I was going the wrong way, so I ran back and finally caught up with a few people who were running toward a slope deep in the jungle. The trail was slippery, and had turned muddy from the rain. I continued running and slid along the mud. I lost control and the cassava roots, which were supposed to be my dinner, fell out of my hand. I figured I would have to eat vegetation and leaves again. I still heard lots of shooting. It sounded like a battlefield.

I ran down the slope for about fifteen minutes and ended up at a small river where I hid. I heard people running in my direction, and soon I met up with them by the river. Then, the rain came and it came hard. It was cold. Most of the people who made it to the river had nothing. Only a few people had escaped from the abandoned village. Then, it started to get dark fast. All I could hear were raindrops hitting the leaves, but I could not see anything. I sat by the tree hugging my knees to fight off the cold. At the same time, I was scared that the people would abandon me in the dark forest. When the rain started to wind down a little bit, I tried to look for the people in my group, but I only saw Kheng and Sophat, my two best friends. The two boys had traveled with me from Veal Renh. They were twelve and thirteen years old. Kheng was the older one. I was told that they were born in the province of Takeo. We were happy to see each other, but everyone else was missing.

It rained off and on all night long. I was dirty from the mud and my clothes had been ripped into pieces from being tangled in shrubs and tree branches. The two boys and I stayed there for the night. I slept under a tree trunk, while I covered my body with my father's scarf and some wild elephant ear leaves. I could not sleep at all that night because it was too cold and I was so frightened. I tried to check on the people around me to make sure they would not leave me alone in the forests. I also could not sleep because I was afraid that the gunmen who had committed the massacre at the abandoned village would find and kill us all. At that time, I did not trust anyone except for my friends Kheng and Sophat, with whom I had been traveling. I imagined all the terrible things that would happen to me that night, including tigers, snakes, and scorpions. Although none of those creatures bothered me, land leeches were everywhere. They were small and jumped very fast. I blocked my ears with pieces of rag from my clothes so they would not get into them while I lay on the ground trying to rest. I continued to do that every night throughout my journey in the forests.

By dawn, the rain had finally stopped. I saw gibbons swinging from tree branches above us. The sun began to rise, penetrating the thick forest canopy. We moved to another place. I went into the river to wash myself and took the opportunity to look for crabs, but could not catch any. Wasting no time, we moved on quietly and quickly. This time Kheng, Sophat, and I were traveling empty-handed among strangers. Run and the rest of our group did not show up, and we never saw them again. From this point on, we survived on fruits and wild vegetation. I ate anything that the adults said was not poisonous. We began to see a trail in the rainforest that had been cleared by people ahead of us, and we followed the trail for about another week, but it seemed like we had gone nowhere.

Kheng and Sophat could not travel anymore. Sophat was too sick to move on, while Kheng was suffering from an infection in his leg. Kheng did not have the energy to fight the thousands of land leeches sucking the blood out of his wound. It seemed that there was no more blood left inside of him, it had all gone to the hungry leeches. My fragile friend Sophat was sick with malaria. He looked yellow and his eyes had turned a cloudy gray color. During the day, he had a fever and at night he was cold; his teeth shook until they almost fell out from banging against each other. When they pleaded for me to continue, my heart broke to leave them behind. Still, I had no other choice but to go on.

Once again, I was lonely and scared. This time, all the people I traveled with were strangers to me. I was afraid of them, and fearful of being eaten by these strangers, although it never happened before. It must have been a week since Kheng and Sophat had forced me to leave them. My heart was still broken with the loss of everyone in my group and I was depressed at the scenes of abandoned babies and their dead mothers. I kept hearing Sophat begging me to leave him, "Go ahead and leave me here. I'm too tired. I can't go on." I, too, was scared of being not able to finish this desperate journey. I began to feel regret for not having stayed with my family in Chouk. I started to pray to my ancestors, my grandparents, and my mother. I also reminded myself not to give up hope of staying alive. I had been through a lot of dangers already and did not fear any obstacles that laid ahead of me. I kept reminding myself that I had to be strong and had to live. Every time I thought of my mother, I seemed to gain strength and felt the wind pushing me along. I began to feel that I was not alone and that thought motivated me to be brave and keep going.

I had been traveling for over four weeks now in the rain-forests in the mountains. I convinced myself that the Khmer-Thai border had to be ahead of me. Even though I had no more energy left, I had the desire to live. Every night, I slept sitting up with my back against a tree and covered my body with my father's scarf. I hugged the scarf and sniffed it every day and every night trying to get the scent of my father. It was my only companion. I cried so much on this journey. I felt that I had no more tears left.

One day in the late afternoon, we reached a huge river in the middle of the jungle. The water was high and the current was strong and looked dangerous. I saw at least a hundred people with small children camping on both sides of the riverbanks. Many families had made fires to cook their food. I was so happy to see all these people and saw an opportunity to get some food. I saw men making rafts out of tree branches and bamboo sticks to transport their small children across the river. I found a couple of logs and tied them together with my father's scarf to carry me across the river. One of my hands held tight to the logs. With my other hand and both of my legs, I pedaled and kicked in the water to cross to the other side of the river. As I made the crossing, I felt some satisfaction with my survival skills.

But at the same time, horrible things continued happening all around me. While people were crossing the river and others eating dinner, a group of men, armed with M16 automatic rifles started to shoot at the crowd. Refugees were murdered in cold blood on both sides of the river. It was a massacre. I witnessed dozens of people die and others get wounded. Children and the sick died on their rafts in the middle of the river. Some fell in and drowned. Others jumped off their rafts and were carried away by the strong current. I held on to my logs and pedaled my feet as fast as I could to get to the other side. I hid under a big root by the edge of the riverbank. As I had done previously, I grabbed a handful of dirt to put on my head and asked for Mother Earth's protection. I also prayed for my own mother's spirit to protect me. I closed my eyes, sank with only my nose above the water, and held tightly to the root of a tree. I survived. I believe that my mother's spirit has always been with me.

The shooting stopped after about five minutes. I continued to hide there until things quieted and then got out of the water. I saw people running everywhere looking for shelter. Almost everyone still in the water had died and I heard women and children crying for their loss ones. About half an hour later, I climbed up the riverbank and found a pineapple on the ground among the dead and the wounded. I ate it quickly and ran along the trail as fast as I could. Since then that river has been named *Steng Vietnam* (Vietnam River) because people were convinced that the Vietnamese soldiers had murdered the refugees to prevent them from leaving Cambodia. Years later, I was told that it had been Thai soldiers patrolling the border who committed the massacre.

Now I was all alone. I followed the trail for about thirty minutes and then I heard the sound of motorcycles and vehicles ahead of me. I did not trust my ears. I stepped away from the trail into the woods trying to listen carefully just to be sure that I was not hallucinating. I also was afraid that the gunmen in black would ambush me. So, I stayed there for about ten minutes until I was sure I was safe. Trying to escape the Vietnamese and living with Khmer Rouge soldiers, I gained many survival skills.

I was happy and knew the danger was over. "Thank you, Lord Buddha! Thank you *Maek* for leading me to safety," I said proudly. When I reached the border, it was around 4:00 p.m. But it seemed dark to me because I was still in a state of shock. There were some refugees already at the border when I got there. Thai soldiers, who were patrolling wanted to shoot me, but I raised my hands in the air and then kneeled on the ground begging for mercy. They finally motioned for me to stand up. They searched my tattered, ragged clothes for jewelry or watches, but found nothing. One of them kicked me on my left side and I fell to the ground. He was yelling *ton* (get up) in Thai.

That afternoon, I witnessed Thai soldiers robbing other refugees. The soldiers demanded that men hand over their watches. Also, farmers who lived at the border took advantage of refugees. They would give them only a few rambutan fruits in exchange for jewelry. It hurt me so much to see such things happen to my fellow Cambodian refugees.

CHAPTER 7

Permanent Scars

*B*efore sunset, Thai soldiers herded all of us at gunpoint onto the pavement of Route 3, heading south. They walked up and down the line of refugees and continued checking everyone for watches and jewelry. I saw some women and girls cry and men clench their fists and bite their lips in anger. After about thirty minutes of walking, they made us turn right onto a dirt road heading into a campsite. It was the Thai Red Cross Association's Center of Khao Lan. It was located in the southeast corner of Thailand on the border with Cambodia, between the Cardamom Mountains and the coast of the Gulf of Thailand, in the province of Trat.

That first evening, I saw two Thai armed guards with M16 rifles strapped to their backs riding on their dirt bikes zooming through the campsite. They circled and disappeared. Children and women ran inside their tents. I wondered what was going on, but did not bother to ask anyone about it. That night, I had nowhere to go and knew no one to stay with, but finally, I found a place next to a family's tent and slept there for the night without food. I had very little sleep because it was so cold and my stomach churned with hunger all night long. I did not have anything to cover my body. I had lost my father's scarf when I lashed it to the makeshift raft and it was swept away in the *Steng Vietnam.*

The next morning, I wandered around and discovered a small Thai market near the campsite. I helped one of the merchants unload her produce from a cart, but then she shooed me away. I did not leave and continued to help her until the job was done. I did not ask for anything. I just walked away. Then I heard her call out, *chay lek ma nee* (little boy come here) in Thai. I turned back without hesitation. She handed me a few rambutan fruits and one orange. I thanked her in Khmer with a *sampeah* and continued to look for other work. I went to the white-sand beach by the campsite and helped a fisherman unload his fish and crabs from his boat. The fisherman was kind and did not shoo me away. After the work was done, he gave me a few fish and blue crabs. Again, I thanked the man.

Now, it was about noon. I decided to go into the bushes at the edge of the campsite to look for edible vegetation. I picked a handful of wide baby ferns and then went back to the tent where I had slept the night before. I was happy to know that I would not go to sleep with an empty stomach again. I ate the orange and gave all my rambutan fruits to the family near where I had slept the night before. After seeing they were happy, I took the opportunity to ask if they could make fish soup with fern and boil the crabs for dinner. To my surprise, they agreed and I thanked the family for their kindness. I did not know their names because in our culture it is impolite to ask strangers for their names.

Most of the time we would address an older person as *bong, pou, ming, oum, yeay,* or *ta* depending on how old they seemed. For someone younger, we would address him or her *p'oun/oun* or *khmuoy.* To be more specific, we would add *oum pros* or *oum srey* (for an uncle or aunt who seems older than a father or mother). *P'oun/oun pros* or *p'oun/oun srey* (for a younger brother or sister); *Khmuoy pros* or *khmuoy srey* (for a nephew or niece).

According to my culture, it is disrespectful for a younger person to call an older person by his or her first name. This would be taken as an insult. Although the family of three had just a little bit of rice, they still shared it with me. I enjoyed it with the soup and boiled blue crabs. That night, I also told them that I was alone and had no place to stay. So, they allowed me to sleep next to their tent for another night.

The next morning, I wandered around and spotted a man wearing a white shirt in a bamboo house in the middle of the camp. He looked busy. I also saw people stop by and then leave. I wondered what was happening. The man was going through some papers. I went up to him and I told him about my situation. He wrote my name down and asked me in Khmer with a heavy accent to come back within one hour. I thanked him. And I continued to walk around the camp looking for anyone I might know, but I had no luck. One hour later, I went back to the bamboo house and saw two white people (foreigners) and a few Asian workers in the office. I told them that I had arrived at the camp two days earlier and was alone. I also told them that I was hungry and scared. They listened to my story patiently and seemed to take me seriously. By this time, I started to see more refugees like myself coming to the office.

After taking my information, a foreign man went to the back of his pickup truck and got a big plastic sheet, a green silk-like scarf, a short-sleeved shirt, a pair of shorts, and a can of milk. I could not believe what I saw. Before accepting the gifts, I thanked him with a *sampeah* and he nodded his head with a slight smile in response. Before I walked away, I thanked him again with a bow, bending my body very low. This time he had a big smile on his face as he watched me. When I looked back, he seemed to be proud of what he had just done. *"Awkun lok"* (Thanks, sir), I murmured as I walked away with great excitement. At that time, I had never met anyone so kind as this foreigner. I thought that I was dreaming like I was in heaven. I was glad that I had gone to the bamboo house. He was the first foreigner I had seen up close and he happened to be my savior. However, I regret to this day that I did not learn his name.

I went back to the family and asked if I could make a tent next to theirs. Again, they agreed. I collected a few poles and tied the plastic sheet to the family's poles to make a nice home for myself. I went to wash myself at a pond near the bushes and put on my new clothes. I looked completely different. It was the first time in four and a half years that I finally did not look like a skinny raven without feathers. I threw my black tattered clothes away in the bushes, the symbol of Khmer Rouge and Pol Pot. I did not want to see them ever again. That depressing color had brought me nightmares too often. I was glad that they were gone from me forever.

For a few weeks, during the day I snuck out to beg for food at a nearby village. Also, I continued to help Thai fishermen carry fish from their boats in exchange for some rice grains, fish, or crabs. After one month, my life began to improve significantly in Khao Lan due to the involvement of the International Committee of the Red Cross (ICRC), the United Nations International Children's Emergency Fund (UNICEF), the United Nations High Commissioner for Refugees (UN-HCR), and the World Food Program. They started to distribute food supplies to all the refugees. Also, I saw the young Princess Sirindhorn of Thailand who flew in a helicopter to visit the camp. It was quite an event that day when her helicopter landed in the middle of the campsite. Everyone ran to take a closer look at her. I, too, had the rare opportunity for a glimpse of the princess.

After her visit, the international relief agencies came to distribute rice, sardines, canned cabbage pickles, and milk to refugees once a week. Children like myself were allowed to get more milk at the bamboo house. We had the choice between liquid and condensed kinds of milk. I went to the bamboo house every day and mostly chose condensed milk. I liked the sweetness and fondly remembered eating the baguette with condensed milk when my family had had our one vacation years before.

We would stand in line for hours in the scorching sun or soaking rain to receive humanitarian aid. I remember that the food trucks came every Monday and people would fight to be the first in line. I, too, fought for the first spot but never won. To indicate that we had received our portions for the week, they marked our right ear with a permanent marker. I did not like this, but I was happy to receive some food. Armed Thai soldiers were assigned to stand and guard the line with M16 rifles and police batons in their hands. Their watchful eyes scared us so much. They were ready to beat us with their batons if we either cut in or stepped out of line.

One day, I got hit on the head with a baton because I was trying to get a second helping of food. A guard came straight at me and yelled, *hyud* (stop) in Thai. My knees trembled. I knew right away that I was in big trouble. I was about to run, but I was grabbed by the arm. When he started to inspect my ear, I began to faint. After seeing that my right ear was much cleaner than the other one, fast like a lightning bolt, the armed guard beat me on the head without a warning because he knew that I had already received my food. I fell to the ground and blacked out. I attempted to get up but was unable to because I was dizzy and could not see anything. I felt warm blood rushing down my face.

The nice foreign lady who was handing out the aid was shocked. She ran to pick me up and wiped the blood off my face and head. Everyone was scared, but no one made any attempt to step out of line and help me. I covered my head and took off from the scene as fast as I could. By myself in the tent, I cried with disappointment and anger. I did not understand why people who looked like me had never been nice to me. Twice in less than one month, I felt that only foreigners truly cared about me.

I saved up my condensed milk to sell to my fellow refugees so I could buy a pair of cheap flip-flops and new clothes and bought another plastic sheet to give my tent a little more privacy. I also used my savings to buy some sea salt. I used a tin can to cook my food. Between the small poles, I hung a tin can above a fire pit to boil my rice or vegetable soups. Since one tin can of grains a week was not enough to feed a growing and hungry boy like me, I made porridge instead. Sometimes, I made vegetable rice soups that I had learned how to cook from my mother. I kept my sardines to eat with my porridge. When I got more rice from helping the Thai fishermen, I treated myself to rice, canned cabbage, pickles, and grilled fish.

Very often in the late afternoon, other children and I would wait by the road for Thai merchants or motorists who had traveled from the local market in the Klong Yai district. We hoped that they would throw some food at us. They usually did. They enjoyed watching us fight over their leftovers. Most of the time, they tossed rambutan seeds to us to fight over. They ate all the meat and left only seeds for us. We would take the seeds to our tents and roast them in my tin can. Because we were noisy, drunk Thai guards would chase us children away, and sometimes the slow ones were kicked by the guards' big, heavy military boots. The guards were upset with us because we had disturbed them while smoking marijuana, drinking alcohol, or sleeping with prostitutes. Like many other children, I was kicked by those drunk guards for fighting over rambutan seeds and leftover food tossed to us from Thai sellers.

When the relief workers left the camp, the guards would drive their dirt bikes into the camp searching for pretty girls so they could come at night and gang rape them. We called these people, *Puok Moto Trai* (Dirt Bike Gangs). They came as a group with their fast and loud motorcycles to intimidate us. Some nights, I heard young girls desperately screaming for help. It hurt me so much to hear such unforgivable crimes committed against my people by such ruthless human beings. These girls had suffered enough, from losing their loved ones to other tortures, and now they faced traumas that would scar them for life. My anger built up, but I could not do anything to help them. Those girls were caught between the tiger and the crocodile as the Khmer proverb says, *choh teuk krapeu laeng leu khla.* They had escaped the genocide of the Khmer Rouge and now faced rape by armed Thai guards.

I once witnessed a man tied to a tree and beaten severely by the camp guards. He had stabbed one of the guards during an attempt to rescue his daughter from being gang raped. I noticed that all the girls slept between their parents for safety at night. One day when I snuck out of the camp to find work, I ran into nine Thai soldiers gang-raping a Cambodian-Chinese girl. When they saw me one of them shot at me, but missed. I ran back to the camp telling one of the nurses who was working in an open plastic tent medical aid station. She ordered a group of men to help her, but it was too late to save the girl. She died from losing so much blood.

Every morning, I saw Thai merchants come to the camp and call out asking if anyone had gold or silver to sell or trade.

The desperate refugees would either sell or trade their hidden jewelry at a loss for food or fruits from the Thai merchants. Those merchants made fortunes out of Cambodian refugees during their first months in the camp.

After we had lived in Khao Lan for two or three months, the Thais decided to send us back to Cambodia. At first, we thought we would be transferred to a new refugee camp. They provided each of us with a few tins of rice grains and then loaded us onto their trucks. After I got my rice grains, I saw that the soldiers were busy controlling the crowd. Yet I got away with running back to the camp. This time I had enough rice to sell, so I could buy a long-sleeved shirt and long pants. When I wandered around the camp, I never left my belongings in the tent. I always wrapped them in my scarf and carried them with me at all times in fear of them being stolen.

A week later, we were told that the truck would come again and asked refugees to volunteer to leave. I volunteered and stored the grains they gave us in my scarf. I attempted to run back to the camp but got caught. We were forced at gunpoint to sit and wait for a truck to arrive. When the vehicle—a dumpster truck—did arrive, I had no choice but to climb onto it just like everybody else. I was nervous because I had no idea what would happen to me next. I had flashbacks to all the depressing scenes I had witnessed in the mountains. I could see myself like those people who were blown up by land mines and shot by the Khmer Rouge or Vietnamese. I also flashed back to the day that I first got loaded onto the back of a Khmer Rouge truck at Sre Ambel. I wanted to jump off and run to the nearby mountains, but I was afraid of being shot in the back like the Vietnamese had done to many of my friends and the Khmer Rouge soldiers in the battles of Veal Veng and other places along the way to the river by National Route 48. Once again, I let fate decide my destiny. I stopped worrying and tried to enjoy the new scenery.

The truck sped up on Route 3 heading north. It was mid-morning on a weekend in November 1979. It was hot and it smelled bad in the truck. Everyone was standing in the back holding onto each other for balance. Children were crying from exhaustion and hunger. I was at the very back but was pleased with my position because I could admire the beauty of the landscape.

It was my first ride since I had left the base at Aural Mountain ten months earlier. This time, I rode on a smooth and paved route and had no fear of an ambush by enemies. But the driver drove like a maniac. He went fast and seemed not to care about his passengers who were falling on top of each other in the back. I felt like we were pigs being transported to the slaughterhouse.

About a half hour later, we reached the city of Trat and the truck slowed down. I was fascinated with all the stuff that was for sale at the market. I had not seen anything like this since my last visit to Kampot with my family before the war. After we passed the Trat marketplace, the truck started to speed up again. About five hours later, we approached the Thai military garrison of Ban Len and the truck stopped at a checkpoint. After a thorough search through the vehicle, the truck started to slowly roll and then picked up speed again. After a quick ride, the truck came to a stop by a small river near a thick jungle of bamboo.

Two men in military uniforms with M16 rifles got out from the front seat, opened the back of the truck, and motioned for us to get off. I was among the first ones to exit the vehicle. When some people with families refused to leave, the driver lifted the back of the truck and dumped them out like rubbish. It was late afternoon, around five o'clock. The sun was starting to go down and we felt the darkness on its way. The men in uniform pointed to the bamboo jungle on the other side of the river and said in a demanding voice in Thai language, *pai tee nan thidin Kheme* (go over there, it is Khmer's land). We did not resist and started to march forward toward the river.

We crossed the small river and took shelter on its banks in the thick jungle of bamboo. Once again, I found myself in the land of darkness in Cambodia. This time it was in the jungle of northwest Cambodia, somewhere near the strongholds of the Khmer Rouge in the Dangrek Mountains. I had risked my life walking across rainforest mountains in southwest Cambodia seeking safety, and now the Thais had sent me back to another danger zone in the northwest. But I promised myself that I would find a way to get back to Thailand someday.

It was dark when we crossed the river into the jungle. Refugees started to settle in and make fires for cooking their food. I did not have anything to eat that night. I spread my plastic sheet on the ground to sleep on and covered my body

with my scarf feeling regret for everything. It was cold that
night and my plastic sheet and my scarf were wet from the
nighttime dew. I slept folding my arms curling my knees together and crying softly. The moon shone through the thick
leaves and branches of the bamboo trees, and I could see my
fellow refugees sleeping and sitting in the area. It was a clear
night with lots of stars in the sky. I counted the stars and tried
to name a few, which I had learned from my village's elders.
I thought of Run, Kheng, and Sophat. I wondered if I would
ever see them again or if they were alive from the long journey
in the jungle of southwest Cambodia.

That night I felt so lonely and scared. I could not sleep
at all that first night. During the day, I stayed around the river catching frogs, crabs, shrimps, and snails. I also wandered
around the riverbanks looking for lizards and insects to eat for
lunch and dinner. I cooked what I caught with bamboo shoots.
Although there was no salt or ingredients to add for flavor, the
soup was still tasty.

Every day refugees died from stepping on land mines,
falling into booby traps, malnourishment, and diseases such as
malaria and diarrhea. A couple of times I was caught by Thai
soldiers patrolling the border when I encroached on their
territory to look for food. They put me in an outdoor cell at
Ban Len for the day and then sent me back to the other side
of the river. At night, I followed my fellow refugees crossing
the river into Thailand to steal corn, tomatoes, cassava roots,
and peanuts from Thai farms near the border. We were very
good thieves. We taught each other how to get the roots while

leaving the plants standing and how to break the ears of corn without making any noise. We assigned some people for the lookout and spread around the gardens like fans. We stayed flat on our bellies digging with our fingers to break only one or two roots from each cassava, tomato, or peanut plant. As for corn, we kneeled low in the middle of corn bushes and held the ears with both hands firmly to break them in two.

We were all determined to stay alive and to find food. Many times we heard the farmers shoot their rifles in the air, but we always stayed put. This worked for months and no one had ever been caught. Sometimes, though, the farmers out-smarted us. They would hide in their huts or behind bushes waiting for us to sneak into their gardens and then they would start to shoot at us, but they always missed. On top of that, the fighting between the Khmer Rouge and the Vietnamese happened almost every day. Refugees died in the crossfire and from rockets everywhere, but the Khmer Rouge still held onto their territory. For months, I was stuck in that deadly area and witnessed so many deaths and depressing scenes. At first, there were hundreds of Cambodian refugees just dumped in the bamboo jungle area. By the time I left, almost the entire population had died.

As I described at the beginning of this account, one evening under a full moon in January 1980, I was caught while digging for roots in an open field on a peanut farm. I saw a shadow and was scared because I thought that it might be an ogre coming to eat me alive. When I turned my head around and looked up, a man was standing above me, pointing his shotgun at my head. He pulled my head up by my hair and was ready to pull the trigger and said *tai* (die) in Thai. I kneeled and begged for mercy, closing my eyes. I gave him a *sampeah* and pleaded in Khmer, *meta kom somlab khnhom oum khnhom khlean pek* (please don't kill me, uncle, I'm too hungry). At the same time, I asked my mother's spirit for protection. Shaking from fear, I heard the farmer sigh. He put down his shotgun and pulled me up to a standing position.

He hugged me and then led me to his tiny thatched hut at the edge of his farm. He fed me cooked cassava root and an ear of corn: This was a moment in my life that I could never have expected in any of my late-night dreams. He put his shirt on while looking at me, but I was too afraid to look up. I could not eat because I was still shaking from fright. That evening, I heard multiple gunshots near a cornfield on the other side. He looked in the direction of the gunshots and shook his head, but did not say a word.

After hearing the nearby farmer's cock crow, the man led me to his white pickup truck and drove off. He was short and stocky and looked like he was in his early fifties. Before we got to the military checkpoint, he told me to hop in the back and I covered up under a basket. It was predawn and the road was still relatively quiet. A soldier came out of a sandbagged bunker, took a quick look in the front seat, and let us go. Later, when the man bid me sit in the front seat, he smiled and said in Thai, *thahan Thai di* (Thai soldier is good). I gave him a *sampeah* without saying anything because, despite his help, I was still frightened by him.

CHAPTER 8

The Illegal Guest

*A*bout an hour later, we reached the town of Lum Puk in the province of Buriram, in southeastern Thailand. I saw people walking and getting ready to open their shops by the route. I saw students in white uniforms lining up in front of a school building and saluting the flag. The man pointed to the school building saying in Thai, *rong reiyn.* I responded in Khmer, *bart Oum.* That was the very first word I said to him since I last begged him to save my life. He also pointed to the market and said, *talad.* I smiled at him and he reached out with his left hand and rubbed my right shoulder. We passed a school and the market and I saw houses and fruit trees on both sides of the route.

After a short while, the man pulled into a long dirt drive-way. I saw a banana farm, with rows of Thai eggplants, chili peppers, and cassava plants. After parking his vehicle, he asked me in a heavy Khmer accent to wait for him. I began to feel comfortable because I knew that he spoke my language. He went up the steps into the house and a few minutes later, I saw him come down with a little light-skinned middle-aged woman and walk toward the vehicle. I got out of the vehicle and knelt on the ground giving a *sampeah* directly to the woman. She tapped my shoulder but kept her other hand on her hip. I stood up and then she said in Thai, *chay di* (good boy).

They walked me to a big rectangular wooden table under the house and asked me to sit on it and wait. The man took off somewhere into his garden and the woman went back up to the house. I heard her doing something, which sounded like preparing a meal. By this time, the sun had risen over the tree-tops. I kept sitting there all by myself for hours. I was not bored because I took the opportunity to observe everything around me. The house was very nice, a traditional wooden Thai house. It was built on stilts with a tin roof and fine wooden walls with lots of windows with shutters. There were also gutters around it and a few downspouts attached to them.

Besides the couple, there was a young pretty lady, who seemed to be in her early twenties, and two teenage boys. One boy seemed a little older than me, but the younger one was around my age. I was not invited to go up into the house because they did not yet know who I was. All the children looked healthy and clean compared to me. Everyone had their hair cut short including the young lady. They all looked more like their mother with light complexions. They seemed to be open and welcoming. The young lady introduced herself in Thai, *chan chue* Malee (my name is Malee). She continued, *khun chue arai?* (What is your name?). I responded with a broken Thai, *phom chue* Vibol *khap* (Yes, my name is Vibol). I told her my fake name. She continued to ask if I was Khmer Rouge, *khun kheme daeng mai?* I shook my head and said, *mai chai khap* (No, I'm not). She added, *kheme daeng mai di* (Khmer Rouge is bad).

The mother then asked if I spoke Thai, and I told her that I did not. At this, they all started to laugh. I understood everything they said. I had learned just enough to communicate in a simple conversation when working for the Thai fishermen in the village near the Khao Lan refugee camp.

The young lady went up the steps into the house and soon came down with a full tin plate of white rice accompanied by a grilled fish and a piece of dried meat. She placed it on the table and left, and then the mother said, *kin khaw khun chay* (eat rice, child). The phrase "eat rice" is used for meals such as lunches and dinners by Cambodians, Thais, and Laotians. For example, one would ask, "Have you eaten rice yet?" instead of, "Have you eaten lunch or dinner yet?" Or one would say, "Come to eat rice," instead of "Come to eat lunch or dinner."

Everyone went up into the house to eat their lunch, leaving me to enjoy a delicious meal on my own. I did not leave a single grain of rice on my plate and chewed all the fish bones as well. I drank rainwater from a big ceramic vase by a spout below the gutter, using a silver bowl to scoop the water from the vase. I had not tasted such delicious food nor had clean water for a very long time. I quietly thanked the family for their kindness. To this day, I still do not leave any food on my plate if I am eating at home. In public, I try to leave a little on my plate just to fit in. After all the years I spent hungry, I value food very highly.

After lunch, the boys and their father took a nap while the mother and daughter washed dishes and cleaned the floor. I washed my plate and spoon with the rainwater and left them on the table. Then I walked around outside the house, to the barn, and then to the garden.

By late afternoon, everybody came down and hung out around the table under the house. The two teenage boys took me to the lake and showed me a good tree to climb in their garden. They introduced themselves to me, as Malee had earlier. We felt like brothers right away. Although they spoke only Thai, I understood a lot because it was a simple conversation. I did not talk much, just listened and nodded my head in agreement because I did not want to make mistakes. I did not want my first impression to be a bad one. I had evolved quickly from nearly wetting my pants when their father almost shot me at the peanut farm the night before, to brotherly love the next day. These boys brought me hope and made me feel like a normal child once again. I no longer felt afraid like I had the day before, and I thanked Lord Buddha for leading me on a path to safety.

After eating dinner alone with a simple meal of rice and vegetable soup at the table that first evening, the father came down and tied up a hammock for me to sleep in. I thanked him and fell asleep right away. However, I woke up in the middle of the night because it was cold. I had no blankets or anything to cover my body. My plastic sheet had been left behind in the bamboo jungle and my scarf had been lost in the peanut farm near the border. That night the wind and rain of the monsoon season made it even colder, and I could not go back to sleep. I started to think of my fellow refugees who were at the farms with me. They probably thought that I was dead. We stole just enough food for us to stay alive day by day but for no longer than that. We did not attempt to destroy or sabotage the farmers' crops. While I was in deep thought, a rooster crowed in the family's barn. It was still dark, and I knew that the sun would rise shortly. I got up washed my face and was ready for a brand new day in a new place.

The family lived in a wooden house with a huge garden of chili peppers and Thai eggplants. They also owned banana and cassava farms near the house. Houses in the town were far apart from one another. The boys went to school in the morning and came back home in the afternoon, while the young lady stayed home helping her mother. The father spent a lot of his time at the farm near the border. He would leave very early in the morning and come back home after dark.

There were two *sdao* (bitter-tasting quinine trees) in the middle of the garden near the house. The trees seemed to flower all year round. The family boiled the flowers of *sdao* every day for dinner. They dipped the *sdao* in a bowl of shrimp paste placed in the middle of the circle for the family to share and ate it with rice. Thai eggplants were also a big part of their diet. At first, I could not eat their food because the boiled *sdao* was too bitter, the raw eggplant tasted funny, and the shrimp paste was too spicy. For the first few days, I ate plain rice, but sometimes I had fish sauce. The boys and the young lady always encouraged me to eat like them. However, it did not take me long to learn how to eat their spicy food. Soon enough, I ate whatever they ate. After two days of my stay, I was allowed to eat with the family in the house.

The man and his wife spoke Khmer fluently, but with a heavy accent, and I found it hard to understand. Many people in this area were ethnic Khmers. They had had a presence in the area since at least the time of the Khmer Empire, which lasted from the ninth century to the fifteenth century. With the fall of the Angkor, the Khmers in this region were subject to increasing Thai influence. In the eighteenth century, the Thai kingdom officially annexed the former Cambodian provinces of Surin, Buriram, Sisaket, and many others in this region and eastern parts of Thailand. The couple's children spoke only Thai. In the evening, after chores which I helped the family do, I took a bath in the lake by the gardens. The family had built a wooden boardwalk on the edge of the lake. We all sat on it and used a bucket to scoop the water from the lake and pour it over our heads. I bathed like this every evening before dinner. The family also taught me how to sing in Thai. I was told by the family to sing wherever I was in public so everyone would know that I was one of them. They also taught me how to speak Thai and had me work in the barn feeding their pigs and chickens. And they also had me help them to chop firewood for cooking. I was happy with my new life.

Malee liked to play with me the most. She helped me clean the barn every morning before going to the market with her mother. She called me *lek chay* (little boy) and I called her *phi saw* (big sister). I addressed the man *Lung* (uncle in Thai, older brother of father and mother) and the woman *Paa* (aunt, older sister of father and mother). They called me *khun chay* (an affectionate term for boys). Besides going to the market, Malee was always in the kitchen cooking and cleaning. The two boys, who always wore their school uniforms, never helped around the house. They only focused on schoolwork. I went up to the house only to eat or to bring water to fill up the tank in the kitchen.

One day when *Lung* took me to a barber shop near the school, he told me to pretend to be mute. I did not look or talk to anyone. He asked the barber to shave my head keeping only some hair on top. I was proud of my new look, and everyone seemed to be pleased with it, too. Malee played with my head and took me to the lake to take a bath. She pushed me off the boardwalk and when I swam back and tried to get up, my shorts slipped down to my knees. She pointed at me turned around and laughed hard. Realizing that I was naked, I jumped back into the lake and refused to come out of the water.

She ran back to the house laughing all the way home and left me alone. I was very embarrassed. I came out of the water when Malee left. When I got back, she was still laughing and told everyone about it. Somchai, whom I called *phi chay* (big brother) pointed to my private parts and laughed. After I changed, Somchai took me to his school to watch his fellow students play soccer. I wore my black and white striped sports pants and the flower-pattern short-sleeved shirt that Somchai gave me. I also wore my new white flip-flops that Malee had bought for me from a local market. It was the first time in five years that I felt free and dignified, a great feeling. I sang a song that I learned from the family. Somchai smiled and sang a duet with me, while we walked and waited for a ride. Somchai praised my voice, *khun khamrong di* (you sing well), then he put his arm on my shoulder like buddies do and we continued walking. We took the back seat of a motor tricycle taxi and got dropped off on the road by the soccer field. We tried to avoid eye contact with police officers who were standing by the school's playground. We kept moving and did not stay in any one spot for long. I was scared but did not show it.

I had been living in Lum Puk for more than one month and word had gotten around town of my illegal status. One day around noon, I saw a police officer come to the house and talk to Malee and her mother. I hid in the barn and peeked through a crack on the wall. If he came to the barn, I could hide in a haystack. That evening when *Lung* came home from the farm, he asked me to sleep in the house. I thanked him. After dinner, he grabbed his flashlight and drove off. *Paa* lit up a lantern and we all sat around the lamp and I noticed that everyone looked at me with sadness on their faces. After a while, the mother said we should all go to sleep.

Arthit, the youngest boy, set up his mosquito net and told me that I could sleep with him that night. I was so happy to finally have company again. Since leaving Veal Renh one year before, I had been sleeping separately from other children. Sharing a mat and mosquito net with Arthit brought back good memories of the time I shared with my friends back in the labor camps in Cambodia. I was excited, so Arthit set up a sleeping station. Somchai also set up his mat next to ours. That night all three boys, including me, slept on the floor in the middle of the living room.

The mother and Malee slept in their separate bedrooms. Arthit snored all night long and his arms and legs were all over me. I barely slept that night. By midnight, I heard the father come back, but he did not come into the house. He slept under the house. Everyone was sound asleep and Malee snored the loudest. I could not sleep because I knew that the family must have made some kind of plan for me. I started to feel sad and worried. I liked the family and wanted to stay with them forever. All my life, I wanted a big sister or big brother. I felt that Lord Buddha had granted my wishes, and had given me Malee and Somchai. I began to feel that I had a stable place to stay and did not have to worry about my next meal. Most importantly, I felt safe. No more Vietnamese or Khmer Rouge could harm me. That night for the first time since I left the bamboo jungle, I thought of my family in Cambodia.

I worried that they might decide to travel west and make the deadly journey that I had. I knew the suffering they would face if they decided to travel to Thailand. The chances of surviving in the mountains were slim. I also hoped that they would have proper ceremonies for my mother, my brother Mouch, and my grandparents. I also was thinking of a plan to run away to avoid being sent back to the deadly ground in the bamboo jungle of the Khmer-Thai border. I was thinking of my mother and wondering if she was still looking down on me. I stared at the ceiling through the mosquito net for a long time, with tears rolling down my face. I was quietly calling on my mother, telling her that I missed her and loved her very much. I asked if I could see her again.

The night was getting late and it was pitch black outside. The dogs howling in the distance reminded me of when I was a small boy living in my village hearing my neighbors' dogs. I was so tired that I finally fell asleep. That night, my mother appeared to me in a dream. I saw that she was holding a baby in her arms and was sitting under the banyan tree at the Buddhist temple in my village of Chi Kha, a sacred tree. She was smiling but did not say anything. In my dream, I tried to call my mother to get her attention *Maek! Maek!* But she did not respond. She continued to smile and then she disappeared. I woke up gasping with disappointment at not being able to communicate with my mother. I felt sweat on my forehead. I could not go back to sleep. I thought to myself that my baby brother Hing had died, and the baby in my mother's arms must have been him. I felt horrible and saddened at the thought. I did not know what to do but cried alone in the middle of the night. I had not cried for a long time because I had no more tears left, but that night I cried so much over the fact that I might have lost another member of my family. I had felt joy for the past few months, but now I felt deep sorrow.

The next day, after Somchai and Arthit left for school, *Paa* and Malee went to the market, *Lung* asked me to get into his pickup truck. I asked him where he was taking me. He told me that we were going hunting for animals in the woods. I told me that I did not want to hunt and asked him to take me back home. He refused to turn around and continued driving. I started to get scared. I thought that he would take me to the woods and abandon me in the wilderness to be eaten by predators. When he saw that I was ready to pull the door handle, he stopped the vehicle. As soon as his pickup truck came to a complete stop, I pulled the handle and the door swung open. I jumped out and started to run to the back of the vehicle. He stuck his head out of the window and called me to come back. "Come back don't be scared, boy." I stopped, but shook my head and cried out in fear. He called and motioned me to get back into the vehicle, but I continued to cry. Noticing that I was crying, he got out of his pickup truck and walked toward me to ensure my safety. "Don't be foolish, I'll never hurt you, son," he told me. I wiped my tears and walked behind him back to the vehicle.

About ten minutes later, we got to a tiny hut in the woods. Bushes and short trees were growing on one side of the hut and dense, tall grass in a field on the other side. It was not as scary as I had anticipated, but it was still very remote. While I was standing by the hut with my eyes scanning the surroundings, an older man, skinny and tall walked toward us. He had a big smile and was carrying a shotgun and a rabbit. His teeth were kind of rotten. The two men exchanged greetings. I gave the old man a *sampeah*. He handed me a dead rabbit and said in Khmer, "Rabbit meat is very good." *Lung* handed me a machete and asked me to skin the wild rabbit. I hung the poor animal upside down on a tree and cut and peeled off its skin. I cleaned the skinned rabbit in a small brook, while the two men made a fire. I stuck a stick through the rabbit's body so we could roast it on top of the fire pit. This was about mid-morning. As the rabbit meat turned brownish, my mouth started to water with hunger. We ate the roasted animal without rice. Although there was no salt or ingredients to add for flavors, it was still very tasty.

After eating the rabbit meat, the two men took off with their shotguns leaving me alone in the hut. I was not scared because I knew that they would not abandon me. Besides, the truck was still there, so I was convinced that they would return. A few hours later, I heard multiple gunshots. By midafternoon, they came back with a dead wild boar that they both carried on a wood pole on their shoulders and they also carried a couple of gigantic rats and a rabbit. They skinned the animals and then cleaned them in the small stream in the woods. They took only the meat and loaded it in the back of the pickup truck. They burned the remains of the animals and put the fire out before we left.

At dusk, we came out of the dense forest. We went our separate ways. *Lung* and I went back to Lum Puk, while the old man went a different way on a motorcycle. I was so happy that we finally were out of the woods. I had no intention of going back there. Seeing the woods had traumatized me. When we got home, a meal had been prepared for us. It was rice with grilled fish and spicy shrimp paste with vegetables and eggplants. We ate our late dinner on the table under a fluorescent lamp that was operated by a generator in the barn. The mother came down from the house and took the meat that we had brought back up into the kitchen. She stayed up later than usual that night. She laid the meat out on banana leaves and then sliced the meat into smaller pieces. She salted it and left it out to dry.

Having seen *Paa* do that, I missed my mother so much. I remember when my father or my uncle and I brought home fish and animals, and my mother would stay up all night cleaning and salting the meat to make sure it would not go bad. I also missed my mother's special dish of *samlaw kawko* with either fish or chicken. She would ask me to pick a few *phle mareah* (bitter melons) from our garden and collect a handful of *bramat dei* (bitter spinach) from a dried-up pond to add a nice, mildly bitter taste. That was my favorite dish and my mother knew it. I would eat it until I could not move. I also remember that when I came back from fishing in the evening, my mother would leave some dried fish and rice for me. *Paa* had done for me exactly what my mother had done for me and my father.

After dinner, I washed myself with the rain water in one of the ceramic vases and then *Paa* told me to go to bed. That night I snuck inside Arthit's mosquito net again. He did not even notice that I had invaded his space because he was in a deep sleep and snoring like a baby pig. I envied him but felt blessed by his kind heart. Even though we were probably about the same age, I considered him my little brother because of his innocent nature. Again, that night I felt clean and my stomach was full.

The next morning, I noticed that the father and mother got up at the first crow of the rooster, and before dawn, they woke me up as well. After I washed my face, I saw Malee walk out of her bedroom like a sleepwalker. Her hair was all messy and her eyes were only halfway opened. She dragged herself into the kitchen. I quickly got out of her way to avoid being bumped into. I thought that was strange, and wondered. "Why did they wake me up so early, and why did Malee have to get up, too?" I asked myself. Malee started the fire in the kitchen for breakfast, while her parents were outside. It was still dark and the roosters in the barn continued to crow. About ten minutes later, Malee gave me breakfast of rice porridge and dried fish. Then, she went back to her room and left me all alone to sit on the kitchen floor to eat.

By the time I finished my breakfast, it was dawn and the roosters had started to flap their wings and crow as they competed with the neighbors' birds. I went down the steps to go to the lake to water new plants in the garden. After I finished watering the plants, I went back to my morning chores in the barn. I fed the birds with rice grains, swept the barn with a straw broom, and picked up chicken poop to make compost for fertilizer. Then, I chopped up some pieces of downed banana trees and mixed them with rice hulls. I also added some water and poured the mixture into the trough near the barn to feed the family's two fat pigs. By sunrise, my job was halfway done. While I was sweeping the dirt floor of the barn, Malee came in and took me by the hand to the house. She put my head on her shoulder. She started to cry and then ran upstairs. A few minutes later, she came down with two plastic bags and put them on a big rectangular wooden table under the house. She hugged me and said, *khob khun* (thank you). *Mai pen arai khap* (it's okay) I responded. *Khun lek di* (you are a good boy) she added. She took off quickly into the house and I never saw her again.

In one of the bags were my old clothes. On the other was some meat wrapped in banana leaves. When I saw my clothes in the bag, I knew that the family was sending me to live with a different family, but was not sure with whom. I believe it was the weekend when Somchai and Arthit took the opportunity to sleep late. I believe that they did not even know that their family was sending me away. I wanted to say goodbye to them, but they were still asleep.

Soon enough, I saw a motorcycle approaching the house. When it got closer, I realized that it was the old man that the father and I had spent time hunting with the day before. When he got off his motorcycle, he asked me how I was doing. I told him that I was fine. The old man reached his hand to touch my head gently and with a smile showed his rotten teeth. I did not move away or say anything to him. The mother told me in Khmer and Thai, *khun chay eng taw chea muoy phi* Nan (child, you go with big brother Nan). I shook my head and told her that I did not want to go with that man. I told her that I loved her family so much. She covered her face and nodded with understanding. The father said that Nan was a friend of the family, and I would be safe staying with him because in Lum Puk there were a lot of police who unless I moved might find me and send me back to the bamboo jungle at the border.

After hearing that, I agreed to go with the old man but thought that it would only be temporary. I thanked the couple for everything that they had done for me. I hopped on the motorcycle behind the old man and hugged my bags. When Nan turned his motorcycle around getting ready to take off,

I turned to take a last look at the couple. "*Awkun oum pros oum srey*," I thanked them for one last time. "May Lord Buddha bless you," said the mother. At that moment, I saw her cry while her husband wiped his eyes with his shirt.

We took off, approaching the paved road, and turned left toward the bamboo jungle. It was a beautiful morning. The road was quiet and we went fast. I held onto Nan's waist as tight as I could but also had my bags to hang onto. I was scared because it was my first time riding on a motorcycle. We had no helmets. We passed the market, barber shop, and school. We did not talk. I hid my face behind Nan to avoid the morning air. About forty minutes later, we turned right onto a small, unpaved road. There was farmland and a few small houses with gardens scattered on both sides of the dirt road.

Nan stopped his motorcycle in front of a small farmhouse that was built on stilts with a tin roof. It was surrounded by several trees of edible fruit—mango, jackfruit, guava, papaya, sapodilla, banana, and coconut. I went to sit on a table under the house and observed my surroundings. The ground was soft from the rain. It was a depressing environment. After all, I was still a child, only thirteen years old. However, I understood that it was nobody's fault. I had been born in the wrong place and at the wrong time, but I still did not want to accept this reality. My desire was not to live in huts and work in the swamps anymore. I wanted to wear nice clothes, eat well, go to school, and have a loving family. I wanted the lifestyle of Arthit and Somchai.

I saw that every family in that village seemed to be very poor, somewhat poorer than my village before the war. While

I was in deep thought, Nan asked me to go up into the house. There was a bedroom and a kitchen attached to the hall room. In the kitchen, there were pots, pans, and dried meat and fish hanging on the wooden walls. The odor did not bother me. Inside the house, there were no photos of family members, only some posters of Thai celebrities and a picture frame of King Bhumibol Adulyadej hanging on the wall where the bedroom was.

While I was sitting on the floor folding my legs and looking around the house, a short and skinny woman came out of the bedroom and asked me slowly in Khmer what my name was. Again, I gave her my fake name, Vibol. She told me that Vibol was a good name. She went into the kitchen and brought Nan and me breakfast. I told her that I was not hungry, and she did not insist I eat. The old couple was nice to me that morning. They were calm and patient. They spoke in soft tones of voices. I was not afraid but was unhappy to be there.

I went outside to stand by the coconut tree and admire its fruits. I looked up and wondered how sweet they were. I had not had any coconut since the Khmer Rouge entered my village in April 1975, and I wanted some. Having seen me looking up at the coconut fruits, the short and skinny woman stuck her head out of the kitchen window and gave me her permission to climb up and pick some if I wanted to. I did not expect it, but was so excited. I immediately climbed up the tree, reaching my hand to twist a fruit to detach it. I got one coconut and dropped it to the ground and then attempted to reach for another one. My hands got tired from holding onto the tree for so long, that I slipped off and fell to the ground. The fall knocked the wind out of me, and for a moment I could not breathe. I lay flat on the ground next to the picked coconut fruit.

When the old couple saw what had happened, they ran down from the house and picked me up. They tried to help me into a standing position and rubbed my chest. It hurt so much. After a minute or so, I finally was able to open my eyes and started to breathe. I jumped up and down slowly and went up to the house to lay down on the floor. After seeing that I was okay, Nan grabbed his shotgun, hopped on his motorcycle, and took off. The old lady cracked the coconut shell a little and emptied the juice into a silver bowl. She then broke the shell in half scraped the meat from the shell and put it into the bowl with the juice. At that moment, I felt very spoiled! The old lady made me think of my mother and grandmothers, who used to spoil us children when we were sick. I felt comfortable and regretted the negative feelings about her family the minute I entered her house. Her kind heart had changed my mind quickly. I felt like I was a child again. I lifted the bowl from the floor and thanked her sincerely. I drank the whole bowl, but slowly because I wanted to enjoy it. It was so delicious.

Nan spent a lot of time hunting animals. He did it for a living. Almost every morning he would take me with him to the woods to hunt. We would come home in the evening and sometimes late at night. Nan's wife was the seller. She would take meat, vegetables, and fruits to sell at the local market. Although I wanted to help, she never let me go with her. Every morning before going to sell her products, the old lady would pack us food, mostly rice and dry meat or fish. To me, she was a perfect wife and a caring mother. She rarely talked. I hardly hear the couple discuss anything. They seemed to know what they were supposed to do when they got up in the morning.

I spent a lot of time in the woods with the old man. He taught me how to set up traps to catch animals, but he never let me use his shotgun. I set up all kinds of traps to catch rats, lizards, rabbits, and even wild boars. When we got to the woods in the morning, we always saw animals caught in our traps. For the big and dangerous ones, Nan would shoot them before we attempted to get closer. However, the small and less dangerous ones, he would hit them with a stick. We never came home empty-handed. We took only meat home. Sometimes we camped in the woods to hunt wild boars, but I never liked doing this because I had had bad experiences in the wilderness.

The experience made me feel sick and depressed every day due to the violence towards the animals. I started to eat less and less. I always had a stomach pain. I noticed that my skin had turned yellow and my feet were starting to swell. I begged Nan to take me back to Lum Puk, but he ignored my pleas and started to get annoyed. One day, he screamed at me and said in his impolite manner in Khmer, *anh som eng mork thweu kon anh* (I asked you to be my son). I cried, shaking my head repeatedly, and said nothing in response. Although I appreciated his good intentions, I preferred a different lifestyle than his. Within three weeks of living with the old couple, it seemed like I had already been there a lifetime. Every day, I was either in the woods with Nan or carrying water from the pond to water the family's crops. They never took me anywhere for fun or bought me anything. They were not mean but were always boring. As time went by, I got sicker. I wanted to run away but did not know where to go. I started a hunger strike. I stopped talking to the couple, though I continued doing my chores. I cried often, feeling hopeless and lonely.

Noticing that I had stopped eating, Nan's wife started to worry and tried every possible way to make me start eating again. But her attempts failed. I noticed that the old couple started to fight daily. I also realized that the wife ignored and tried to avoid her husband. I felt the stress and pain they were going through. I felt bad to see them fight because of me, but I knew that it was not my fault. I did not bring any problems to them. All I wanted was to go back to Lum Puk.

After the third day of my hunger strike, Nan asked me to pack my belongings. He told me that he would send me to live with another family. His announcement gave me mixed feelings. I was somewhat happy and scared at the same time. In my mind, I was convinced that he would let me go back to where he had taken me from. That evening, I expected *Lung* would come to pick me up. I sat by the doorstep waiting for him to arrive. My heart started to swell with excitement. I imagined that *Paa,* Malee, Somchai, and Arthit would wait for my arrival welcoming me back with open arms. I could smell the delicious dinner that Malee would have ready for me. My stomach started to crawl. I also imagined that Arthit would have already set up his mosquito net waiting for my company. I could not wait to jump into the lake to take a bath and the next morning,

I would just go back to do my routine chores. All the happiness that I shared with the family in Lum Puk would return.

I sat impatiently by the doorstep waiting for *Lung* for at least an hour. It started to get dark. The old lady lit a lantern lamp for me and then went into her room without saying a word. I continued to wait, but he never showed up. My heart sank. I unrolled my straw mat set up a mosquito net at my usual sleeping spot and crawled inside the net to lie down. That night, Nan and his wife went to bed much later than usual. I heard them whispering until midnight, but I could not make out their conversation. I did not care and just tried to get some sleep in the hopes that *Lung* would come to pick me up the next morning.

Early in the morning, the old lady put her meat in a basket and went to the market. I also woke up but still lay on the mat. It was so hard to get up because I was tired and starving. When I heard Nan go outside, I forced myself to get up, rolling my mat and taking down my mosquito net to put them away. I washed my face and brushed my teeth in the kitchen and went outside to water the plants behind the house. My eyes kept looking to the driveway desperately hoping for *Lung* to pick me up. The sun rose above coconut trees in the distance, but still no one came. I was very disappointed and started to hate everyone.

When I was almost finished watering the plants, I heard Nan call me. I came over and he asked to get my stuff. He started up his motorcycle and told me that he would take me to live with a new family. I still hoped that he would take me back to where I had come from. Nan did not yell or show any anger towards me. He told me to hop on his motorcycle behind him. A half-hour later, we approached the entrance of a pathway by a huge rambutan farm. I saw a man wearing a straw hat waiting by the road holding onto a silver pickup truck. I had butterflies in my stomach because I thought that it was *Lung.* But I wondered why he had not picked me up at Nan's house himself. As we got closer, I saw it was someone else. My heart sank. We came to a stop and I got off from the motorcycle to stand behind Nan. "What's going on?" I asked myself quietly. A Chinese-looking man in his early forties exchanged greetings with Nan.

Then I saw the younger man reach inside his pickup truck pull out a handful of paper currency and hand it to Nan. After putting the money in his motorcycle seat, Nan told me that I had to stay with the Chinese-looking man to help him with his work. I did not respond. Nan pushed me gently toward the Chinese-looking man, who tapped my head and opened his pickup truck's door to let me get in. I did not say anything, just climbed into the vehicle and sat still. Within minutes we drove into the middle of rambutan farm and then stopped between a hut without walls and a wooden house with walls and windows. It was very quiet and it was far away from the road.

After putting my belongings on the floor of the hut, I wandered around a little bit to admire the beauty of the rambutan. I saw the man get out of his pickup truck and go straight behind the house and soon came with a young girl with a light complexion. She looked like she was fourteen or fifteen years old. As soon as she saw me, she tried to wipe off the sweat from her forehead. She seemed to be a little embarrassed about her appearance.

She looked confused. Perhaps she wondered why there was a new little boy at the rambutan farm. I did not pay much attention to her because I thought that she was the man's daughter, and did not make any attempt to ask her name or introduce myself. I began to walk toward the hut, but the girl, who was standing like a mannequin, spoke out in perfect Khmer, *kout chmos* Pinya (his name is Pinya). I turned around and saw that she was pointing to the man. She also told me that she was a Cambodian living with another Thai family in the next village over. She assured me that no one would know that I lived with the man on the farm. After she finished telling me this, the girl quickly went back to the kitchen in the back of the house.

Later, Pinya showed me different parts of the farm. In some sections, the trees were newly planted and some had just started to flower, while others bore fruits. We went to a tree that had ripe fruit in colors of green and bright red. I was hungry and wanted badly to pick some, but wanted to make sure that I first had permission from the man. I was impatiently waiting for Pinya to give me the go-ahead to pick some. When he did so, without hesitation I put a few in my shorts; the others I peeled and popped into my mouth right away.

Oh, Lord Buddha, the fruit was so good and juicy! Having seen me gobbling it down like a hungry wolf, Pinya broke a

branch that was holding more fruits and handed it to me. I just
stopped walking and stood in one place popping the peeled
fruits into my mouth munching the meat and spitting out the
seeds. After my stomach was full, I ran to join up with Pinya
at the edge of a river. He showed me how to operate the water pump, and how to use the hose to water the trees. He also
showed me my room. I had my bedroom in the house. It was
for the first time in my life that I had my room. There was a
foam mattress, a pillow, and a blanket, all neatly arranged in
my bedroom. I touched all the luxurious things in my room.
Everything was soft and magical.

That day around lunchtime, I heard a truck approaching.
Pinya told me to take my belongings into the house. I quickly
grabbed my stuff and ran up the steps into the house. He followed me and told me to hide in my room. He told me in Thai
while pointing to my room, *ah meaw khun nang tee nan* (little
one, you sit over there). Soon enough, the sound of a dumpster
truck came to a stop on the pathway a little far away from the
hut. I heard some people speak Khmer and some Thai. I heard
the little girl ask for some strong men to help her carry food.
At the same time, Pinya came up into the house to check on
me just to make sure that I was not going to come out. When
he saw that I was sitting still, he whispered to me that I was
a good boy. I nodded my head and then he left and closed the
door behind him. I was bored and about half an hour later, I
fell asleep in a seated position with my back against the wall.
When everyone had left, the man came back and woke me up.
It was almost dark. After coming down to the hut, I looked

around, but everyone was gone. It was quiet, but still better than spending time in the woods with Nan because Pinya had a fluorescent lamp to light the place and alleviate the nighttime darkness.

That evening we had sandwiches for dinner. It was my first time eating a Thai sandwich. The sandwich was made of French bread with meat, slices of cucumber, scallions, and mayonnaise inside. It tasted different, but I loved it. After dinner, I went down to the river to take a bath and brush my teeth. The water was nice and cold. That was the first night I had a good sleep because my mattress and pillow were very comfortable. My back and my head did not hurt and the blanket kept me warm. The lights from the living room made me less scared. Pinya slept in his hammock in the hut with a shotgun on the floor next to him.

I woke up at dawn every morning. The first thing I would do was go straight to the river to wash my face and then put gasoline in the generator and start up the water pump. Next, I would water the trees, especially the new plants. I watered at least one thousand rambutan trees a day in my daily routine. By nine or ten o'clock, I had completed my work. It usually took me between five to six hours to water all the trees. After that, I pulled weeds and took away any dead trees and branches. I ate so much rambutan fruit until I was sick of it. I lived on the rambutan farm for about two months and did the same thing every day. After work, I spent most of my days hiding out in my room or in the woods by the river to make sure no one saw me. I felt lonely and missed Malee, Somchai, and

Arthit every day. Sometimes, I heard the sounds of big guns at the border because we were not too far away from the bamboo jungle.

Then one day I got very sick. That night I lay down on my mattress and began to shiver. I kept holding my knees together and piled a blanket and clothes over myself to keep me from shaking. I was hot and my temperature skyrocketed. Pinya came, put his hand on my forehead, and sighed deeply. That night my fever caused me to have a seizure. Pinya was panicked. He sprinkled cold water on my body, but it did not help. All night long my condition kept changing from shaking with cold to feeling very hot with a high fever. I could hardly bear the pain.

The next morning Pinya drove me to a clinic in the next town over. The nurse asked for my identification, but we could not produce it for her. Pinya told the nurse that he would go home and get it for her. Then he took off fast. The nurse and I waited for hours, but he never came back. The nurse gave me some medicine and liquid IV hydration. A couple of hours later, my temperature went down, but I was still shivering. I started to shake a lot. My stomach hurt and my teeth chattered. Since no one came to discharge me, I had to stay overnight at the clinic. I was disappointed with Pinya for abandoning me. I had no clue where I was, nor what I should do next. I was very scared, of everything and everyone. At that moment, I trusted no one. I was afraid that the nurse would finish me off just like the Khmer Rouge nurses did to their patients.

During the Khmer Rouge era, when a sick person went to a clinic this meant they were going there to die. Khmer Rouge nurses had no medical training, and they were only trained to bury their patients. They did not believe in helping sick people because they thought it was a waste of their food and resources. Every time I saw the nurse come check on me, I was scared and thought that she had come to inject me, to kill me, and then toss me out, to lie in the sun.

The next day around noon, I saw a few police officers in gray uniforms with pistols on their hips come to the clinic. The most senior police officer asked me in Thai if I was a Khmer. I told him that I was. He continued to ask if I had any family or knew any other Khmers in Thailand. I told him that I did not have any family in Thailand and did not know any Cambodians living there. He asked me how I got to Thailand. I told him that I had escaped the fighting at the border. He thanked me and turned to his lieutenants then hopped on his motorcycle and took off. Two officers took me by my hands and helped me to climb up onto the back of the police pickup truck. They did not say a word and I did not ask them anything. In my mind, I knew that I would be going back to where I had come from, a deadly place in the bamboo jungle of Cambodia. I did not have any more hope of staying alive. I was still sick and weak. I had not had any food for two days. The police officers got in the front seats and sped off. I sat in the back of the pickup truck. I felt so cold from my sickness and the wind. Again, my teeth chattered. It was a smooth ride on a brand-new paved road, but I was dizzy and threw up on the floor. Again, I wanted fate to decide my outcome.

Knowing that I was throwing up in the back of their truck, the officers pulled over and stopped by the roadside. I was surprised that they spared me. I did not get beaten or kicked. I sat on the ground by the side of the road waiting for them to finish cleaning up their vehicle. I had a migraine headache and started to throw up again. They handed me a menthol tiger balm *(breng khrala)* to sniff. I shook my head, refusing to accept it. And then they gave me a hard candy. Again, I shook my head. They also offered me water, but I ignored them. I did not talk or smile because I did not trust them.

When the truck was cleaned, I managed to pull myself up and climb into the back of the vehicle. I was still shivering. The police officers began to lose their patience with me and drove very fast. About two hours later, we approached a military police checkpoint and the vehicle came to a stop in the middle of the road. I saw an armed officer with MP (military police) written on his helmet, emerging from a concrete bunker. He walked toward the two police officers in the front seats and gave a quick salute. Both officers returned the gesture. After a brief conversation, the military police officer walked to the back of the pickup truck and checked on me. He then walked back to open the barrier and let us go through.

About five or ten minutes later, the vehicle pulled to the right of the road and came to a complete stop by a military post. Two middle-aged men emerged from the post carrying M16 rifles, dressed in military uniforms. Again, they exchanged salutes and greetings. One of the soldiers signaled for the officers to get out of the vehicle and led them to their posts, leaving me alone in the back of the pickup truck. I looked over to my left and saw rows and rows of shelters behind the gate of the military post, and on my right across the street, there seemed to be new construction underway. I immediately knew that this was nowhere near the border. I did not hear any sounds of big guns. Instead, I heard people's voices behind the post.

Ten to fifteen minutes later, a soldier and both police officers came out of the post and told me to get out of the vehicle. I did as I was told.

CHAPTER 9

Refugees

*L*ater that afternoon, the gate opened for me to enter the camp. I was shocked. I saw hundreds of my people in a red dusty area surrounded by barbed wire. The Kamput camp had originally been used as a holding center for the Khmer Rouge who were seeking refuge after losing to the Vietnamese forces in 1979. Later that year, the camp was converted to a processing center for Khmer refugees who were fleeing the fighting between the Khmer Rouge and Vietnamese forces.

I was led to a wooden house that was built on stilts with a tin roof. I saw a lot of soldiers stationed in it. There was a flagpole in front of the house and a big megaphone tied up high near an antenna. When I looked around, there were a lot of eyes staring at me. These were all Cambodian refugees whose eyes were filled with hope and sorrow. I saw some of the soldiers in the house drinking alcohol and could smell that they were smoking marijuana. Some were playing cards. I was told to stand by the flagpole. I was still sick and tasted bitterness in my mouth. I was shivering and my stomach hurt.

The sun was about to set and the chilly air made me even colder on top of my sickness. I saw one of the soldiers jump down from the house; he held a black baton and was in full uniform. He came up to me and said, *pai tee nan* (go over there) pointing in one direction. He led me to a storage building close by. He unlocked the iron door of the building and told me to get inside. I did not hesitate to go in because I had been a captive before. I had been in a cell twice at the Ban Len military garrison. He locked the door and said, *non tee nee* (sleep here) and then he went back to the house.

That night, I slept on the ground, folding my arms and knees together tightly to control my shivering. There was no mat or blanket. I missed my mattress, my pillow, and my blanket at the rambutan farm. Somehow, I did miss the kindness of Pinya and the soft heart of Nan's wife. I still missed the company of Arthit and even the snores of Malee. Although they were not my blood relatives, at least they had provided me comfort and a warm place to sleep at night. That night, I slept without food or water. I was all alone in the darkness of a storage building. I was scared of the dark, and of dangerous creatures that might be in the building such as snakes, wasps, fire ants, scorpions, and especially the scary eyes of geckos. I stayed awake all night feeling pity for myself. I prayed for the morning to come soon and hoped that something good would happen to me then.

The next day, early in the morning, the Thai national anthem played from the gigantic megaphone at the guard's house. I noticed that everyone, including the refugees who were outside their shelters, stood saluting the Thai flag. Around noon that day, a guard brought me a plate of rice with spicy chicken curry and said, *kin khaw chay lek* (eat rice, little boy). I was able to get my taste for food back. It was my first meal in three days, and it was very good. About an hour later, he came back with a bowl of water and took the plate away. I thanked him, *khob khun khap*. He halted and turned back. I saw his eyes were wide open. He unlocked the door and asked me in Khmer if I knew how to speak Thai. I told him that I could understand some. I also told him that I had been sick for a week and needed medical attention. He could tell that I was not lying because he heard my voice was weak and saw that my body was shaking. In addition, he noticed that my eyes had an unusual color of white and my skin was yellow. He was convinced and nodded his head in belief. To my surprise, he took me by the hand led me to the guard's house, and gave me some medicine. He also gave me a plastic sheet and a cloth that was big enough to cover my body.

The next morning, I saw a white SUV approach the guard's house and then come to a stop by the flagpole. Three people got out of the vehicle and walked toward my cell. When they got closer, I noticed that they all had special badges hanging from their shirts. There was a white male with a beard, a white female wearing a long skirt and a blouse, and an Asian woman in a professional black suit. Both foreigners seemed to be in their fifties, tall and slender. When they got to the cell, I stood up and greeted them with my *sampeah* through the bars of an iron door. They smiled and the woman asked me in a foreign language, how I was doing. I told her that I was fine, but wanted to get out because I was sick and scared. The man said something and I saw that they all nodded in agreement. The short Asian woman with a pretty face told me in Khmer with a heavy accent that they would bail me out that day, so I could live as a free boy. After hearing their assurance of my freedom, I started to feel happier.

I watched them as they left, wondering whether they just said what they did to make me happy or if they meant what they said. As an optimistic person, I convinced myself that everything would somehow turn out in my favor. I saw the refugee children playing and wanted to join my fellow Cambodian refugees very much. I could hardly wait to get bailed out. I missed speaking to my people and being around them. I stood by the door looking outside, waiting for the two foreigners and the Asian woman all day. By late afternoon, my patience had run out. My negative thoughts about other people came back. I sat down on my plastic sheet and started to think that I could not trust anyone anymore. All people were evil, I thought. Even the foreigners who had promised me my freedom were liars. I began to think that they tricked me like all those others.

The sun was on the horizon, and the kind guard brought me dinner. It was rice and pork chops, mixed with pickled cabbage and a bowl of water. I asked him if he knew whether those foreigners would come back for me. He said he did not know. I ate my dinner while the guard was patiently waiting for me to finish it. He asked if I wanted to go to the bathroom, and I told him that I did not need to. The truth is that I needed to pee badly, so after the guard left, I peed in one of the corners of the cell. At that time, the only person that I could call a friend was the guard. At least he fed me. Soon I stopped thinking, and again, told myself that fate would decide what happened to me. It was late and everyone seemed to be asleep. I tried to quiet my mind and go to sleep.

On the third day, early in the morning, the national anthem song played and this time I stood and watched to see if the white SUV would come back. Sure enough, soon after the song ended the SUV came to a stop by the flagpole. This time there were only two people who got out of the vehicle. I did not see the Asian woman. These were the same foreigners who had come yesterday. I saw them walk to the guard's house and a few minutes later, they came with the most senior guard, walking fast toward my cell. My heart rose in hope. I stood by the door impatiently waiting for them to arrive. When they got closer, the foreigners had big smiles on their faces, which seemed to be a good sign. The guard unlocked the door and gave me a signal to come out. I did not rush and took some time to come out of the cell.

I was led to the white SUV. Hundreds of eyes of my fellow refugees watched me. I sat in the backseat by myself. The man drove and the woman sat beside him in the passenger seat. About an hour later, we reached Aranyaprathet in Sakeo province near the border of the Cambodian province of Battambang. I entered a relatively small building accompanied by the two foreigners. The office was close to a market in a Cambodian refugee camp. A middle-aged foreign man interviewed me through an Asian translator. Both men were pleasant and patient.

The foreign man first introduced himself as an American. He said he worked for the International Rescue Committee (IRC), but I do not remember his name. He may have been the first American I ever met. He sat behind a desk with a pile of papers on it. The translator sat on a chair next to mine in a tiny room across from the American's desk. Both men seemed to be sincere. I felt very comfortable sharing my story with them. The American man asked for my history. I told him my real name, but could not figure out my date of birth. I told him that I did not know how to spell my name because I had never seen my name on any document. He smiled and then flipped through a few pages of documents on his desk. He also checked with his colleagues, and they came up with Uok Leang Hong, exactly the sound I told him. I told him that I was born in October of 1967, but was not sure about the exact date. "Pick a date, any date that you like," the man told the translator to tell me. Both men waited patiently, while I tried to scramble through numbers in my head.

"Fifteen, I will pick number fifteen," I proudly spoke out in my child's voice.

"Very nice," the American man said with a smile. "Why are you choosing number fifteen?" he asked.

"Because number fifteen is in the middle of the month and it should be easy enough for me to remember," I responded. The translator smiled and said Khmer, *khmeng chlat* (a smart kid). He told the American what I had said and about his comment. The American man smiled and said in a broken Khmer, *leak aw nah* (very good). He added my date of birth to the form. "Now, it is official," he said.

He pulled out a Polaroid camera from under his desk and asked me to smile. I forced myself to smile just a little bit, but he had not taken the photo yet; he asked me to give him a bigger smile. I did as he asked. He snapped his camera as I held my big smile. He pulled the picture out and let it dry. After a few minutes, he showed it to me. It had been six years since I had seen my face. I could not remember if I had ever seen a photo of myself before. Until the Khmer Rouge came to power, I used to see my face in my aunt's mirror. My uncle and I would quietly sneak into her room and look at our reflections in it. I thought that I had not changed much. I was shy about seeing my face, and giggled at the picture, while the American man looked at me with sympathy. The interview ended after only twenty or thirty minutes. He took the photo back and attached it to the form and placed it carefully in a folder for safety. To me, this man did his job with pride. He had a big heart, I thought.

I was driven back to Kamput soon after the interview ended. Everyone in the camp lived in long wooden shelters that looked like horse barns with high ceilings and tin roofs. One day, I was told that foreigners were looking for orphans like me to live with them. I went to a small office of the IRC near the market at the edge of the camp to register. It seemed like I was among the first ones to have learned about the program. The IRC officials began to register children who had no parents. Soon, they set up an orphanage. I lived with ten to twenty other orphans in a barn. We were provided new clothes and two meals a day, lunch and dinner. Many refugee families tried to register their children with the orphanage center, but they were denied because they intended to get free clothes and food. The Americans in the IRC assigned one of the guards, who spoke Khmer fluently, to watch over us. His name was Sayan and he lived in the province of Surin. Every night, he taught me how to sing Thai songs, but most of the time I preferred to sing in Khmer. He never went against my wishes. Instead, he encouraged me to continue singing in my language. Every evening after dinner, all my friends at the center would ask me to sing in exchange for sweets. Sayan bought me a notebook and a pen, so I could write my songs in it. I thought I had a good memory because I could remember the whole song by practicing it only four or five times. The first song I learned how to sing was *Meul Duong Dara Ras* (Watching Starlights).

I began to teach myself how to write and read in the Khmer language with the help of Sayan and other children. I learned how to write my name in Khmer and chose my new last name, Neth. Besides my interest in music, I loved to listen to talk shows on the radio and read novels. The IRC opened a small library in the camp and they collected many good Cambodian books for us to read. I was moved by the romantic novels and sentimental stories such as *Phka Srapoun* (A Faded Flower) *Kolab Pailin* (A Pailin Rose), and *Sophat.*

Most of the Thai armed guards in Kamput were mean. Many of them had committed some sort of crime. They were sent to beat us refugees in the camp. They were constantly being moved from camp to camp. I saw new guards all the time, and it seemed like they were all mean to us. If we got caught failing to stand when their national anthem played, or for not wearing our identification cards, the guards would beat us severely. They would hit adults with rifle butts or batons. They would kick children on their backs with their heavy military boots or would hit or kick us in our backs or ribs. I asked Sayan what had happened to the nice guard who fed me when I was in the cell. He told me that all the nice ones had been either transferred or sent to be retrained. Sayan told me that he would eventually be transferred away, too. It was just a matter of time. I was saddened to hear that. I asked myself why my people always suffered so much.

During the day, I wandered around the camp looking for relatives. I also hung out at an outdoor market watching Thai kickboxing and soap operas on black and white television that some Thai merchants had. It was the first time I had ever seen a television. Before the Khmer Rouge came, I had watched outdoor films in the schoolyard in Chi Kha, but I had never seen a TV set. I ate strange fruits like white grapes and yellow apples for the first time in my life that were given to me by a generous Thai merchant. I went to her stall every day to watch TV, and she would give me sweets and fruits. She never asked for my name and I never asked for hers either. She was a little chubby and had light skin. Her stall was covered with a big plastic sheet and had no walls. She sold radios, cassette players, musical tapes, magazines, candies, and toys. Other vendors around her sold clothes, shoes, vegetables, fruits, and different kinds of foods. Very often, I heard vendors yell at the refugee children for stealing their products and the guards would kick them and chase them away. Every day when I heard the guards yell, *pai* (go), I would prepare to run. They would kick anyone who was in their way.

One afternoon, I went to look at the photos that were posted on the bulletin board by the side of the red gravel dike near our shelter. I took my time and scanned each photo. To my pleasant surprise, my eyes came across a black-and-white picture of a boy that looked familiar. I looked at it for a while and decided to read the brief biography that was attached to it. My heart started to rise with excitement. I recognized the large eyes. I slowly read the name, age, date of birth, place of birth, parents' names, and names of siblings. I read over and over again the paragraph under the photo. Name: Cheng Hai. Age: 14. Place of birth: Koh Kong. Father: Cheng. Mother: Khan. Siblings: Cheng Muoy and Cheng Yong.

After gathering all the information, it became clear that this was my uncle Tse-hai. It was the happiest moment for me in six years. All of a sudden, my happy memories with my uncle flashed back. I did not wait. I quickly grabbed the page with my uncle's information and ran to the IRC office to tell the worker the news. I pointed to the picture and the worker pulled out a thick folder with thousands of photos attached to information and compared the page that I showed him. He assured me that my uncle was living in the Mairut holding center in Trat province. Very quickly, the news reached my uncle and he took the chance to believe it was true.

The holding center at Old Kamput got overcrowded; a new and bigger one was needed. After living for two months in Old Kamput, in May 1980, my fellow refugees and I were transferred to a new processing center, New Kamput, just across the street. It was quite emotional to say goodbye to Sayan and the kind merchant lady at the market. But I did not miss the other guards, who had beat us day and night for the past two months.

In New Kamput, I was placed in the section named Hang, which was named after a Southeast Asian mythological bird. New Kamput was a much bigger camp than Old Kamput. There were bamboo and wooden houses all along the sides of the red gravel dikes. All of the houses were brand new built on stilts and had tin roofs. No more mean Thai guards were hitting us, beating us, kicking us, or raping our women anymore. We children lived in houses among fellow orphans. Depending on the size of the families, families either shared a house with other families or lived as a nuclear family. Unlike Old Kamput, there were more Khmers doing business with their fellow Khmers. Throughout my stay there, I was arranged to share a house with some of my fellow orphans from the Old Kamput and some new ones. Many were transferred from different holding centers to New Kamput. We slept in groups of four orphans. I shared a mat with three other boys: Ol, Vinn, and Nhean. Very quickly, we became close friends.

In the new camp, there was a music class, a dance class, a play or show class, and a Khmer language class in a big house within walking distance from where I stayed. After attending the Khmer language class, I always found the time to watch adults acting and singing. I was fond of modern musical shows. When the time came for a performance, I would run from my class or the shelter and take a front-row seat. The duet singing between lovers fascinated me. I sang along with them. They often took notice of my sweet and tender voice, but they never gave me a chance to join them. The costumes the characters wore were simple but fancy. To me, it was such a pleasure to watch, especially for a child like me who had lacked such pleasures.

Some of my fellow refugees were trying to become economically more self-reliant by buying and selling items. Soon, I started to spend less time fraternizing with the artists and started my own business. After class, I would burn charcoal for sale to other refugees. I built an in-ground oven out of clay by the barbed wire fence at the edge of the camp. I collected wood and stumps that had been thrown out by the contractors who built the houses in the camp. I burned these in my oven, covering it all up for a few days to allow the burned wood to turn into charcoal.

My three closest friends were completely different from one another. Ol was a gentle boy and was kind to me. He had a soft voice and got along well with me. Vinn never talked and always seemed sad because he missed his family and wanted to go home. Nhean was rough and showed no emotions, but loved to paint and draw. He made most of his money from selling his paintings and drawings. But Nhean was also sometimes annoying and I cried often because he teased me. Every time, he made me cry, I would tell him that I would move away to live with my uncle in Mairut. I always told him that he was a mean and annoying boy. My cursing encouraged him to give me a much harder time. The things that Nhean did to upset me the most were when he peed on my charcoal ovens and hid my books which made me late for my Khmer language class. The teacher would punish me by making me stand in front of the class, which made me ashamed for being late. At that time we were only taught how to write and read in Khmer. Since I was upset with Nhean so much, I stopped going to class hid myself under the shelter, and built a new oven.

I spent most of my days collecting wood near the barbed wire fence and stayed under the shelter blowing the flame. Soon my face was covered with black smoke from the burning charcoal. Ol and Vinn jokingly gave me a new title: *Thawke thyoung* (a wealthy charcoal owner). Nhean would comment about my title that I was black just like my charcoals. I tried to be patient with him, but I wanted revenge so badly. I had made up my mind that I would avoid him as much as I could. I had still not been reunited with my uncle, whom I hoped to live with someday soon. I continued to hide under the shelter to make charcoal. Also, I kept visiting the office to see if I could leave this place soon.

Months went by, but it seemed like a lifetime to me. I thought that the foreigners had forgotten about my desire to reconnect with my uncle. Every time that I was upset with my friends, I would tell them that I would leave very soon and go to live with my uncle. I told them that my uncle was tough and would beat up all the boys in the blink of an eye. They seemed not to take my words seriously. They said that I would not have a chance to go anywhere. Soon, I began to believe them. I started to lose hope of being reunited with my long-lost uncle.

However, one day in September, my wishes became a reality. One clear midmorning while I was busy blowing onto the flame in my oven, I heard Vinn call me, "Hong! Hong! *Barang*

is looking for you." I was so excited about the presence of a foreigner. I immediately stood up and hit my head on the ceiling
above me. I was knocked out. I fell forward, landing on top of
my oven, and breaking it to pieces. Luckily, I was not burned.
Vinn noticed that something had happened and ran to pull me
out to an open area. When I opened my eyes, I was told that a
foreign man and an Asian translator were waiting for me by the
steps of the house. I was so happy to see the American man and
Asian translator who had interviewed me in the IRC office in
Aranyaprathet a few months earlier. I thought I was dreaming.
The American man gave me a choice; did I still want to go to
Mirut or have my uncle come to the New Kamput? Just like my
previous decision, I stuck with it. He also told me that my uncle
was living with a family, but I still did not change my mind. I
told him that no matter what, I wanted to go to live in Mirut
with my uncle. I saw the smile on the American man's face. Although he did not promise me anything, I could see by his smile
that he was sincere. I believed that he would grant me my wish.

My eyes followed his tourist van as it was speeding away,
sending red dust into the air. I decided not to repair my oven
because I knew that I would be leaving this place soon. I put
out the fire and covered the oven with dirt to make it per-
manently disappear. I took the remaining charcoal to sell to
my regular customers. I made enough money and was ready to
start a new life with a member of my own family. That day, I
treated myself to a stick of ice cream made of jackfruit. I had a
flashback to when I was very small and lived in the village and
my friends would race to the ice cream man. We would all line

up and wait impatiently for him to pull out ice cream sticks from a metal ice cream box. The steam coming out from the ice box in the heat of the scorching sun excited us. We had to lick the ice cream fast before it melted.

That evening after dinner, I took my time to wash my body and hair with a bar of soap. Although my hair was still greasy after washing it, I felt clean. I also brushed my teeth and washed my old clothes, spreading them out to dry. Then I lay down on the mat at my usual sleeping place next to Ol wearing the brand new clothes that I had just changed into. I did not hear Vinn mention anything about the meeting I had with the American man, so I decided to keep it to myself. The next day, I went to the IRC office and was told to get ready to leave. I was so happy with the information but continued to keep it a secret because I wanted to surprise everyone.

The next day at midmorning, I saw a gray minivan come to a stop on a dike close to our shelter and my heart started to beat fast. I knew that I was about to be reunited with my uncle. The same men came directly to me and asked, "Are you ready to see your brother?" the American man asked through his translator. I corrected him and said, "No, he isn't my brother, he's my uncle." He smiled at this. While many of my friends were circling the two men, I went up the steps into the shelter to pack my stuff. When I finished packing, I went under the shelter, dug out a log, broke it, and took out a handful of Thai paper currency and some coins. All my friends were stunned. I put my money in a plastic bag with my clothes and said nothing.

I walked to the parked vehicle while the two men waited inside it. Many of my friends were alongside me. It seemed like I was being escorted to a limousine while my chauffeur and bodyguard waited in the vehicle. At that moment, I felt like I was an important person like Princess Sirindhorn paying her visit to Khao Lan. She had been escorted by heavily armed bodyguards while getting off and boarding a helicopter. After seeing I was leaving, Ol started to cry. He tried every possible way to make me change my mind. He refused to believe that it was real. He kept asking if I was leaving. I was sad and emotional as well. My tears fell, but I was not crying like Ol was. Nhean too was sad to see me leave and he hid in the back of a shelter crying with regret. When I got to the minivan, I wiped my tears and opened the door to take the backseat. I waved for the last time to my friends and said goodbye. That was the last time I saw them.

After looking at me through the rearview mirror, the American driver asked me why I was crying. I told him that I would miss my friends, but I was excited to be reunited with my uncle. He smiled and sped up. By noon, we reached Aranyaprathet. We stopped at the market and our translator bought me an orange soda that was sold in a clear plastic bag with a plastic straw in it. The plastic bag was tied with a couple of thin rubber bands to secure the liquid from being spilled. I sipped the liquid through the straw very slowly, while the minivan sped southwest. I enjoyed the taste of the cold drink.

By mid-afternoon, the vehicle stopped at a military checkpoint. The guard took a quick look at us. After seeing the two men in the front seats showing their badges, the guard opened the gate to let us go through. As the vehicle passed through the barrier, I turned around and looked through the back window to examine the guard and wondered if the guards in Mirut would be as mean as the ones in Khao Lan and Old Kamput. I had a bad feeling that they would be the same because I remembered what Sayan had said, that the kind ones were transferred and retrained. I knew I had to prepare for the worst. As we made our way into the center of the camp, I noticed that it was quite different from both the Kamput and Khao Lan camps because there were a lot fewer houses. There were no red gravel dikes like in Kamput, only white sand and dirt like at Khao Lan. I saw rows of barn-like buildings and houses scattered around. They looked like they had been built a long time ago.

As the minivan came to a stop in front of an office building, I looked through the window to my right and saw a boy with large eyes, wearing long pants and a short-sleeved shirt sitting next to a middle-aged man. Suddenly, my heart beat fast and I had butterflies in my stomach. I felt nervous and anxious at the same time. When I pulled the handle to open the door, I saw my uncle and the man stand up. They were waiting for me to get out. When the door swung open and I stepped out of the vehicle, the skinny boy looked at me with his large, curious eyes and seemed confused. He was not as excited as I had antic- ipated. I also noticed that he neither smiled nor attempted to greet me as I had expected. "What's wrong with him?" I mur- mured to myself. But the man who stood next to him reached out his hand to me. The American man asked me through his translator if the boy standing in front of me was my uncle. I told him that he was my uncle because I remembered his large eyes and his light skin complexion. Then, he turned to ask the boy the same question. I saw the smile finally appear on the skinny boy's face and he nodded his head in agreement. This was a huge relief. After knowing that we were related, the two men proceeded into the office building and the three of us got ready to leave. It was a joyous day for us.

My uncle introduced me to the man next to him and said that his name was Yun and that he had been living with him. Yun smiled and led us home. My uncle reached over to carry my plastic bag so that I could walk freely. His caring and consideration were the same as before. Even when we were small and lived in our village, my uncle always tried to take all the burdens upon himself. He always felt that he had an obligation to keep me safe because he knew that he was much stronger than I was. I always felt that he was my savior and protector. I was so thrilled to finally be with my uncle. I knew from that point on, I would never be alone again and felt safe with him nearby. We held hands like new lovers do and followed Yun to his shelter. Yun introduced me to his wife who had much darker skin than he had. They seemed to be the same age, in their late thirties. Yun said that his wife and he did not have any relatives; so he said that the four of us could live happily as one family. I thanked Yun and his wife for taking me in.

Yun was a Khmer Rouge soldier and had been stationed in Sre Ambel. He escaped the Vietnamese forces by going to the rainforest of Koh Kong and then, settling in Mirut at the beginning of 1979. Yun had seen that my uncle Hai was too young to wander around in the camp by himself and out of the goodness of his heart, Yun took him in. The two of them had lived together until Yun's future wife came along. When Yun was sick with malaria, she took care of him. After he realized that he needed a partner, Yun married the nice lady who had nursed him. Although Yun knew that she was not beautiful, her caring and kindness toward Yun won his heart.

Many Cambodian refugee families in Mirut shared space in the long open barn-like buildings. Like in Old Kamput, each family divided up an area for themselves. Hai and I slept in the hallway while Yun and his wife slept in a small room that was blocked off with plastic sheets. During the day, Yun would look for work to get some income for the family, and his wife cooked. Everyone used outdoor charcoal stoves to prepare their meals. Hai and I chipped in to help Yun and his wife in any way we could. We never took advantage of them because we appreciated that they treated us like their blood relatives. For that reason, I began to believe that not all Khmer Rouge people were cruel. At least I knew that Run and Yun were decent ones. Kou, Run, and Yun had never committed any crime against humanity that I knew of.

To sustain our family economy, we grew our vegetables and raised our chickens. There was plenty of land for gardening around the building. Hai and I cultivated a small plot of land near the manmade well. We planted lettuce *(spei)* and water spinach *(trakuon)*. We used water from the well to water our vegetables. We watered them twice a day, early in the morning and the evening. We used our pee and chicken poop to mix with water for fertilizer. Our lettuce and water spinach grew tall and plentiful. When they were ready to harvest, we cut them and sold them to vendors at an outdoor market by the entrance to the camp. Also, we raised a couple of chickens in a coop beneath the shelter's floor. We fed them with leftover rice grains, insects, and termites. We ate only our vegetables, but we raised chickens to sell. We got up before the sun rose to prepare our fertilizer and by dawn, our vegetables had been watered. After our chickens were fed and our garden had been taken care of, Hai and I would sneak out of the camp to collect *smao ach kok* (a type of weed that has white flowers with long thin stems that grow in the bushes) which we sold to Thai merchants at a flea market. People used the weed's flowers as an herbal medication. The best time to collect these weed flowers was after it had rained because then they looked fresh and clean, and they were easy to spot among the grasses and bushes.

Following one rainy day, I spotted a bunch of the plummy flowers of *smao ach kok* standing out among the wet bushes. I was so happy. It was my lucky day, I thought. I did not alarm Hai because I wanted to surprise him. I did not hesitate and fast like lightning, I was right on top of the weeds grabbing a handful of them and pulling them out from the bush. All of a sudden, I felt a burning sting on my lips. I was not sure what it was, but soon noticed a dozen angry hornets bursting out from the bush charging at my face and head. I knew that I had just accidentally pulled out their nest.

I felt the burn on my lips getting worse so I cried out loud and ran to a nearby puddle of water. I dipped my lips into it. I must have looked like a duck drilling his beak into the swamp for a leech. Standing in the distance, Hai began to laugh very hard. Besides the pain, I became irritated with Hai laughing at me. My lips started to swell. When I stood up to curse Hai, I could hardly see him. Seeing my thick lips covering half of my face, Hai ignored my cursing and laughed even harder. He laughed so hard that he could not talk. He started to cough violently and I noticed that he held his stomach to stop the pain that caused him to laugh so hard. I had no sympathy for him. Instead, I continued to curse him. "You know Lord Buddha can see everything. I pray that one day you will face the consequences," I said to him. I demanded that he stop making fun of me, but he would not stop. I started to walk back to the camp. He ran after me and pleaded with me to stop being angry. It was afternoon and we decided to call it a day.

Within a short period, we made good money from selling our chickens, vegetables, and *smao ach kok.* I had enough money to buy my dream clothes, a white long-sleeved shirt and a pair of long khaki pants. Ever since the first time I saw my teacher's uniform when my mother had introduced me to him on my first day of school in my village, I had been dreaming that one day I would dress like him. Now, that day was about to come. But I waited for the right time to purchase the shirt and pants. I felt that my wish was about to happen.

However, things began to change. We noticed that Yun and his wife argued over us daily. The wife wanted us to give her all our hard-earned money, but the husband felt that we should keep it because we risked our lives for it every day. Besides, the domestic violence among other refugee families in our shelter was too painful for us to witness. One of the men who lived next to us had been beating up his pregnant wife every single day. He kicked, pushed, punched, and whipped his wife every day, causing her great pain and making her head bleed. We were horrified by the violent acts; we constantly worried about the poor woman. We wanted to help, but we were scared of the consequences that we would face. Most shocking was that no one seemed to care about making any attempt to prevent the violence.

I learned that the majority of the adult males who lived in our shelter had been members of the Khmer Rouge armed forces. Therefore, the violence they had witnessed or committed was deep-seated in them. Although I had never seen Yun beat up his wife, the yelling and screaming frightened me. Besides, Yun's wife whom we called *Yeay Khmao* (black grandma) was jealous of our presence. One day, Yun told us that he was about to have a family of his own, but his pregnant wife feared that he would pay more attention to us than his family. To avoid causing trouble between Yun and his wife, and seeing the domestic violence around us, we decided to move. At this time, Hai and I decided to stop doing our usual business. During this stressful period, I secretly visited the IRC office seeking a way for my uncle and me to join the orphanage. After getting a green light from the office, one day I asked Hai to tell Yun that we would join the orphanage. Even though it was sad for Yun, he agreed that it would be best for us to leave his family.

Like in Kamput, orphan children in Mirut were taken care of by international relief agencies. Food, shelter, and clothing were provided. I convinced Hai that we would have a brighter future if we joined other children living in an orphanage center. With the consent of Yun, the process went smoothly and soon we were on our way out of his guardianship to pursue our new lives. After living with them for one month, we left Yun and his wife. It was the right decision, to move out of a small adoptive family to join one big family of thirty or more children at the orphanage center. Although we were among strangers, we were happy. During the day, international relief workers were watching us, many of whom were American, French, English, Japanese, and Thai. But at night we children took care of each other. We were brothers and sisters. Chhay Sarim was my closest friend. We slept next to each other and sometimes talked all night. We talked about everything. Sometimes, we talked about girls. I told him that I wanted to marry a city girl. We giggled and teased each other about who would fall in love first.

Foreign workers spend a lot of time teaching us about living abroad. They taught us geography by showing us a map of the world. They also taught us science, but I did not believe them that the earth was round that it traveled around the sun, and that the moon traveled around the earth. It completely differed from what I had previously heard the elders tell us, children. Also, they introduced us to blue jeans, boots, and t-shirts. The Asian workers, especially the Japanese, taught us about technology. They showed us pictures in magazines of automobiles, airplanes, computers, and watches.

Flashlights were very popular among us children. We would save up our earnings to buy a flashlight, to compete with each other for who had the brightest and sharpest beam. We also used flashlights to create our puppet shows by shining beams on walls or white sheets. I liked to make my friends go, *"Oooh! Aaah! Wow!"* when I made a shadow of a rabbit which I had learned from my father when I was a little boy. It was the only kind of show I was good at. I would beam my flashlight through a mosquito net to make a shadow with my palms, using my fingers to make a rabbit's legs and ears. Because the orphanage center was at the edge of the camp, at night, Khmer Rouge fighters would come down from the mountains and abduct children from the center to join them in fighting the Vietnamese forces. Some of the children were convinced that by joining the Khmer Rouge to fight the invaders this would help them to receive high-ranking positions. Many of them left the center to join the Khmer Rouge and then died in the mountains. These incidents frightened and concerned the international relief agencies and led them to find other places to resettle us.

The international workers decided to transfer the rest of us to the kitchen hall to live. From that point on, we were not allowed to roam around at night and flashlights were temporarily banned to avoid being seen by Khmer Rouge abductors. In the 1940s, 1950s, and 1960s, Cambodian children living along the eastern borders of Khmer and South Vietnam faced the abductors of *Bramat Bramong* of Vietminh. Now, in the late 1980s, children in refugee camps at the western border of Thai and Khmer faced *Krom Chab Khmeng* of Khmer Rouge. Because of the Khmer Rouge incidents, relief workers started to stay with us at night. Also, we were assigned to take turns to stay on guard at night.

All of these happenings now reminded me of those earlier times when I had escaped the Vietnamese in the Cambodian jungles. Back then, Run had assigned one of his men and one of us children to take turns being on the lookout for enemies at night while the rest tried to get some sleep. If we saw anything suspicious, a guard would get ready to shoot and the other one would quietly wake everyone up to get into position—ready to either run or attack. For us at an orphanage center, we wanted to make sure that the *Krom Chab Khmeng* would not sneak in at night and abduct us. Soon we were told to get ready to be transferred to a new holding center of Khao-I-Dang, in northeastern Thailand. If I remember correctly, there were no more than fifteen of us left to be resettled because of the abductions. Our transfer was kind of secret and fast. There was no time for us to say goodbye to friends who were not living among us.

One breezy morning in January 1981, we were asked to line up in front of the main office for a head count. Soon a white tourist van driven by a young Thai man came to a stop before us. The vehicle seemed small, but we all fit in because we did not have much to carry. Most of us weighed less than one hundred pounds and each of us was less than six feet tall, so the space was enough for roughly fifteen of us. Our van sped up along a paved road and headed north. It was the first time I had ridden in a vehicle with a group of people whom I trusted. It was the best ride ever. We talked, we sang, and we laughed. We did not care too much about the scenery. Our four-hour ride seemed like a quick one because of our joy. By late afternoon, our vehicle pulled left onto a red gravel road and came to a stop at a checkpoint. After a brief exchange of paperwork between the foreigner who had followed us and a Thai guard official, the barrier was lifted to allow our vehicle to go through. We were dropped off in front of an open bamboo building by the entrance to the camp. But it was too late for us to continue to our final destination when our entrance passes had been cleared.

That night, we stayed in an open building, *Montipet Kandal* (central hospital), run by the

International Committee of the Red Cross. Khao-I-Dang camp was situated at the foot of Khao-I-Dang Mountain on the Khmer-Thai border. The camp was administered by the Thai Ministry of Interior and the United Nations High Commissioner for Refugees. The next morning, we were transported by van to the camp. Bamboo huts were clustered along the red gravel road. They were built of straw and stood on stilts along man-made ditches. After a quick ride, we got to our final destination the Children Center Section One *(Koma Komprea Sangkat Muoy).* The center was located by the water tower and was surrounded by ditches and road-like dikes of red gravel. The center was my home for one year and eight months from January 1981 to August 1982.

Every day, I saved my fruits and crackers to sell to vendors at a local market so I could get some money to buy clothes, and English textbooks such as *Essential English,* and to pay for English lessons. Private English classes were taught in the evening near my center. The class was taught by one of the two famous Khmer refugee teachers named Srun. The two best-known teachers at the time in Khao-I-Dang were Srun and Prok. Although I attended both Srun and Prok's classes, I spent more time learning from Srun because his class was close to the center where I stayed. Every evening before he started his lesson, Srun would go around the classroom to collect his fee. People who could not afford to pay him would sit outside the classroom. If they were lucky, they would find a hole in the wall to peek through to see what he wrote on the blackboard. Like many of my friends, I could not afford to sit in the classroom often. I decided to study outside the classroom by going through the pages of *Essential English I* and listening to Srun pronounce the words. Outside, I would repeat after him.

At first, the English language was outlawed by the Thais. But by 1981, they lifted the restriction, and quickly it became very popular. We wanted to learn English because we were hoping to be able to write letters to the Western embassies in Bangkok or to communicate with foreigners. Every time we saw them come to the camp, we would surround them and hope that they would pick us to go to live in their countries. The English language seemed to be the only passport for refugees to escape from behind the barbed wire fence.

In addition, sports were big for us, especially soccer, volleyball, and ping-pong. We could hardly wait for the weekend's
soccer and volleyball matches between Cambodian refugees in
Khao-I-Dang and Thai athletes from Aranyaprathet. The soccer field in Section Five was always packed with refugees to
cheer our fellow Cambodian refugee athletes. My heroes were
T-28 (an American fighter jet), *Stang* (hawk), and *Kaphleung
Thom* (big gun), these were their nicknames because they were
fast, quick, and strong. We never learned their real names. Every time our team got the ball, we went crazy cheering for them
to make the Thais angry. Sometimes, the Thais played dirty.
They would kick the Cambodian players with their cleats. The
Cambodians would try to defend themselves. *T-28's* position
was a winger, *Stang* was a center forward, and *Kaphleung Thom*
was a defender. *T-28* would steal the ball from the other team,
and pass it to *Stang,* who almost always would make a goal. *Kaphleung Thom* would never let anyone get by him if they came
his way. If someone did get by him, he would make them jump
and kick the ball back, all the way to the other end zone. However, the competition was never fair. Although the Cambodians played much better than the Thais did, they had to let the
Thai team win to make the guards happy so that they would
not beat up the prisoners. The only crimes the prisoners committed were either getting caught by sneaking out of the camp
to do business with Thai merchants or sneaking into the camp
illegally. There were a few times when the Thais lost to the
Cambodians. The guard's captain, whom we called *Ah Sak Bei,*
would beat up the prisoners severely in retaliation. It was also

the same with volleyball games. The final scores were always in favor of the Thais. We all knew that they had cheated, but we were just happy to see the skills our teammates exhibited.

Many of us also had a small business. With the money that I saved up, I bought a baby chicken and raised it by myself. I made a small coop from bamboo to keep it inside. I always left a few grains of rice for my chicken. I also collected insects, particularly termites, to feed it. After a couple of months, my chicken had grown healthy and big. I took it to a flea market known as *Phsa Deihoy* (a dusty market) in Section Nine and sold it for 90 baht of Thai money, a little over three U.S. dollars. I spent some of my money on a cold drink and my favorite snacks of *nom pum* (a waffle) and *nom cheung chrouk* (a fried cake made out of flour and green beans that is shaped like a pig's toe).

On my way back to the shelter, I saw a six-year-old boy who was a dealer of *labeng kreab ampil* (a tamarind seed game, more like dice, or what I have since come to know in the United States as three-card monte). He was encircled by a crowd of boys and young men betting on the game. I stood there observing his trick for a few hands. After seeing he was small and seemed to be naive, I started to count my money. I had 70 baht left. Out of greed, I decided to play and was sure that I could make double just in the blink of an eye. I waited for one more hand and this time I was ready to play. I tried to concentrate on his hands before I decided to make a bet. I did not blink, fixing the seeds and the tin can. I saw he inserted two tamarind seeds under the tin. He took his hands off and called for bettors to place the money on the plastic sheet with a handwritten number from one to six. I was so sure that the two seeds had been placed under the cover by the dealer. Without thinking further, I threw my remaining 70 baht on number two. The majority of bettors started to bet on number two, too. My heart was pounding with excitement. All I wanted was to bet just once and walk home with plenty of cash. That was my goal.

I fought to put my hand on top of the cover and win. "I'm going to hit a jackpot," I said. The boy asked us, "Are you ready?" We all said, "Yes," with a big smile on our faces. "One, two, three," the little boy counted. After "three" he lifted the cover and we all saw, only one tamarind seed left on the plastic sheet. We did not let that boy get away with it easily. We demanded he show us his hands and fingers just to make sure that he had not hidden another seed in his palms or between his fingers. The poor kid stood up, shaking his pants and showing his hands, but nothing was found. I had nothing to argue about. I just walked away screaming, "I hate gambling."

Hearing that Cambodia's Prince Sihanouk, accompanied by his wife Princess Monique, his daughter Princess Bopha Devi, and his former Prime Minister Son Sann were coming to visit Khao-I-Dang, I pushed my way through the crowd to the front, where I waited anxiously for the prince to come by so I could touch his hands, which I had heard were soft and smooth like cotton. Some people said his hands were boneless. Sure enough, I was able to see him up close and reached my hands to touch one of his. It was smooth and soft like I was told. After touching his hand, I rubbed my own on my head and my face because I heard that he was a divine king. God chose him to come here to give us blessings and bring hope to us refugees. I was convinced that by touching the divine former King Sihanouk's hands I would receive good luck. I felt like I was the happiest and luckiest boy in the whole world that day. When I got home, I bragged that I had touched the god prince's hand and my bragging continued for days.

One day in the afternoon on the way home from school, I decided to stop by the *Phsa Deihoy* as usual, looking to buy my favorite snack of *nom cheung chrouk.* I ran into an old man who was staring at me. At first, I tried to ignore him. After seeing the fixed gaze of the old man, I began to think that he must have known me from somewhere. I decided to approach him. After giving him a *sampeah,* the old man grabbed my hand and asked for my name. I asked him if he knew me, but he did not respond. He looked at my face and then he started to read my palm. I knew exactly what he was doing. I did not resist. I let him read both of my palms patiently. *Chaw eng mean samnang* (grandchild, you are lucky), said the old man. He continued saying that I would be traveling far away soon and would become a leader someday. I did not believe him but thanked him anyway for the energy and hopefulness. I told him that I was just a poor orphan. He smiled and said, "You'll be all right."

Listening to international news was huge in the camp. No one had television, but we listened to the radio. Everybody was hungry for news about the future of us refugees. We all wanted to leave this barbed wire cage to seek a better future in another country, especially in the West. The Voice of America (VOA) was perhaps the only reliable source of news at the time. The news was broadcast on the radio twice a day, early in the morning and in the evening. The shelter that had a radio became the center of information. News listeners and sellers would gather there regularly.

We boys took turns bringing water home for cooking, bathing, washing our faces, and brushing our teeth. Every morning while standing in line waiting for the water trucks to come and fill up the tanks, I would listen to VOA broadcast live from Washington, D.C. The newsmen talked about world politics. The man who lived near the water tanks turned up the volume of his radio every morning so we all could hear VOA. He only turned on his AM/FM radio during the hours when the news was on to save the batteries. The broadcast was in the Khmer language. Among all the world leaders I heard on the radio, I mostly remember Jimmy Carter and Ronald Reagan. VOA mentioned the American policy toward Cambodian refugees. Although I did not know much about the American and Western policies toward Cambodian refugees, I knew that they were trying to do something to bring us to their countries. We called them *Brates Tibei* (third countries). Everybody anxiously waited and hoped to be chosen to resettle in a third country. I, too, impatiently waited to leave the camp but was not sure which country I wanted to go to. I thought about Australia. The majority of refugees wanted to resettle in America. I went to the water tanks every morning, so I could hear the news.

One day Sarou, an assistant director at our center, came to get me from school for an interview with a foreigner. We met in the bamboo office and Sarou was the translator. After getting details of my background, he asked me which country I would prefer to be resettled in. I told him that Australia would be my first choice because I liked the name of the country. He smiled and said he had lived in America. He also said, "America is a beautiful country." I thanked him and then gave him a *sampeah.*

After a month went by, one night I had a dream thinking that our shelter had burned to the ground. I woke up from this dream and screamed out loud that the shelter was on fire, causing everyone to get startled awake. I was sweating. That night I could not go back to sleep. I heard people say that having a dream of burning a home was a bad sign and something awful could happen to me any time. I was so frightened and thought of all the horrible things that were possible. The next day, I did not want to go anywhere. I told Hai about my dream, but he seemed not to take it seriously. Unlike me, Hai had never been superstitious. He believed in facts and his abilities. That morning, I was late for an arts and crafts class where I was learning to sew clothes. While I was in deep thought, Sarou came running, and out of breath was calling me to hurry to the center. "Oh! Lord Buddha! Something is going wrong with me," I murmured. I stood there hesitating, unsure if I should follow Sarou. After getting permission to leave, I slowly followed Sarou out of the classroom.

"Is something bad happening?" I asked.

"No, in fact, it is good news, come on, hurry up," he replied. I felt relieved and ran after him.

When I got to the office, our director asked me if I wanted to leave the camp. I started to cry. In my mind, I was thinking that they would send me back to the border and would abandon me in the minefields. He asked, "Why are you crying?" I begged him to let me continue staying at the center. "You have been selected to go to live in *Brates Tibei*," he continued with a big smile on his face. At first, I did not believe him. I looked at Sarou and he assured me that I would get picked up by a driver soon. My body felt so light, it seemed like I was flying. I stopped crying immediately and wiped away my tears. I would be among the first few orphans to leave Khao-I-Dang. I asked our director if my uncle would be leaving with me. He said he did not know. I wanted to tell Hai about the news, but he was still in school.

About thirty minutes later, a white pickup truck arrived and stopped on the red gravel road by the entrance to the center. After spotting the vehicle, Sarou grabbed me by the hand and asked me to hop into the back. He rode in the front with a Thai driver who said he was taking me to an interview. I felt like I was in heaven, and tears of joy rolled down my cheeks. But they dried quickly from the wind from the speeding pickup truck. Everything reminded me of the day two years earlier when I had been in the back of the Thai police's pickup truck going to the first refugee camp Old Kamput. All of a sudden, everything was quite emotional for me.

I tried to remember everything about my family and the events that happened. During the short ride, the vehicle stopped on the road in front of the office of IRC. I entered the office very anxiously. But I was ready because I had been through this kind of process before when I had an interview with the wonderful American IRC officer in Aranyaprathet. In the office I sat quietly, trying to gather lots of information into my head just in case they required me to provide it to them. I tried to look for Sarou, but he was gone. While I was in deep thought, a Thai lady with a heavy accent asked me to follow her. I took a deep breath and walked closely behind her and then, sat down in a chair across from her desk.

The first question that came from her mouth was in Khmer: *ah meaw eng see sva reu see svay?* (Little one, do you eat monkeys or mangos?) That was a weird question, I thought. I was not prepared for that one. I stared at the ground trying to find an answer. *Khnhom awt see sva te* (I don't eat monkeys), I said.

She said good, and continued, "Did you attend your parents' wedding?"

"I never saw them get married," I answered.

"Are you married?" she asked.

"No, I'm not. I'm too young," I replied.

"Do you have a girlfriend?" She stared straight into my eyes.

"No, I don't have a girlfriend," I replied with a shy smile and then looked down at the ground.

"Is your family waiting for you at home?" she asked, shuffling through her papers.

"No, I'm an orphan," I told her.

"Why do you want to go to America?"

To this, I said, "I want to eat a lot of ice cubes. I also want to learn English and ask people in power to tell the bad people in my country to stop killing innocent people and to start doing good things for them."

She laughed and then said, "You're a good boy." I thanked her and then gave her a *sampeah* of goodbye.

When I walked outside of the office, I saw Sarou joining a crowd of people checking names that had been posted on the bulletin board. These were the people who had so far been approved to leave Khao-I-Dang.

CHAPTER 10

Hope

*A*fter the IRC interview, I began going to the office every day to check for my name on the bulletin board. I began to miss some classes because I had a lot of hope that I would soon be going on a long journey to freedom.

A week later, the good news came. I saw my name posted on the bulletin board with the instructions that I was to go to Phanat Nikhom Transit Center. My final day arrived in August, after twenty months of long waiting in Khao-I-Dang. That evening, we, the music lovers, including Hai stayed up later than usual. We sat in a circle by a garden with beautiful flowers under a clear sky. We did not talk, only sang and played acoustic guitar. It was a sad night for many of us. Among us who cared deeply about music, only I was planning to leave the next morning and go to a faraway land.

That evening, I sang a farewell song with my close friend at the center named Dara. It was a duet titled *Lea Heuy Sumatra* (Goodbye Sumatra) written by President Lon Nol in the early 1970s when he went on a state visit to Indonesia. He fell in love with the island of Sumatra and was attracted to one of the Indonesian women while on his state visit. Upon his return to Cambodia, he wrote the song to express his emotions about leaving the island.

The next morning, a few of us packed our bags and said goodbye to our friends. We walked to the bus stop in front of the performing stage in Section Two. There were hundreds of new faces and many refugee families with small children who were waiting to be picked up just like us. It was exciting to see such activities. We clung to our group of orphans from Sections One and Nine. Soon, two or three jumbo buses arrived. Quickly, we showed our documents to foreign workers who checked them and then we got on the first bus. After everyone had boarded a vehicle, our bus traveled south at full speed. About four hours later, we arrived at our destination of Phanat Nikhom in Chonburi province. We were led to a one-floor stucco building with a tin roof and lots of windows. I picked a sleeping spot on the concrete floor and then began to wander around. It would be quite an adjustment from sleeping on a bamboo floor to now sleeping on concrete. But I did not complain. It was not new to me, as I had slept on cement floors before during the nightmare era of Pol Pot in Chi Kha and Veal Renh.

After a few days of resettlement in Phanat Nikhom, I had another interview. I was asked about my life before the Pol Pot regime, during it, and then after it was overthrown. They also asked me about my escape to Thailand and all the places I had lived as a refugee. By this time, I had become an expert at telling my own story.

Chonburi was much smaller than Khao-I-Dang. Many of the shelters in this new camp were built out of stucco and wood. Every morning, I attended a class in basic English that was

taught by volunteers from the Catholic Office for Emergency
Relief and Refugees. They taught us how people in America,
Europe, and other developed countries use toilets, forks, and
knives. They also taught us about the governments of the U.S.,
Canada, Australia, New Zealand, and the countries of Western
Europe. I looked at the map of the world every day—especially
America, trying to learn the names of each state and their cap-
ital cities. Every evening we gathered on the grass watching an
outdoor movie about the life and struggles of Jesus Christ.

To help me from missing the fun times I had with my
friends, I decided to copy into a notebook the songs I had sung
at Old Kamput and Khao-I-Dang. Some nights I wrote letters
to Hai, Dara, and Sodavy in Khao-I-Dang. Every time I received their letters, I would read them over and over again remembering the fun times we had together. Their letters made
me so emotional. I only read them at night. Sometimes I cried,
but sometimes I laughed, it all depended on the contents of the
letters. Showing emotion like this, some of my new friends
thought that I was a bit crazy.

Dara always complained that she and her two young
brothers, Veng and Chhan, were like birds who, despite living
in an open cage, could not fly away. She also mentioned that
she missed duet singing with me and entertaining our friends.
Sodavy complained about how he felt losing me and said that
he had no energy to go to school. He started to skip classes and
was punished by our director for that. He said that he missed
me every night. He refused to allow other children to sleep in
my spot. Hai worried that he might not be able to see me again

soon, which did not happen until after I arrived in America. He told me in a letter that Phany had been sleeping on his lap singing sad songs every evening. He also wrote that Phany complained that she and her younger siblings Phally and Sambath seemed like the talking birds of *sarika keo* (a family of mynah birds) that are caged. Phany was the goddaughter of the former Cambodian Prime Minister Long Boreth, who had served under the Khmer Republic. He had been murdered at his residence in Phnom Penh by the Khmer Rouge soon after they entered the city.

Hai had been always shy with girls. He never showed any feelings toward any of them. I could imagine how strange it must have been for him to have a teenage girl sleeping on his lap singing sad songs. This part made me smile and sometimes laugh out loud. Sodavy and Dara always ended their letters by asking me not to forget about them. It was the first time that I understood the value of friendship and family.

All the refugees in the processing center of Chonburi were required to have physical examinations, which required us to be naked. Everyone had to take off their clothes to allow the examiners to take a good look and to make sure we were free of skin diseases. I saw many women and young girls refuse to take off their clothes. Some cried with embarrassment, while some complained that it was the first time strangers had seen their naked bodies. Some said that they would feel ashamed fearing that people would talk about them.

When it came to my turn for my physical exam, I un-buttoned my shirt while standing in line in the center's large stucco building. I saw two Asians: a man and a woman, and one male foreign doctor sitting in the small examination area walled off with white curtains. When I entered the examination area, right away, I took off my shirt and dropped it on the floor, and, then, I pulled down my shorts to my ankles. I spun around very fast so that they could check my naked body. I was very shy, particularly with having an Asian woman nurse inspect my body. It reminded me of when Malee pointed at my private parts and laughed. I did not want it to happen again. So, I quickly pulled up my shorts and ran out very fast. When I came outside, one of the men in the long line, pointed at me. Immediately, I realized that I was still half-naked and shirtless. After realizing that my shorts were not completely covering my private parts, I turned around and went back into the room as fast as I could. One of the men asked me in Khmer to drop my shorts again, and the doctor ordered me to turn around and I did as I was asked. After seeing a nod from the examiners, I picked up my shirt from the floor, pulled up my shorts all the way, and slowly walked out of the room with great relief.

About a week after the physical examination, I had to go through another round of interviews. This time it was regarding the United States of America. The day of my interview, I walked into a stucco building and sat down face-to-face across from a big tough-looking American man with a crew cut. He started by giving me his name and title with the Immigration and Naturalization Service (INS). He told me through his translator to answer only what was asked and to be brief and clear. I was very nervous about the way he looked and the tone of his voice. He also said that if he liked all of my answers, he would let me go to America. But if he did not like them, then he would send me back to Khao-I-Dang. After hearing that, I was scared of him. I saw that he looked through my file very carefully. I tried very hard to stay calm and hoped that I would remember all the answers that I had given at my previous interviews. *Now, I understand why America is so powerful because her people are tough like this man*, I remember thinking to myself.

"Where is your father?" he asked.

"I don't know," I answered.

"How about your mother?"

I said, "She died."

He continued, "Do you have any siblings who are alive?"

I said, "I don't know."

"Have you ever been to America?"

"No, I have never."

He asked again, "Would you like to live in America?"

I answered quickly, "Yes, I do, sir."

He went on, "What do you want to do in America?"

I told him, "I want to go to school to learn your language."

He smiled and continued, "What do you want to be when you grow up?"

I said, "I don't know, perhaps to help people who are in need just like you are doing now."

I saw the smile on his face grow and he said, "I would like to tell you, that you are going to America. What do you say, big boy?"

I thanked him warmly. Seeing he was happy, I took the opportunity to ask him about having my uncle Hai also go to America with me. I told him through our translator that he was the only family I had left, and I hoped to live with him in America. I saw him pull out a notepad and write down my uncle's information on it carefully. I thanked the two men and gave them my *sampeah* of goodbye.

I ran back to the shelter to tell the good news to my friends. At the shelter, many of my friends surrounded me when I shared the news. Some pushed and others punched me with joy and envy at the same time. While I was taking my shirt off, one of the boys pushed me so I did my spin kick, but I lost my balance and fell. I used my left hand to protect my head from landing on the cement floor. Then, I heard a pop like someone had broken a peeled stick of sugarcane. I saw the boy who had pushed me, look at me in panic. I got up, looked at my arm and I saw that my wrist was bent at a 90-degree angle. A bone was sticking out through my skin. I pulled my hand and the bones came back together. It hurt so much. One of my friends yelled out, "Go to the clinic, now." I held my arm, ran quickly to the clinic, and told an Asian nurse what had happened. She looked at my arm and yelled in an angry tone, "You're such a dummy." She said that I would have to stay there until my arm healed. I started to cry and begged her not to tell the Thais and foreign workers about the accident. She did not respond. She asked me to follow her to an X-ray station. After the X-ray was finished, she put a cast on my broken arm. She told me to come back to see her very early the next morning before the clinic opened.

I thanked her and left very disappointed with the foolish antics of my friends.

That night, I could not sleep because I was worried that they might make me stay behind to take care of my arm. I waited anxiously for the morning to come. At around six the next morning, I went to see the nurse at the shelter as she had suggested. She gave me a plastic bag with my X-ray in it and some pain medications to take. She suggested that I not let the examiner in Bangkok know about the incident. She further warned me that I would have to stay behind if anyone found out about it. I thanked the kind nurse with respect and went back to my shelter. For the whole day, I napped and took care of myself. That night, I asked my friends to help me pack my belongings and then, I tried to get some sleep to gain strength.

At midmorning the next day, I was told to go to the building across the street to wait for the bus. My heart was beating fast with excitement and worry at the same time. At the station, many people were waiting for the bus, but I did not know anyone. And my arm hurt. There were all ages of people waiting for the bus. It was another emotional morning in which I would be saying goodbye to all my friends with whom I shared many memories from the past two months of living in Chonburi. Unlike other occasions, this group of friends did not cry. Among the refugees were Cambodians, Vietnamese, Laotians, and Hmong. I saw some older men with bamboo marijuana bongs on their backs.

As soon as the bus arrived, I got on, carrying the plastic bag with my belongings, while hiding my broken arm inside my shirt. I sat close to the back trying to comfort myself. I did not care about the scenery this time. My mind was full, thinking about my friends, my arm, and the future ahead of me. About two hours later, we got to the capital city of Bangkok. I looked out the window. I saw things that I would never have imagined. The city was indescribable. It was big; it was noisy with motorcycles, cars, and buses; white smoke was coming out of factory buildings; pedestrians were walking freely everywhere. The rivers, bridges, highways, buildings, markets, and motorists made my head spin. After thirty minutes of fighting the afternoon rush, we came to a stop at the temporary holding compound for refugees, Lumpini. After getting off the bus, we were led into the camp, which looked like a prison. The compound had been used as a prison for those who had committed serious crimes.

There were concrete walls and tall fences of barbed wire around the compound. There was tall grass and piles of trash all around the long rows of low bungalows. The smell of raw sewage and pollution made us choke. As soon as I walked into one of the bungalows, I saw some of my old orphanage friends. We were given sandwiches for dinner that evening and bottled water. It was my first time drinking purified water. I saw small children crawling under the bungalows looking for things. Some came out and showed their families that they had found some Thai coins. I saw some elderly Hmong inhaling liquid marijuana through bongs just like the guards did at Khao Lan. Others smoked joints. Unlike the guards at Khao Lan, these men were quiet and peaceful.

Soon, the sun set and night came. I saw lights in the distance. I heard the sounds of sirens and airplane engines. I saw
red and white beams of lights circling above in the night sky.
I realized that I was very close to the airport and that soon I
could be on my long journey to a "third country." I was convinced that the old man at the flea market in Khao-I-Dang was
half right about my destiny. I walked away from the building
toward the bright light in the distance. I stood there for a long
time counting the red lights on buildings in the distance and
timing the circling lights. I thought of Hai and all my close
friends at Khao-I-Dang and wondered if they were still singing and playing their acoustic guitars at this hour. I tried to
think of everyone I could, the good people and the mean ones.
I quietly said my goodbyes to all of them. Since I did not know
with whom I would live, I tried to imagine what my new family might be like. I had many questions: what kind of people
would they be? What would they look like? Would they like
me? Would I like them? How would they treat me? Would they
take me in as a member of their own family? Also, I prayed
to have older siblings. I wanted to be a younger brother so
that I could be spoiled. Being the oldest had never been fun.
I was the one to blame for all the bad things that my younger
siblings did. Certainly, I wanted to be different in my new life.
I thought of my mother and wished that she was next to me.

At the same time, I tried to remember all the deceased
members of my family, including my grandfather Cheng, my
grandmothers Khan and Kuoy, my brother Mouch, and especially my beloved mother Muoy. I searched for their faces

among the stars. Although I did not see them, I made up some constellations to represent them. My tears started to come down, and it got very dark. Suddenly, I heard a voice from the building behind me announcing, "We're boarding the plane tomorrow." My mind clicked right away and I remembered what the nurse had said to me the day before.

Many of the refugees could not sleep because of swarms of mosquitoes. I told one of the children who was lying next to me that I had to go to the bathroom, which was quite a ways from the bungalow building. It was dark inside. I was thinking about what to do to make sure the physical examiner would not notice my broken arm. Something came to my mind. I had to find a way to take the cast off. I found a stick and a rock by the bathroom. I sat by the long cement water tank soaking the plaster in the cold water waiting for it to become soft and loose. After a few hours, the plaster was still bonded firmly to my arm. I decided to poke it with a stick and gently hit the plaster with a rock to break it into pieces. I did not give up. I sat in the bathroom alone all night soaking, poking, and striking the plaster to make it soft so it would break off. Sure enough, before dawn, I was able to remove it from my arm.

By dawn, everyone was up, and around nine or ten o'clock, the examiner came asking us orphans to line up so she could check our bodies. I was in the back of the line. Everyone took off their shirts and pants just like we had done in Chonburi. I could not wait for my turn. I was so anxious. I was not shy now. I wanted to get it over with as quickly as possible. When my turn came, I spun around slowly, putting my hands on my hips so the examiner could not see that one of my arms was broken. The new nurse nodded her head. "Very good," she said.

After dinner, I gathered all my belongings, putting them in a big white plastic bag that had written on it "ICM" (Inter-governmental Committee for Migration). In the bag were my travel documents, a copy of my arm X-ray, my pain medica-tions, and my fancy gray colored pants—they looked like the ones Kong Samoeun wore in the movies shown in Cambodia before the Khmer Rouge—and a white short-sleeved shirt like the ones students wore to school in Cambodia and Thailand. I had bought them in Khao-I-Dang. These were my dream clothes. The kind of clothes I had begged my father to buy for me. I had never worn them and had kept them for special oc-casions.

I promised myself to wear them in America to impress American girls. While I was imagining and feeling my beauti-ful clothes, the bus came. It was dark. We were asked to line up for a name check and head count.

I boarded the bus and sat in a comfortable cushioned seat waiting for everyone else to board. I looked into my bag one last time to make sure I was not missing anything. I hugged the bag and waited patiently. The bus started to move and my heart beat fast. The Bangkok night was breathtaking. I had never seen such beautiful, colorful city lights in my whole life. About fifteen minutes later, we were dropped off at the door of an airport terminal. We were divided into small groups and then walked inline into a huge glass building with a shiny floor. There were escalators and elevators taking people up and down which confused me. When I looked around, many of the people who had been with me were gone and were all somewhere else. I felt confused and a bit lost. I was kind of nervous because I saw some Thai travelers look at us with disgust and shoo us away.

I went and sat alone by an escalator, holding my bag and my swollen arm to avoid getting in their way. I was hurting inside and out. Around ten or eleven o'clock, a young, slender American man came to tell us to move closer to the ticket counter to get ready for check-in. He said with a Boston accent through a translator, "Hello folks, my name is Mark, and I will be helping you get on the plane tonight." He told us to stick together and then he left. While we waited in the waiting area, I noticed some Thai airport workers demanding one of the elderly Hmong men to give up his long bamboo bong, but he refused. After a while, he was escorted out leaving his family behind to wait for him. I did not see him return.

CHAPTER 11

Flying Angels

*A*round midnight, we finally entered the gate and walked onto a double-deck Boeing 747 jumbo jet with the word, *"THAI"* on it. It was big and beautiful inside. There were many rows of comfortable-looking seats. As I was led to my row, I looked around and only saw foreigners and strangers putting their stuff away, or adjusting their seat belts. All my friends were gone. There were only adults in nice, clean outfits; I was assigned to a seat between two foreign men. I greeted them with *sampeah,* but they only smiled back at me. Neither of them spoke my language.

Thirty minutes after midnight, the plane slowly moved away from the gate and then took off. I looked through the window and saw the city was bright with a lot of different kinds of lights. "Wow! I can't believe that I'm flying," I said to myself. Soon we were in the sky. Although I did not believe in angels, I tried to look for them anyway, just in case they were real. I remember when I was a young boy, I believed angels were playing and swimming in the sky above me. The elderly people in my village told us children that when we heard the sound of thunder it meant the angels were playing and that when it rained, they were swimming.

Soon everything was quiet on the plane. I looked around and saw that people had either closed their eyes attempting to sleep or were reading newspapers or magazines. After a little while, a flight attendant came to offer me a drink, and I ordered an orange soda. I expected to see it in a plastic bag with a straw-like an Asian translator had offered me when I was on my way to reunite with my uncle in Mirut. I was very happy with what I received. Soon enough, dinner was served. The young steward reached his hand over to pull out a tray table and then he placed a tray of food on it. There was a fork, a spoon, a knife, a napkin, and some food. I had never seen anything like this before. So clean and neatly arranged. In a bowl, there was some white rice, chicken curry, and vegetables. There was also something sweet in another bowl; it was mango pudding.

I was now the only one in my family who had ever flown in an airplane and who had received a magical meal that did not need to be cooked. All the flight attendants had to do was just open a rolling box, and out came food and drinks. But before I started to do anything with my food, I observed the people around me. I did exactly what they did. I ate very slowly, trying to enjoy the delicious meal. Everything was perfect. After dinner, I asked one of the stewards to show me where the lavatory was. He let me get out of my seat and then led me to the nearest lavatory. He also showed me how to open and close the door. His kind gestures inspired me. Besides, I thought he looked better than Deap (my first teacher) in his suit. I began to feel like Prince Puyi of China. Just hours ago, I was shooed away, just like Puyi had been forced to abdicate on February 12, 1912, after the Xinhai Revolution. Then, all of a sudden, I was treated like the last emperor of China when he was briefly restored to the throne by the warlord Zhang Xun from July 1 to July 12, 1917.

Everything seemed to be perfect, but one thing that made me feel a little strange was sitting on a metal toilet bowl. Although I had been taught about this in Chonburi, I had never actually sat on one. All my childhood, I had squatted to poop and my butt had never touched a toilet seat. It felt weird, but I was proud of myself for being able to figure out everything without any help.

After coming back to my seat, a young female flight attendant was waiting for me. After making myself comfortable, she handed me a red rose with a big fat stem. I struggled to lift my hands to give her a *sampeah* and then thanked her for her thoughtfulness. "Am I dreaming? No, this is real," I reminded myself. For a brief period, my life felt like that of a prince of Siam. I had completely forgotten that I was still a poor little Khmer refugee with a broken arm, riding high above the surface of the earth in an airplane.

The warm blanket made my arm feel so much better. I took a last look around and saw all the window shades were down and no one seemed to be paying any attention to me or even cared what I was thinking. Finally, I came back to reality. After all, I was just a fifteen-year-old Cambodian boy, sitting in a flying machine on my way to meet a new family whom I had never seen or spoken with, on the other side of the planet.

I noticed that more than half of the passengers on the plane were already asleep. I, too, tried to close my tired eyes and join them.

While I was in a deep sleep, I was woken up by an announcement from the captain asking us to buckle our seat belts as we were preparing for landing. The lights came on and the window shades were opened. I saw a beautiful sunrise in the distance above a blanket of white clouds. Again, my eyes were scanning for angels but I saw nothing. I began to believe that we were the angels. I looked through the windows and saw only rain; it was early morning. Soon, the plane landed and I heard an announcement from the captain, "Welcome to Frankfurt." After fourteen hours or so, I set foot on the land of another late dictatorship, that of the Nazi regime under Adolf Hitler. Knowing that I was in Germany, I felt my skin crawl. I remembered how the Khmer Rouge of Pol Pot praised the power of Hitler's Nazi Germany. I learned a little bit about the transformation of Germany into a totalitarian state under Hitler while I was in Chonburi.

When the plane came to a complete stop at the gate, I tried to look through the windows again, but I saw no soldiers with weapons. This was a relief. Even so, when I was told I could leave the plane, I was frightened. Yet when I was led out of the plane into a spacious glass building, I saw no pushing or yelling. I started to believe that I was in a peaceful place. A German airport worker checked my ICM plastic bag and the documents inside; he knew exactly what to do. Next, I was led to sit in a huge waiting area by the gate. I watched with amazement as many planes took off and landed. "How do heavy machines like that fly like birds?" I asked myself. Around six or seven in the evening, I was taken to a different airplane. I expected to see the kind Thai flight attendants, but when I got to the door of the plane, my heart sank. Everything was completely different because there were no more Asians, only foreigners on the plane.

A nice, tall man examined my boarding pass and showed me my seat. It was by the window and I was very happy with it. I thanked him in my broken English, "Sang-you wary mach mis-ter." He answered with a smile in his perfect English, "You're welcome." If I remember correctly, I saw his printed badge, "Pan American Airways." At this time, I came to realize that I was now in an American aircraft. Again, I began to think about how my new family would look. I could not wait to meet them. My eyes were scanning the inside of the plane and looking through the window, trying to see as much of Germany as possible, before getting to my host country.

After about thirty minutes in the air, American flight attendants came around taking orders for drinks and dinners. There was a variety of choices. I tried to listen to passengers who sat close to me to hear what they were choosing. For drinks, I heard the words: water, Coke, ginger ale, and tomato juice. And for dinner, I heard the words: beef, chicken, and fish. I wanted to try "tomato juice," but it was too difficult for me to say. So, I ordered Coke for a drink. For dinner, I wanted to order chicken, but it was also too hard to pronounce, so, I asked for fish, instead. After my order had been placed, I saw people around me put down their tray tables and I did the same. It was my first time having a Coca-Cola. I was so proud of myself for copying the other people. I also had no problem with using the lavatory this time. I did not look outside because the sky was dark. After brushing my teeth, I made myself comfortable in my seat and went to sleep.

Pictures From My Life

Meeting with Hai at the Bradley International Airport in Connecticut on the evening of his arrival in America, December 1982. From left to right: Hai's new parents Karen Seiffert, David Seiffert, Hai, me, and Sovann Duong.

With my American father and brothers in South Hadley, Massachusetts, in 1983. From left to right: Richard, Nicholas, me, and Patrick.

Playing music with my brothers at home in South Hadley, Massachusetts, in 1986. From left to right: Patrick, me, Loeun, and Nicholas.

With my band members, the Golden Eagle in West Springfield, Massachusetts, in 1988. From left to right: Hoeut Pen, Sina Ung, me, Chead Sim, and Him Pen.

With my parents Richard and Michaela Johnson at my graduation at
Umass in Amherst, Massachusetts, May 1993.

My surviving siblings with my aunt, Yong. From left to right: Kun,
Yong, Srey, Horn, Hing, and Suon. The photo was taken in my village,
Chi Kha, 1994. My youngest half-sister Leng is not in the picture.

With U.S. Ambassador Charles Twining in Phnom Penh, Cambodia, 1994. Mr. Twining was the first American ambassador appointed to Cambodia since the fall of the Khmer Republic of Lon Nol's government in April 1975.

Me and Minister of Tourism Veng Sereyvuth touring the Singapore delegation at Angkor Wat, Siem Reap, Cambodia, in April 1995.

With the Johnsons at Grandpa J's 90th birthday in Omaha, Nebraska, June 1995. Grandpa J, Cecil is in the middle row wearing a black suit sitting between Nadyne and his wife Harriet. I am the second one sitting on the far left in the first row.

With family and friends at my wedding ceremony in Billerica, Massachusetts, in September 1998. My mother Rev. Michaela Johnson married us and she is standing behind me wearing a white robe.

Dancing with my bride at my wedding reception at Park Cafe in Lowell, Massachusetts, in September 1998.

Me and Thavra with our babies Anna and William at Umass in Lowell, Massachusetts, 2002.

My co-campaign manager Harry Schnur briefing me before giving a speech at Old Tyme Restaurant in Lynn, Massachusetts, in June 2011.

My co-campaign manager Michael Ouk high-fives me on my victory night for city council at Mitapheap Restaurant in Lynn, Massachusetts, in November 2011.

Me and Thavra with the Seamans family at a charity fundraiser in Salem, Massachusetts, 2013. Toby and Stella-Mae Seamans whom I have so much respect are sitting in the middle in the front row.

With U.S. President Joe Biden in Lynn, Massachusetts, 2014. He tells me he still remembers my brother Nicholas' father-in-law, Richard Poole.

With Massachusetts Governor Deval Patrick in his office at the State House in Boston, Massachusetts, 2015. He is the first black governor in Massachusetts' history.

Throwing the first pitch to start the North Shore Navigators' game opening day at Fraser Field in Lynn, 2015.

Honoring those who have served on Veterans Day in Lynn, Massachusetts, in November 2015.

Speaking at a Memorial Day in Lynn, Massachusetts, in May 2016.

Vacationing with my family in Siem Reap, Cambodia, in July 2016. The photo was taken by a local photographer in front of the gate to Angkor Wat.

Attending a well-respected political commentator, Dr. Kem Lay's funeral in Phnom Penh, Cambodia, in July 2016.

Speaking at a fundraiser for the homeless in Lawrence, Massachusetts, 2017.

A ribbon-cutting at a grand opening for a doctor's facility in Lynn, Massachusetts, May 2018. Mayor Thomas McGee and Dr. Sokharith Mey look on.

PART II

My New Life

CHAPTER 12

Freedom

*A*fter ten hours of flying over Europe and the Atlantic Ocean, I was awoken by an announcement asking us to buckle our seat belts, as we were approaching John F. Kennedy International Airport. When I opened the window shade, I saw a beautiful morning sun shining above a blue body of water. As the plane got closer to the New York harbor, I saw everybody extend their necks to look out the windows. I heard passengers say, "Look, there is the Statue of Liberty." I, too, looked and saw the stunning statue of Lady Liberty, welcoming everyone to America, and I knew that I was going to be welcomed into her country. I had heard so much about her when I was living in the camps. "I'm going to visit her someday," I had promised myself. Looking ahead to my right, I saw an amazing sight of the Manhattan skyline: the East River Bridges, the Twin Towers of the World Trade Center, the Empire State Building, and the Chrysler Building. I kept turning my head and straining my neck to follow the breathtaking views from one window to the next until we landed.

The Pan Am Boeing 747 gently touched down on the smooth runway of JFK International Airport. Then, the captain announced, "It's six: thirty Eastern Standard Time in New York City." The plane moved slowly and then, came to a complete stop. After watching everyone get out of their seats, I grabbed my bag and walked out along a jetway bridge, leading to the terminal. I followed the crowd and stood in line waiting to be called by an immigration officer. When I got to the counter, I saw a serious-looking American man in a uniform. I was scared and my knees began to tremble. He said something to me, but I did not understand. So, I showed him my ICM plastic bag and he immediately knew what to do.

He took out my travel document and looked it over and placed a rubber stamp on it. "Welcome to America," he said to me with a smile. I felt so relieved. I took it as my 15th birthday present. It was a beautiful morning; the date was October 29th, 1982, and I had just had my birthday less than two weeks earlier. Another officer came and led me to where some other refugees were waiting outside the customs area. We were led into a separate room. When our paperwork was completed, we were asked to go to the other side of the room, to a long table which had boxes under it. Behind the long table, there were many smiling faces. I was amazed by the gentleness and sweetness of the people greeting me. Their appearances were completely different from the INS officer in Phanat Nikhom Transit Center. They welcomed me with open arms. All I heard was, "Welcome to America" over and over again. I smiled and said, "Sang-you wary mach," to every one of them.

At that table, I was given a new pair of sandals and a blue winter jacket with a hood. A kind American man with a smile examined my feet and my body. He asked me to try on a new pair of sandals; they fit me perfectly. Then, he helped me put on the blue jacket. Although it looked bigger than my body, I felt comfortable and warm. He smiled and said, "You're a big boy! It looks great on you." Then, I was taken by bus into the heart of New York City. I felt like I was in a deep jungle again. But this time it was filled with endless skyscrapers. I was excited and frightened at the same time. When I looked up, it seemed like the buildings were going to fall on top of me. I kept turning my head, straining my neck, following all the moving yellow taxis and swarms of people on foot. I got a bit dizzy looking up at the tops of skyscrapers against the midmorning blue sky, and down at the moving vehicles on the streets and over at the shop windows filled with many fancy display items. Everything was like a dream. I had never imagined that I would see such things. I had heard of New York City and had seen some photographs, but never imagined anything like this.

I was taken to a building not too far away from the World Trade Center and told to wait there for a ride to my final destination. All day, I kept looking through the windows at the activities on the streets. Everything seemed so big, even the police officers. The uniforms they wore and the sirens on their vehicles were intimidating. After a dinner of sandwiches, I got picked up to go back to the airport. New York City at night is like heaven on earth. The city lights were beyond my imagination; Bangkok was no match for it. Around 7:00 p.m., I walked out of the terminal and boarded a light aircraft. Unlike the Boeing 747, I had been on, this flight was bumpy because this plane was lighter. Up in the air, I looked down and saw lights extending in all directions.

After a short flight, the aircraft landed at the Bradley International Airport in Windsor Locks, Connecticut. The twin-engine aircraft moved slowly and finally came to a complete stop outside of its gate. I was told to get off and walk through the door leading to a waiting area. My heart was beating fast and my eyes were bleary. I stopped for a little bit to get my vision back. Finally, I was able to see smiling and anxious-looking people in a spacious waiting room in the terminal.

There was a tall young Asian man and a tiny Asian boy sitting among the people beaming at me, as refugees boy. As I got closer to the people, I heard my name called out. "Hong?" I raised my hands and walked toward the voice. A pretty middle-aged American woman extended her arms and hugged me. I pushed her away gently while holding my broken arm. I saw everyone look stunned, their eyes looking for an explanation. A young man stepped in and introduced me to the family. "This is your new family, the Johnsons." I apologized to my American mother for rejecting her. I explained to the young man that she squeezed my broken arm very hard. The young man relayed my message to her. She looked sadly at me. I attempted to give them a *sampeah,* but was interrupted by a handsome middle-aged American man. My new father hugged me gently and tried not to squeeze my left arm. I dropped my plastic bag on the floor and hugged him back. Then my mother tried her luck again and reached out her arms gently to hug me. It worked this time. I hugged her back with my right arm very tightly and for a long time. She kissed me affectionately on the head. My American parents turned to the two tall boys standing next to me, my American brothers Nicholas and Patrick. They introduced themselves and I introduced myself.

After we exchanged handshakes and hugs, the young man from the refugee agency introduced himself. "I'm Sovann." Then he turned to a woman who said, "I'm Marlena Brown. I work for the Lutheran Services. Sovann is a social worker. He'll help you with anything you need."

Soon, with great joy, I walked out of the airport building accompanied by my new family. In the car, Interstate 91 northbound was a smooth highway. Hundreds of small cars, medium cars, big cars, and all sizes of trucks seemed to have lives of their own. I looked outside, and there were no rice fields or cardamon mountains. There were only beautiful colors of green and gold tree leaves and traffic lights everywhere. Everything seemed so clean and organized. No dirt or dust on the highway. I did not see one passenger riding on the back of a pickup truck or the roof of a vehicle like in Cambodia and Thailand. Every vehicle carried only a minimum of passengers and traveled very fast. In the backseat of our vehicle, I was sandwiched between my seventeen-and fifteen-year-old new brothers Nicholas and Patrick, who were six-feet-one inch and six-feet-two inches respectively. In the car, Patrick asked, "Do you play soccer?" I wondered what he meant by soccer, but I understood the word "play." I thought he meant hacky sack. I hesitated a little but said, "Yes," even though I had never played it before. Nicholas tried to get my attention by pointing to the beautiful Connecticut River, the Springfield Bridge, and the beautiful light of downtown Springfield, Massachusetts.

I saw our father's happy smile through the rear mirror, knowing that his boys were already getting along well. Our mother turned around and gave us a gentle smile.

We passed through the city of Holyoke. Then, we passed South Hadley High School on the right. About ten minutes later, on the left, we turned into a small paved road called "Faculty Lane." Then, we went left onto a street called, "Ashfield Lane." Nicholas pointed to a big red house in the woods saying, "That's our house." Our father took a sharp right turn and then left, drove up a gravel driveway, and came to a stop. "Welcome to the professor's house," said our father with a beautiful smile. The address was 27 Ashfield Lane in South Hadley, Massachusetts. Later, I was told that every family who lived on Ashfield Lane worked at Mount Holyoke College and that many of their children went to Ivy League schools.

When we entered the house, we all went straight to the living room. While I was standing there, our father said, "Patrick, show your brother where to put his jacket." Patrick took off his jacket and threw it on the rug in the middle of the living room. Without thinking, I unzipped mine and tossed it on the rug next to Patrick's. Nicholas shook his head and then laughed. Our mother picked them up and said, "Patrick, that's not the place to put jackets!" While she was putting them away, she asked if I would like some milk. I quickly said, "Yes!" Then she suggested the words, "Yes, please!" and I repeated after her.

Soon, she handed me a glass of milk. I thanked her and then took a mouthful, but then I spat it out onto the floor instantly. It tasted awful to me. I had expected sweet and tasty

milk like what I had had in Khao Lan. My poor mother! She
was nervous and quickly took the glass from my hand asking
me if I was okay.

"I'm sorry," I said.

"I hate milk too," Patrick said.

Nicholas and Patrick then took me on a quick tour around
the house. There was a big living room neatly arranged with a
TV, furniture, and a fireplace, a spacious kitchen, a playroom
with a ping-pong table and piano in it, two staircases leading upstairs, three bathrooms, a big studio or study room, a
library, and four bedrooms. Among all the things, I was most
excited about the ping-pong table.

It was close to midnight. Both my brothers said good-
night and went to their bedrooms to get ready to go to school
the next morning. Our mother took my bag to my room and
prepared my bed, while our father showed me all the stuff in
the bathroom. After brushing my teeth and taking a bath, I
put on my very first pair of pajamas, which had a design of
the Incredible Hulk on them. Then, I went to bed and fell fast
asleep. I woke up the next morning after a good night's sleep in
my comfortable new bed. There was a plate with a Golden Delicious apple and a banana on my study desk along with a note
on a yellow sticker, "For you, honey. Love, Dad!" I understood
the words, but I thought that my father did not know how to
spell my name. My name was Hong, not Honey!

After brushing my teeth, I came downstairs carrying the
plate of fruits with the note and greeted my father. Then I
walked to the kitchen and took a seat on a tall chair by the

counter. My father placed a bowl of plain brown rice on the counter in front of me and stood by the refrigerator waiting to see what I would do next. I just sat there staring at the bowl waiting for something else to come, like soup, a piece of chicken, meat, or fish to add flavor. Neither he nor I said anything. After about ten minutes, I gently pushed the bowl away and reached for an apple instead.

My father was confused and took the bowl away to put it in the refrigerator. He reached for a red rotary phone that was hanging beside the refrigerator and started to make a phone call. *Oh, no, what did I do wrong?* I started to worry. "Hello Sovann," my father called out. After a brief conversation, he handed me the phone. *"Chum reab suo bong,"* I greeted Sovann. That was the first time that I had ever spoken on the telephone, and I thought it was so magical. Sovann told me that my father asked him what I would eat and he had suggested rice. I asked Sovann about the two words on the yellow sticker. He explained the meaning of the words, Dad and Honey. He also reminded me to make sure to go to see the doctor about my broken arm. I thanked him and promised to stay in touch. After two days in America, I had already learned two important words, "Dad" and "honey."

After speaking with Sovann, I went to my room to get my X-ray to show to my father. He asked to look at my arm. I pulled up my Incredible Hulk pajama sleeve to show him, and he quickly grabbed the phone and called the doctor's office to make an appointment for me to visit them at once. Luckily, the doctor was available to see me that morning. I went upstairs to change. I went through my brothers' old clothes that were folded and hung for me in the closet. I picked a white T-shirt, a blue stripe long-sleeved shirt, and some long gray corduroy pants. They fit me perfectly, but I needed shoes. It was too cold to wear the sandals on the first day of November in Massachusetts. I went through a pile of boots and sneakers and found a perfect pair of brown boots.

"You look so handsome," my father praised.

"Sang-you Dad," I said with a big smile. He noticed that I pronounced the word "thank" wrong, so he taught me how to pronounce it the correct way by sticking his tongue out between his teeth. I tried after him and got it right on the first try. "You're a fast learner!" His encouraging words made me eager to learn how to speak American English.

About thirty minutes later, we got to the office of Dr. Roger Webber in Amherst, Massachusetts. He did a complete physical examination and inspected my broken arm then placed a cast on it. After having a spaghetti lunch at a local restaurant, my father took me shoe shopping in downtown Amherst. He also registered me as a regular reader at a local institution, the Jones Library. We went from store to store to find perfect boots, but none fit me because we were told that my feet were too wide since I had walked barefoot for so long. My father had no option, but to place a special order for new boots for me. I felt bad for him, but happy to know that I could expect a new pair of winter boots soon. Next, we went to the supermarket to get food. I was delighted to see ramen noodles. My father took every bag off the shelf for me.

That evening, my new grandparents came to see me. I was shocked by my mother's gestures. She introduced her parents to me by putting her hands on top of their heads. "This is my mother Elsa and this is my father, Erwin," said my mother while tapping their heads gently. I was speechless and afraid to look. I thought that it was so disrespectful on my mother's part. My new grandparents Erwin Memmedoff and Elsa Martmann were German immigrants. They had faced discrimination in Nazi Germany and escaped to Paris, France in 1932. In 1933, they came to America and got married that year. In Germany, Erwin had been a lawyer, while Elsa was a chemist. They lived in New York City when they first arrived and then moved to Albany. Wanting to continue to practice law in America, Erwin took classes at night while working for the Winthrop-Steam Chemical Company during the day. He eventually made his American Dream a reality. Both of my new grandparents were kind, gentle, quiet, and shy.

For the first two weeks, my parents took me around to introduce me to their neighbors and friends. I visited my parents' offices and met their co-workers. At the time, my mother was working at Mount Holyoke College as an administrator before going back to graduate school. I visited all my Cambodian friends throughout western Massachusetts who had come to live in American homes like myself. We had all come through the Lutheran Social Services (LSS) of Framingham, Massachusetts, and thanks to the hard work of Marlena Brown. The LSS's mission was to help settle unaccompanied Southeast Asian minors in Massachusetts. I began discussing with Sovann Duong, the LSS social worker, and with Marlena Brown, the LSS director, to find an American home in western Massachusetts for my uncle Hai. A month later, Hai came to live in a wonderful American home in the town of Granby, with a family named Seiffert. I went to meet Hai at the Bradley International Airport on the evening of his arrival, and it was a happy moment and emotional reunion for us both.

I had come to America because my new American parents heard through friends at Mount Holyoke College that the LSS was looking for families to take in orphan Cambodian children, whom the Thai government otherwise intended to send back to Cambodia. After contacting Marlena in Amherst, a meeting was held at the All Saints Episcopal Church in South Hadley. Marlena took the opportunity to introduce the program to the families that attended. After seeing the slide show and hearing a nurse from one of the refugee camps speak about her experiences, my parents decided to open their house to one of the orphaned Cambodians. My parents did not decide alone, as they had their two teenage boys, Nicholas and Patrick get involved in the decision and they all agreed. Although my new parents would have liked a girl, a boy was a better fit in a family with two teenage males already in the house. I was the lucky one who was chosen.

My father Richard and mother Michaela Johnson had met at Swarthmore College in Pennsylvania and were married on August 20, 1960. After getting married, they lived in Charlottesville for two years where my father taught English at the University of Virginia. After their first child Nicholas was born in 1965, the family moved to South Hadley where my father joined the Mount Holyoke faculty that year until he retired in 2004. After receiving his bachelor's degree in English from Swarthmore College, my father got his Ph.D. in English from Cornell University in New York and my mother received her master's degree in social work from Yale University in New Haven, Connecticut. My father was a well-known English professor, and Mount Holyoke College's alumni magazine recognized him as one of their outstanding professors. My father was the author of books on modern poetry and English composition. He also authored a book, *Man's Place,* an Essay on *W. H. Auden*, and with his Mount Holyoke colleague Carolyn Collette, a textbook for college-level writing, *Finding Common Ground.* In addition, my father had been an active protester against the Vietnam War.

My father was born on April 18th, 1937 in Washington, D.C. His father worked for President Franklin D. Roosevelt in the Department of Agriculture, and his parents had come from Iowa and then moved to Washington, D.C. during the Great Depression.

My mother was born on August 22nd, 1937 to a family of German heritage in Albany, New York. She was an only child. She attended a boarding school in New York City when she was young. My mother worked as a minister at the Grace Episcopal Church in Amherst, Church of the Messiah in Providence, and Saint Thomas' Episcopal Church in Washington, D.C. My mother had a kind heart but was firm in her decision-making.

Within a week of my arrival, my other American grandfather Cecil Johnson, and his wife Harriet flew from the Mid-
west to come and meet me. Cecil and Harriet asked us to meet
them at their hotel on the campus of Mount Holyoke College,
and they treated us to fancy lunches and dinners. Cecil was
very knowledgeable about world politics. He followed Cambodian politics very closely.

"Now, you tell me about yourself. I have heard so much
about you," Cecil said to me. "You must be very brave and clev-
er to have survived the genocide of Pol Pot and to have made it
to a refugee camp. We did make mistakes by getting involved
in Southeast Asian politics. I'm very sorry for the involvement
that we got into over there. Your new dad was arrested for
protesting against the secret bombings in your country. He can
tell you about it." Cecil had been rubbing and squeezing my
shoulders very hard as he spoke. He certainly had a strong grip.

"Now you're in America. Study hard and one day you
should go back to help your country," Cecil continued.

"Yes, Grandpa, I understand. Yes, Grandpa, I will," I responded.

"Stop making the boy feel uncomfortable, Cecil," Harriet
warned. But no one could stop him from talking and making
comments. Every time he came to visit us, he always reminded
us to work hard, to be independent, and to be generous to others. Cecil and Harriet donated their fortune to churches and
charitable groups and helped with building a cancer center in
Omaha. Sadly, Grandpa J passed away on October 15th, 1996 in
Omaha, Nebraska at the age of 92, on my birthday.

In November, my parents registered me for the South
Hadley public schools as a high school freshman. The first day
I entered the school building, I found myself surrounded by
fellow students. I felt like a foreigner, entering the orphanage center in Khao-I-Dang. It seemed like everyone knew my
name and wanted to touch me. "He's cute! He's so small! He's
cool! He has a broken arm! Why can't I have a broken arm like
him?" some said in the crowded hallway. The new cast on my
arm drew the attention of almost all the students. "That's so
cool! Wow! Can I sign it?" I heard that over and over again
from many students. Soon there was no more room on my
cast left for anyone to sign. I think everyone in town and its
surroundings knew of me because my brother Nicholas wrote
an article about me for the school newspaper. Also, Mount
Holyoke News had news about me on their front page, "Out
of a Bloody Past, Teen-aged Refugee Begins New Life in South
Hadley."

South Hadley High School was small and everyone there
seemed to know each other. There were about three hundred
students in total. There were only six minority students and
all of us were Asians. We Asians played soccer and tennis. Soccer made me a mini-star. With other good players, I found
my name and saw my picture often on the front page of the
local newspaper. Besides being known as a fast runner on the
soccer field, I shocked many students. With Sina, my friend
from Khao-I-Ding, we held hands between classes making everyone giggle thinking that we were gay. But this was what
best friends did, back in Southeast Asia. One day before class

started, I playfully grabbed Sina, putting my arm around his neck as he stood immobilized in my firm grip. I pinched him on the shoulder blade while he struggled to break free. All the boys in the classroom gathered around and shouted, "Oh, you know karate." At the same time, our English teacher Sheila Reis walked in and called the class to order. Quickly, we all returned to our seats, organizing our work to present to her.

Sina and I spent one hour a day with Sheila Reis, running through English grammar drills and dialogues. The three of us would sit at a small table in the special needs resource room. Along the walls were bookcases stacked with books, pamphlets, learning kits, and packets of cards for helping students who needed an independent learning process. She would flip through the pages of words and dialogues designed to help students for whom English was a foreign language. We tried to pronounce the plural of the loaf, but I could not say it. I pushed back my chair twirling my pen in the air and said, "Too difficult." In her soft voice, our teacher patiently encouraged me to try again. She explained the different aspirations that the mouth must make to articulate F and V. Then, she used the words in a dialogue.

Sina and I were the only two Cambodian students in our high school. We became best friends and spent much time at the college gymnasium doing gymnastics, practicing karate, and racing on the college track. Also, every day his mother took us places and made snacks for us after school. Our principal, Charles Kimball, who lived across the street from Sina's home, always kept an eye on us. Every time we saw him, we were on our best behavior because he had the reputation of running a tight ship at the school. My brother Patrick made me practice speaking in front of his classes, telling my story and the struggles of Cambodian refugees in Thailand and America.

As I became more familiar with the American way of life, I began to feel that I belonged to the family. I fought with my new brothers just like we were all born from the same mother. Nicholas introduced me to pizza when he took me to the Holyoke Mall. I thought that it was the best thing I had ever eaten. Also, the idea of material wealth was new to me. I felt so rich when I received my first allowance of $5 from my parents. I kept it in my pocket for days. To earn extra money in addition to my allowance, I helped Patrick deliver newspapers around South Hadley Center. As for my side jobs, I earned money helping elderly people with gardening and mowing lawns in the spring and summer raking leaves and shoveling snow in the fall and winter. I spent most of my days helping Mrs. Holmes and Mrs. Lawson. They owned big properties and had huge gardens. At night, I sometimes babysat our neighbors David and Carolyn Collette's children, Matthew and Andrew. Also, having my room and a stereo was a big deal for me. Most of the time after school, I would shut my door and listen to my tapes with Cambodian songs for the rest of the afternoon.

Often, I had nightmares. I was still traumatized by what I had gone through and witnessed in Cambodia and the refugee camps in Thailand. Also, I was both sensitive and aggressive. I remember that I screamed at my brother Nicholas, and slammed my bedroom door after he had demanded that I eat some strange food—a quiche—that our father had made. I also remember running and hiding under furniture, yelling, "Vietnam! Khmer Rouge! War! Shooting! Bombing! Go! Go! Run! Run!" when I first heard the fireworks of Independence Day. I thought everyone was crazy for not running for shelter and not attempting to evacuate.

After seeing me run around the house panicking and yelling during the fireworks at the soccer field of South Hadley Middle School, my mother tried to calm me down by explaining that I would be safe in America. Knowing that I was still not satisfied, my parents took me to see the fireworks with my own eyes. Although it was beautiful, I was still traumatized by the intense sound and loud explosions. All of a sudden, every battle with the Vietnamese forces that I had encountered came back to haunt me. I saw the body parts of my friends scattered everywhere while the fireworks exploded. I saw blood everywhere on the soccer field. I saw myself running in a crossfire with dead bodies all around me. It was very difficult for me to watch and hear the fireworks, yet I kept reminding myself that I was safe now, in America.

I remember our trip to Florida on my first Christmas vacation in America. One day as we were walking through the thick tropical foliage, I walked far behind everyone and my brothers started to tease me by asking, "Why are you walking so far behind us?" I did not answer them, only smiled and continued walking slowly at a distance. After insisting that I should catch up with them, I explained that I was afraid that land mines might lie in the path. "Those in the front would detonate first," I told my family. They laughed and explained to me that there were no land mines in America, though I was not convinced.

Every time the five of us were at home, our parents would make dinner, while Nicholas set the table, Patrick washed the dishes, and I cleared the table and wiped it clean. I would throw a sponge from the kitchen to the dining room like a frisbee, and it would land on the table every time before I used it for wiping. Among all the delicious meals that our parents prepared, our father's homemade spaghetti sauce was phenomenal. He would cook meat and vegetables the night before. Immediately before dinner was served, he would cook his pasta fresh and perfectly. Instead of tasting it, he would take a piece of pasta and toss it at the refrigerator's door. When it stuck firmly to the fridge, it meant that it was ready and that it was time to rinse it gently under warm water. Our father loved to cook for us, but his usual dinner was a salad made up of spinach, lettuce, carrots, and cucumber, with a blue cheese dressing. At the dinner table, our topics of conversation were always about music, politics, history, and sports.

On weekends, our father always took us to play tennis, squash, and racquetball at Mount Holyoke College. As for music, I enjoyed listening to the Beatles, Simon & Garfunkel, and the Jackson 5. On every holiday, Nicholas would play piano, Patrick would play acoustic guitar, and I would sing the songs of *El Condor Pasa (If I Could)*, the *Sound of Silence* by Simon & Garfunkel, *Yellow Submarine*, and *Hello, Goodbye* by The Beatles in a duet with Patrick who had a beautiful voice. Our father would add his favorite tune *When I'm Sixty-Four.* To me, his amazingly sweet and tender voice sounded just like Paul McCartney's. Our mother always stuck around and praised our talents.

When Nicholas graduated and went off to Yale, I had some influence over my brother, Patrick. We climbed the trees on our property. Our parents almost had heart attacks when they came home and saw us. But we were good at climbing. Also, I encouraged him to watch Chinese kung fu movies with Bruce Lee and Chuck Norris on television on Saturdays and to eat ramen noodles at night. He introduced me to American painter Bob Ross, of "The Joy of Painting," which aired on PBS. After watching movies, we would go outside and practice martial arts. We kicked, punched, and jump-kicked at each other. Most of the time, Patrick was easy on me because he was much taller and stronger than I was. Also, he was quite an athlete. He played soccer, rugby, lacrosse, squash, racquetball, tennis, and ping-pong. He was a long-distance runner, did track and field, and biked across New England. In addition, he was a great chess player and painter. Patrick rarely went out at night. Almost every night, he would read comic books and played chess on his computer until very late. Most of the time, he would beat the computer opponent.

When I turned seventeen, it was quite an occasion. My parents celebrated my birthday at home and it seemed like all my close friends were invited. The celebration took place in our family's playroom. My parents went to all the grocery stores in South Hadley and its surroundings to buy chicken wings for my birthday party. They cooked white rice and mixed chicken wings with soy sauce and Tabasco sauce. The food was simple, but it was quite a feast.

In our playroom, there was a live band which included me and my Cambodian friends who came from refugee camps in Thailand. Seng Ty played drums, Roeun Chea and Thy Oeu played guitars, Sina Ung played bass guitar, and I sang. After performing a couple of Cambodian songs, we decided to try an English song *Jump* by Van Halen. Seng banged on his drums, shaking the whole house. Roeun showed off a new technique that he had just learned from his idol Eddie Van Halen. Sina cranked up his bass guitar volume with Roeun and Thy. The glass doors of the playroom seemed like they were about to shatter because of the sound, making my parents almost panic. For me, I was very good at singing in Khmer. I did my best to kick the air and swing the microphone stand like David Lee Roth. Seeing all the excitement, my new American friends, Michael and Christopher Mancho, two cousins, jumped in to join me in a duet of *We're Not Gonna Take It,* by Twisted Sister. The noise was unbearable and it was too much for my parents, so they had to go upstairs to hide in the library. The next day, another high school friend, Scott Swindale, a tall soccer player took me to his house. He was gentle and well-mannered. His father told me that he had always been interested in Southeast Asia. He sat me down in his living room and apologized to me for what he had done to my native country.

He said, "Forgive me if I caused any harm to you and your family." I said, "I don't understand what you mean, sir."

Mr. Swindale told me that he was a U.S. Air Force pilot who flew B-52 bombers during the Vietnam War and was ordered to drop bombs inside Cambodia. When I heard that, I stood up and pointed at him and said, "So, it was you who created the Khmer Rouge!" He was stunned by my reaction.

He calmly said, "I didn't choose to do it." He continued, "Before I pressed the button, I would always close my eyes and pray that I would miss innocent people and children like you." He repeatedly apologized. I told him that his bombing had angered Cambodians living in the countryside and had compelled them to join the Khmer communist fighters in the jungles. Scott and his mother felt so sad and I saw them cry. After seeing his sincerity, I also apologized for my reaction and said, "I forgive you, sir. I know that you didn't mean to hurt anyone."

Things started to get quiet when Patrick left for Swarthmore College. After receiving his bachelor's degree, Patrick pursued his Ph.D. in physics from the University of Minnesota in the Twin Cities of Minnesota. By this time, our parents sent me to a private school, Holyoke Catholic High School. The high school was more like a college campus. I also changed my name to Hong Net-Johnson. Some of my friends at school would tease me that I was the cousin of Don Johnson, the co-star of the television series *Miami Vice* who played the role of Sonny Crockett in the 1980s. At school, I had to wear a school uniform and we addressed the priest as, "Father" and the nun as, "Sister." They were strict and sometimes mean. Kissing and holding hands between boys and girls was not allowed on the school property. Every Wednesday, we had to attend mass in the school's chapel. Although we were disciplined, the teasing and fighting among us students still happened and so did secret dating.

Michael, a tall and skinny soccer player, very often tried to lure me into fistfights with him. He was curious if all Asians knew kung fu. One snowy day, as we walked out of one of the school buildings, he playfully punched me and made his friends laugh. I told him, "Mike, I told you that I don't want any trouble." However, my warning encouraged him even more to lure me into fighting him. "Come on, Bruce Lee, you wanna fight?" He threw a punch at me, but my eyes caught his arm approaching my face. I turned aside slightly grabbed his arm pushed him into a snowbank stepped on him and said, "Say uncle, Mike! Say, uncle." I continued to twist his arm making him give up. Noticing that no one seemed to care about him, he said, "Okay, okay, I give up." From then on, Michael and some of his friends started to call me Bruce Lee. Some cute girls also began to ask me out. But I was only interested in Desiree Frank who also lived in the South Hadley Center. Desiree and I had become good friends and we spent a lot of time swimming at the Mount Holyoke College indoor swimming pool, and watching movies at the Hampshire Mall in Hadley.

Sister Catherine Kelley, whom we called, *"Sister Sarge"* was strict and mean. She taught the U.S. history and government classes. She made every student cry at least one time. I cried more than once because I was scared and felt intimidated by her yelling. She taught us in a very strict way and tough, but in the end, she became one of my favorite teachers because she made me learn.

Although Sina and I were in different schools, we got together every weekend. We used the five-college bus system. We got off at Amherst College and walked the rest of the way to Rouen's parents' garage to practice our music. The name of our band was The Orphans. We played some American music, but mostly Khmer music. We performed in schools, churches, temples, and private homes. Also, we were invited to perform for the Khmer New Year celebrations and charitable events. I remember when we performed at Roeun's birthday party, we played in the middle of his parents' tennis court in their backyard and drew a huge crowd of neighbors. I could see them wondering about the strange language that was coming from my mouth. "It sounds like a chicken language," someone in the crowd said. But the comment did not bother me a bit.

I remember one day we were invited to perform in an auditorium at the Amherst Regional High School. Roeun, Thy, and Sina played their electric guitars using our medium-capacity speakers. Seng banged his drums. But I used the auditorium's microphone and sang a song that I had made up in both Khmer and English called, "How Can I Live Without You." My solo singing was heard in every single room throughout the school building.

In the summer of 1984, we were invited to perform at a retreat that took place at the Khmer Institute at Hampshire College in Amherst, Massachusetts. All the Cambodian minors who lived with their new families in the northeastern

United States, and some in other parts of the country, came to the retreat to learn about American culture and meet each other. The one-week retreat was full of great memories. We did all kinds of activities. We played sports; we danced Khmer traditional dances and folk dances; and we played music. The last Saturday evening, The Orphans performed. Many children took their chances to show their singing talents. Among the competitors were Arn Chorn-Pond, Charly Chay, and others. I was not allowed to compete because I was a host singer. That evening, I had the opportunity to wear my Elvis Presley/ Kong Samoeun style pants that I had bought in Khao-I-Dang for performances on stage.

On the last Sunday of the retreat, my father picked me up to go to Fenway Park to watch a Yankees and Red Sox baseball game. It was the most boring sport. At the game, I fell asleep when the Yankees were leading. My father and all the Red Sox fans were very downcast.

My father woke me up when Jim Rice hit a couple of home runs which put the Red Sox in the lead. The guy who sat next to me was so upset, he threw his hat onto the ground and started cursing every player. Although I did not enjoy watching the game, I had a great time with my father. However, of all the professional sports, I enjoyed watching basketball the most. I owned all the Boston Celtics big five jerseys and had posters of Larry Bird, Kevin McHale, Danny Ainge, Robert Parish, and Dennis Johnson. It was the time when the Celtics dominated the basketball world.

CHAPTER 13

College Years

*B*y the mid-1980s, all of my Cambodian friends in western Massachusetts had entered their senior years in high school. Loeun Khun's American family moved to Seattle, Washington. Loeun wanted to graduate from Granby High School, where he was a member of the National Honor Society. Both of my brothers had left for college, so I took the chance to ask my parents if they would let Loeun stay with us until his graduation. Out of their kind hearts, my parents agreed without hesitation. Loeun lived with us for one year. After graduation, Loeun did not plan to reunite with his family in Seattle.

We all graduated from high school around the same time. In the fall of 1987, I entered the University of Massachusetts (UMass) in Amherst with a full four-year scholarship. UMass at Amherst is located in the beautiful Pioneer Valley of western Massachusetts.

As soon as I entered university, I showed an interest in politics. I helped in organizing and welcoming the late U.S. Senator Edward Kennedy to speak at the campus. I joined the Student Government Association, co-founded the Cambodian Student Association (CSA), helped to create the Cambodian-American Association of Western Massachusetts, was a member of the International Student Association of Massachusetts, and lobbied to add a Cambodian language class to the university's curriculum.

Sambath Soum was my first roommate. He had been adopted by a wealthy American family in Harvard, in central Massachusetts. He came to school with many luxuries given to him. He owned a brand new red Z-28 Camaro sports car with a mobile phone in it. He had a computer with an Internet connection. He was smart but preferred to play video games on his computer all night. Between classes, he and I played ping-pong at the student union. On weekends, I would have a quiet room to myself because he went home to visit his family.

In the next room over, Cheang Kim and Mengly Chea owned an electric cooking pot. They cooked ramen and Asian noodles every night which drew many Cambodian students to their room. There was Huong Kouch who brought food from her parents' grocery store in Lynn on Route 107. She would add these to Cheang and Mengly's specialties; this would draw even more Asian food lovers to their room. Very soon, Alex Lip became my best friend. We took a lot of classes together and were always debating politics. There was John Gray, who dreamed of becoming a foreign service officer and working in Cambodia. He talked often about meeting up with me and Alex in front of the American Embassy in Phnom Penh when we graduated. Besides making plans for returning to help Cambodia, we played pool after classes and spent time at the Top of Campus restaurant eating and talking politics. In addition to focusing on the American presidential campaign of

George H. W. Bush and Michael Dukakis and the gubernato-
rial race between William Weld and John Silber, we followed
closely the political situation in Cambodia.

We organized our first election, picking those who would
lead the newly formed CSA. Sreng Kouch was elected president, Vannorath Sarin, vice president, Alex, treasurer, and I,
secretary. Boreth Sun had expected to win easily. But he was
defeated by one vote because Yeuy Lip jumped into the race and
spoiled his chance of victory. It was a surprise win for Sreng
because he was more interested in becoming an engineer than
a politician. And it was a hard defeat for Boreth because he
wanted so badly to be the first elected leader. I remember he
cried for days over his narrow defeat. It was my first time organizing a free and fair election. I was proud of that.

While living on campus, I found a couple of work-study
jobs at the Hatch Laboratory. One was helping to raise insects,
including grasshoppers and butterflies for the Department of
Entomology. Paul Ewald, a biology professor at Amherst College tried to groom me into becoming a medical doctor. But
after working for him in a biology laboratory, separating red-
winged black chicks from their mothers and watching some of
the chicks starve to death, I changed my mind. Having experienced family separation myself, I decided to do something else,
something that would help people directly.

In my junior year, I had to pick a major for graduation. The
majority of my friends chose education while others opted for
engineering, computer science, and business. Alex and I were
the strange ones, according to many. They asked, "What are you

going to do with a political science major?" Our academic advisor and my Asian study professor, Lucy Nguyen-Hong-Nhiem suggested that I should follow my friends and major in education or something that would guarantee me employment. She said, "Look, you don't look or speak like white Americans. How can you compete with them? I suggest you think it over." Professor Nguyen-Hong-Nhiem's words rang in my ears for weeks. After encouragement from my father, I decided to go against my academic advisor's wish.

A former U.S. ambassador to the United Nations (UN) Sichan Siv was appointed as President George H. W. Bush's deputy assistant for public liaison in February 1989. He happened to be the first Cambodian-American to be appointed at that level, and I was so proud to share his nationality. Alex and I wrote a letter congratulating him and requested an appointment to visit his office to wish him well. We received a letter from him asking us to meet him in the Office of Public Liaison in the White House. The meeting was scheduled for 9:00 a.m. We were so happy, but neither of us owned a car! I reached out to Sambath and he agreed to take us there. We left in the evening before the meeting and reached the White House's front lawn around 4:30 a.m. We decided to sleep in Sambath's minivan in front of the White House, as we waited for morning to come. We joked that we were sharply dressed homeless people because we were wearing suits and ties. As we got ready to drive to the White House gate, the security guard came and told us that Mr. Siv could not meet with us due to a scheduling conflict. Sambath lost his temper, took off, and left us there, accusing us of lying to him. Then we decided to take a taxi to the Cambodian Buddhist temple in Silver Spring, Maryland and we saw him there waiting for us.

Months later, when the Cambodian Network Council (CNC) organized a world conference to discuss the future of Cambodia at the Johns Hopkins University School of Advanced International Studies in Washington, Sambath offered to drive us again, but we did not trust his quick temper. At the two-day conference, Alex and I had the chance to meet the former Congressman Stephen Solarz of New York, the former Cambodian head of state Cheng Heng, and the first-ever Miss Cambodia, Tep Kennary. There, we also finally had the chance to meet Sichan Siv in person. After congratulating him on his new post, we mentioned the meeting schedule we had had with him at the White House. He apologized sincerely for the inconvenience. The conference showed me that America had played a constructive role in improving conditions for the Cambodian people, especially in refugee camps in Thailand and on the Khmer-Thai border. After meeting them and attending the CNC conference, I became more interested in politics. I learned from them that one way to influence a policy was to make the world know about the elements of a particular issue. I started to think seriously about majoring in political science. Therefore, I took some politics and political economy classes at Amherst and Mount Holyoke Colleges with the connection I had through my father who taught in both schools at the time. Besides my parents, a professor of politics, Stephen Ellenburg at Mount Holyoke College, played a major role in my academic decision.

When Cambodian compatriots such as Prince Sihanouk, former Prime Ministers Son Sann and In Tam, and former Head of State Cheng Heng were seeking support from abroad, especially the United States, Alex and I sometimes skipped lectures to attend their meetings. We helped to recruit people to join the Khmer People's National Liberation Front (KPNLF), a political front organized and led by Son Sann in opposition to the Vietnamese-installed People's Republic of Kampuchea regime in Cambodia. Also, we organized fundraising for their members to campaign for the national election of 1993 under the supervision of the UN. In 1989, peace efforts began in Paris, France with all parties attending; they reached an agreement two years later. The UN was given a mandate to enforce a ceasefire and deal with refugees and disarmament, known as the United Nations Transitional Authority in Cambodia (UNTAC). On October 23, 1991, the Paris Peace Agreements reconvened to sign a comprehensive settlement giving the UN full authority to supervise a ceasefire and repatriate the displaced Khmers along the Khmer-Thai border. The UN began to disarm and demobilize the factional armies and prepare the country for free and fair elections. On March 16, 1992, the UNTAC arrived in Cambodia to begin the implementation of the UN. At this time, the UNTAC grew into a twenty-two thousand-strong civilian and military peacekeeping force tasked to ensure the conduct of free and fair elections for a constituent assembly. In the May 1993 national election, about ninety percent of eligible voters participated in voting to choose their representatives at the polling stations.

While taking classes at Mount Holyoke College, I met many foreign students from Asia. Among them, Oysim Chen was my close friend and study partner. Like me, she loved politics and music. We spent a lot of time at Mount Holyoke College library doing research, attending lectures, organizing international festivals, and watching concerts on campus. After graduating from Mount Holyoke College, Oysim went on to graduate school in New York and became a lawyer working in her home country, Malaysia.

Besides struggling to get good marks in college, I founded a new Cambodian band and was a lead singer. The name of my new band was The Golden Eagle and was based in West Springfield, Massachusetts. It became a popular band on the East Coast of the United States. We performed every Saturday night and traveled as far away as Toronto, Canada. All the band members kept their hair long. For dance parties, we wore long-tailed coats, tight pants, and cowboy boots on stage like Steve Perry of Journey. For weddings, birthday reception parties, and New Year celebrations, we wore suits like John Lennon and The Beatles. All of us were under twenty-five years old and somewhat good-looking. Him Pen was our lead guitar, Sina Ung was our support guitarist and sound technician, Hoeut Pen was our drummer, Chead Sim played bass guitar, Heap Pen played the keyboard, Kalyan Khim was our female singer, and I was the lead singer.

In the spring of 1992, I finally went for my naturalization interview. The INS examiner asked me lots of questions, such as: how many states are there in the United States, (fifty), how many branches of government are there, (three), who makes federal laws, (Congress), how many justices are there on the Supreme Court, (nine), who is President, (George Bush), who are my senators (Edward Kennedy and John Kerry), who is my representative (John Olver), what are the two major political parties (Democrat and Republican), and who is my governor (William Weld), and more questions. Finally, he asked me what my occupation was. I proudly told him that I was a college student. "Okay, I won't need to ask you to write," he said. And that was the whole of my interview process for citizenship!

On July 17, 1992, at age 23, I was sworn in as a United States citizen in the Massachusetts State House in Boston. I was given a package containing a congratulatory message from President George H. W. Bush. Boroeuth Chen and I had our pictures taken as we stood proudly in the State House holding our citizenship certificates and letters from the President of the United States of America. At home in South Hadley, there was a huge banner hanging from the rooftop of our garage congratulating me for becoming a U.S. citizen and receiving a college degree at the same time. My brother Nicholas and his then fiancé, Tina Poole surprised me with the banner. I appreciated their efforts for having traveled from Chicago, Illinois to celebrate my accomplishments.

Nicholas and Tina met at Yale University where they both graduated in 1987. Tina went on to the University of Chicago Law School became an attorney and worked in Maryland. My brother Nicholas graduated with high honors and received a journalism degree from Yale. He went on to Duke University in Durham, North Carolina, and obtained a master's degree in public policy. He worked in Washington, D.C. as a director at the Center on Budget and Policy Priorities, an American think tank that analyzes the impact of federal and state government budget policies.

In January 1993, I was offered a job with the Department of Revenue and I moved to Lowell, Massachusetts to work in their downtown office. In June of that year, Paulina Pen and I got married. I was 24 years old and she was 23. We met when I was playing in the band with her brothers. But after a few months of our marriage, we separated. Paulina lived in Springfield, Massachusetts, and did modeling for the Casablanca agency. By that time, Sina and I had left the band, but the Pen brothers and Chead were still playing in The Golden Eagle. I decided to quit singing in a band for good. I began to focus on community work and helping people to get involved in political and civil processes.

CHAPTER 14

Return to Cambodia

*O*ne night in October 1993, my home phone rang. It was an international collect call. I ignored it. Soon, the phone rang again and when I picked it up, I heard in the background someone saying, "Phnom Penh."

"Hello, who is this," I asked.

"This is me, Ny, my brother-in-law Dy has found your father."

The news made me very emotional. After the phone call, I could not sleep that night. Joy had overcome my sleepiness. I called Phnom Penh and asked Dy to describe and tell me more about my father and his life and everyone else in my family. I called Hai to share the happy news. We talked all night about our childhood in the villages of Chi Kha and Cham Bak.

Within days I was on my way to Cambodia to meet my long-lost family. However, I was shocked and saddened to see the great destruction of Pochentong International Airport in Phnom Penh as a SilkAir plane of Singaporean Airlines made a bumpy touch-down on the runway. Weeds grew everywhere on the runway and abandoned military helicopters were scattered around and inside the airport. A few ceiling fans circled slowly to stir the hot air inside the terminal building. Also, the control tower seemed not to work properly.

The UN peacekeeping vehicles were still inside and outside the city and made the country seem like it was still at war. Many airport workers were working just to handle one passport or travel document. Also, it was amazing to see them taking turns asking for money from travelers.

I walked out of the terminal building, my heart beating anxiously, but with excitement about reuniting with my birth father and the rest of my family. I expected to see them waiting for me outside an exit door of the airport, but I ran into a small shirtless girl who asked me for money. *Pou khnhom som luy muoy roy,* she asked while pulling at my shirt. I thought that she asked for one hundred U.S. dollars, so I said no. Although I felt bad for her, I thought it was too much for me to spare. Later on that day, I found out that she only wanted one hundred riel of Cambodian money which was worth less than ten cents of U.S. money. I came back several times to look for her but never saw her again. To this day, I still regret not finding that little girl. I promised myself that I would return to help my most needy countrymen. For the fifteen-minute ride from the airport to the city, of Phnom Penh, I tried to remember what my father would look like and how the city had looked before the war.

At the time I arrived in Phnom Penh, it still looked like a war-torn city. The only good places to hang out were by the riverside of the Mekong River on Sisowath Quay and in the gardens in front of the Royal Palace. In May 1993, Norodom Sihanouk was reinstated as king for the second time following the national election. Among the few decent hotels in Phnom

Penh was the Sokhalay Hotel, where I checked in and where my family was waiting for me. The hotel had a permanent group of *cyclo* drivers stationed at an entrance. They hoped to pick up a hotel customer. I chose a man of my father's age as my regular driver. *Cyclo* is a very recognizable, iconic part of the transportation system. The driver perches himself on a high seat above the third wheel in the back. He can check on the passenger and has good visibility of the road ahead. A c*yclo* is pedal-powered and the brakes are operated by a hand-pulled lever in front and between the legs of the driver.

Although it was my first time seeing Phnom Penh, I was heartbroken. I was told that it had been so beautiful before the Civil War. It was known as the "Little Paris" of Asia. As I walked to the hotel's front desk to check in, I saw a small middle-aged man who looked Chinese and had a big smile and gold teeth. He approached me and said, "Are you *oun* Hong, from America?" I responded with a smile, "Yes, that's me, *bong."* He reached out his hand to shake mine and said, "I'm Dy. I've been here with your father waiting for you to arrive." Dy found my family with some money I gave to his sister-in-law to enlist his help finding them. The money was to pay for a radio broadcast and some legwork. As Dy led me away from the front desk, the elevator doors opened and there were a skinny man, a woman, and two young girls looking at me from top to bottom. None of us said anything. After Dy had introduced me to the skinny man, my father and I hugged and cried for a long time in front of the door of the elevator. For the first few days in Phnom Penh, my father slept next to me and hugged me every night. He kissed my forehead gently and pulled a blanket over me every night with affection. I knew that he was trying to make up for all those times that he never had a chance to show his fatherly love toward me when I was a young boy.

My aunt Yong told me that people in the village said to her that they had seen Hai and me die in the mountains while escaping to Thailand many years ago. She also told me that our family had had a funeral ceremony for her younger brother, Hai, and me. Yong kept feeling my face in disbelief that I was still alive. I jokingly told her that Hai and I would never die again! People only die once, not twice! My little sister Suon and our cousin, Hech, kept staring at me trying to figure out what I used to look like. Two days later, Dy went to Chi Kha to get my brothers Kun and Hing, half-brother Horn, and half-sisters Srey and Leng to meet me in Phnom Penh. It was quite an emotional reunion after thirteen years. I wanted so much to visit Chi Kha, my village, but I was advised it would not be safe to go.

While I was staying in Phnom Penh, I spent a lot of time with my family taking them sightseeing and eating foods that they had never tasted in the village. For all of them, it was a wonderful experience, especially for the youngsters because it was their first time in a city. Electricity, running water, showers, toilets, beds with foam mattresses—everything was new to them. It was a bit sad that they had never seen anything new or been anywhere beyond our village. But I was very happy to show them what they wanted to see and to teach them how to turn a light switch and running water on and off, and how to use a sink, shower, and toilet, just as I had been taught when I first arrived in America. Also, Dy and my family became very close right away—it was very special. He came from the same town as my mother, Kampong Trach.

While in Phnom Penh, I saw a lot of young handicapped men wearing military uniforms who were begging. They were very aggressive and seemed to blame everyone around them for their condition. Young men with crutches and missing limbs would drag themselves toward me and demand that I give them money because they had risked their lives to defend their country and to work in the K5 Plan. The K5 Plan was implemented between 1985 and 1989 by the government of PRK and its Vietnamese mentors to defend the Khmer-Thai border from a threat posed by the resistance forces, particularly the Khmer Rouge, in its efforts to rebuild the nation and consolidate its administration. The PRK sent young Cambodians to clear the forests, plant mines, and patrol the entire length of the Khmer-Thai border to prevent resistance forces from filtering into Cambodia. Instead, the K5 Plan killed hundreds of thousands, and most of the teak wood that was cut down by the victims was transported to Vietnam by the Vietnamese forces. Cambodians who were sent into forced labor died of exhaustion and disease, and many lost their limbs and lives to the land mines scattered at the sites where they were sent.

After spending two weeks with my family, I spent another week visiting various friends and relatives in other parts of Cambodia. When I was flying to Battambang to visit with some of Paulina's family, I ran into a friend, Margie de Monchy, whom I knew from the time she worked for an international relief agency at a refugee camp in Thailand. We were both flying on a Russian-made airliner that had been given to Cambodia by the Soviet Union. Margie worked as a field director for UNICEF and often traveled around the country. She had adopted a Cambodian girl while she was stationed in Phnom Penh. To Margie, I expressed my interest in coming back to work in my birth country. Margie still had a kind heart. She introduced me to some of her UN friends and a few high-ranking newly elected Cambodian government officials. I made a promise to some of the children roaming the streets of Phnom Penh that I would return to Cambodia someday to help them in any way I could.

While I was still in Cambodia, I went to see several different people about returning to help my people. I visited Mey Samoeun, Under Secretary of State for Agriculture, who had been one of my teachers and advisors at UMass, and asked for his advice. He suggested that I should meet with Thyda Kus, executive director of the Cambodian-American National Development Organization (CANDO). I did as Samoeun advised. CANDO had been formed by the CNC in Washington, D.C., and had sent volunteers overseas to assist Cambodia with the United States Agency for International Development (USAID). Lastly, I met with, Charles Twinning in his office at the American Embassy in Phnom Penh. In May 1994, he became the U.S. Ambassador to Cambodia. I asked him about the possibility of my returning to assist Cambodia. I was inspired by everyone's courage. I was ready to come back to help.

After returning home to the U.S., I began sending resumes to the UN office in Geneva, Switzerland, and in Washington, D.C. for a volunteer opportunity in Cambodia, so that I could help my people. In the spring of March 1994, I was contacted by Sotie Kenmano, the CNC coordinator in Washington, D.C., and offered a job in Cambodia.

Also, in the spring of 1994, Arn Chorn-Pond, a very good Cambodian friend of mine who was from Rhode Island, had just returned to America. He had gone with his American father, Peter Pond, to preach in the Khmer Rouge camps along the Khmer-Thai border. Rev. Pond had been shot multiple times in both legs by the Khmer Rouge for ignoring their warnings not to enter their camps. Luckily, he survived because he was quickly taken by a Thai army helicopter to a hospital in Bangkok for an operation.

When Arn returned to America, he called me and said he wanted to get a paid job in Cambodia. I suggested that Arn contact Sotie. To my great surprise, he was hired on the spot. Arn is a human rights activist and musician living in Cambodia. He founded the Peace Makers and the Cambodian Volunteers for Community Development. Also, he was a co-founder of the Children of War and the Cambodian Living Arts. Currently, he works as a special advisor on Cambodian Affairs of Clear Path International. He has been honored by many organizations for his humanitarian work. He was recognized with the Reebok Human Rights Award in 1988, the Amnesty International Human Rights in 1991, the Kohl Foundation International Peace Prize in 1993, and the Spirit of Anne Frank Outstanding Citizen in 1996.

Arn and I talked a lot about our dreams of seeing Cambodian citizens have the advantages of democracy, education, and economic opportunities. So one day, in the third week of April 1994, we both left for Phnom Penh. At the San Francisco International Airport, I was joined by many young Cambodian-American volunteers from all over the United States. Among the volunteers, we saw a young lady who seemed to be in a panic trying to make a collect call. Her name was Malis Ung and she was from New York. She was about to cry; her wallet had gone missing.

When we got to Bangkok, my anger came back. I remembered the evening I was shooed away by Thai travelers eleven years earlier in the airport terminal as I was flying to live in America. As I got to the immigration counter, I pulled out my American passport and threw it on the table in front of an officer saying, "You know that eleven years ago I was here and your people shooed me away just because I was a poor refugee boy." The officer looked at me like I was out of my mind. After he stamped my passport while shaking his head with disbelief, I gave him $20 and walked away proudly. He was happy with the money and I was satisfied with the way I had released my anger which I had held inside for the past eleven years. After our Thai Airways plane landed in Phnom Penh International Airport, everyone went their separate ways. Most of them got into a CAN-DO's van. But through Malis' connection, I was picked up by the famous Cambodian couple, film producer and screenwriter Nop Sambath and Sam Kol Theavy. To our great surprise, we were assigned to stay in a beautiful villa in an upper-class neighborhood, Boeung Keng Kang, in the Chamkar Morn district.

The house we lived in was built during the French colonial period. All our living expenses were paid for by the US-AID. Besides having free housing, we were provided with a cook, a cleaner, and two security guards who stayed on guard twenty-four/seven. In addition, we were given a generous monthly stipend of $700. This was plentiful at the time, compared to a regular government employee's salary which was between $20 to $80 a month.

Among the proud and amazing young Cambodian Americans we shared the house with were Socheata Meas from Maine, Sokhunthea Sok from Minnesota, Dany Div from New York, and Sovathana Sokhom from California. We all were college graduates from fine American universities and colleges. At first, we were called by our fellow local Cambodians *Ah Nekachon* (Cambodian Foreigners, especially those who had lived in the West). We were not happy to be called that.

Each of us was blessed to have our room with a private bathroom with a flushing toilet, a sink, a bathtub, and a shower. Our living facility had a humongous generator, a nice garden, and a small alligator farm behind the house. All of us were treated like brothers and sisters, and we selected Malis as our residential representative.

However, the government-run electricity was insufficient. Some nights we had to keep our noisy generator on which drove Sokhunthea and Malis crazy because their rooms were next to it. Another downside was that when it rained our main living room and kitchen on the ground floor became flooded. Early each morning we could hear the bread seller riding his bicycle, calling from a distance, *"nom pang! nom pang!"* to alert us that he was on his way. He always stopped at his usual spot in front of the house, and our trusted security guard Heng would make sure that we each had some French bread while it was still warm before leaving for work. On top of that, around 5:00 a.m. there would be a blasting sound of soulful music, from the nearby Buddhist cremation center, Wat Langka. This made it hard for those who worked until late at night to continue sleeping.

Security was a major concern for us. On one of the first days after our arrival in Phnom Penh, I saw a logging truck hit a motorcycle. Two men rolled off the bike and the head of one man was crushed. He was killed instantly on the street near *Phsa Boeung Keng Kang* (Boeung Keng Kang Market) close to our house. I also saw people get shot and killed when they were robbed of their automobiles or motorcycles. The most popular targets for robbers were the Toyota Camry and Honda 100 motorcycles. There were hot markets for both of these in Thailand and Vietnam. One morning while I was riding my brand new navy blue Crystal sports scooter from my teaching job at a branch office of the Ministry of Post and Telecommunications on Sihanouk Boulevard, I saw a man on his Yamaha motorcycle shoot a female student who was riding on her Honda 100 motorcycle. He missed, but I felt the bullet fly over my head. This made me speed up on an otherwise quiet morning on the boulevard of Sihanouk near the Independence Monument. Crystal scooters were fast, but at the time there was no market for thieves to steal them.

At that moment, I was thrilled to see U.S. Ambassador Charles Twining's Chevy Caprice ahead of me, so I hurried and caught up to him. After seeing me right beside his light blue vehicle, he rolled down his backseat window and I briefed him on the incident that had just occurred.

My first assignment was to assist the Ministry of Posts and Telecommunications as an office management trainer. I shared a bureau with Under Secretary of State Kuy Kim Sea, a Cambodian-Australian who had returned to help his country. One day in July during my first few weeks working at the ministry, I was invited to attend the funeral ceremony of the late supreme leader of North Korea, Kim Il Sung at the Royal Palace in Phnom Penh with my boss, His Excellency Kuy Kim Sea. All flags were at half-mast throughout the city. Although I was not too thrilled about honoring the death of the late dictator, it was a big deal for me to have a chance to see King Sihanouk up close once again and to see some officials of the Democratic People's Republic of Korea for the first time.

In Phnom Penh, I worked hard and was committed to helping my countrymen. I taught English to staff at the ministry from 6:00 a.m. to 7:00 a.m. Then from 7:30 a.m. to 2:00 p.m., I helped Minister So Khun with drafting proposal letters to the National Assembly and creating schedules within the ministry. From 2:00 p.m. to 4:00 p.m., I helped with other non-governmental organizations and with educating local Cambodians about HIV/AIDS. We passed out condoms to adults throughout the city. After the UNTAC left the country in 1993 and 1994, the HIV/AIDS epidemic spread among Cambodians very quickly, exceeding the epidemic numbers in Thailand. At first, residents made fun of us for doing different things around the city. They also accused us of treating them like children when we handed out condoms—they thought the condoms were balloons and gave them to their young-sters. Some of them said to us sarcastically, "We're not afraid of AIDS; we're afraid of not having sex." Their comment was sad, but we were not upset with them. We only wanted them to have safe sex and healthy families.

After a month in Phnom Penh, Paulina joined me. But our interests were different, and things still did not work out between us. After coming back to America, she met someone else who shared her interests. She married him one year after our divorce in the summer of 1995. I felt lonely and sad, but my brother Kun came from the village to visit me weekly and kept me company. We shared stories of the past when we had been living apart before our reunion in 1993. Kun said that he only knew what our father told him about me. He thought that our uncle Hai and I were fighting against the PRK and Vietnamese forces with the Khmer Rouge in the jungle. He did not know that Hai and I had been living abroad, receiving a college ed-ucation. Kun joined the PRK armed forces of Heng Samrin when he was very young and fought against the Khmer Rouge. He told me that before he ever pulled the trigger, he prayed that his bullets would miss Hai and me. His story made me cry; my little brother at a very young age had been forced by the government to risk his life fighting the Khmer Rouge.

A couple of months later, I received a second assignment to work at the Cambodian National Assembly. I was to assist Chairwoman Ky Lum Ang with the economy, investment, ag-riculture, planning, rural development, and the environment.

My specific duty at the Parliament was to help the committee chair evaluate proposed laws and to prepare for hearings. Also during this time, I taught English to many Cambodian congressmen, congresswomen, and staff. While assisting Ky Lum Ang, I worked in the provinces with village leaders to prepare them for elections and to help them with choosing effective candidates. I also worked with them by creating revolving loan funds to help villagers become economically self-sufficient. Besides working hard to help rebuild our country after a nearly three-decade-long civil war, we had some fun times together. We went to many places as a group to sightsee and to attend special events. One memorable event that we attended was a one-week retreat in Kompong Som. We occupied every room at the Hotel Koh Pos by the beautiful beach of Koh Pos. Sotie came from Washington, D.C. to join us there, and we became good friends. Every night, many of us sat in a circle on the sandy beach around a fire pit, singing and playing acoustic guitars nearly all night long. It reminded me of the good old days when I entertained my friends in refugee camps in Thailand.

Among the many good songs we sang, I showed off my talent by singing the long-forgotten *Rolok Kompong Som* (Waves at Kompong Som). I started to sing the song at a perfect moment just as the waves were breaking. The song became a hit among us. During our volunteering in Cambodia, some of us young Cambodian-American men found the love of their lives in Phnom Penh. The lucky ones were Boreth, Boroeuth, Sovatha, Heng, and Dy. They married lovely local girls whom they met and brought to America when their work ended. To this day, these couples live happily, some in the United States and some in Cambodia. Like us, Sotie Kenmano also went to work in Cambodia, where she met her husband, William Heidt, who was working at the U.S. Embassy in Phnom Penh. Sotie's husband, William Heidt was nominated by President Barack Obama and confirmed by the Senate to become the U.S. Ambassador to Cambodia, where he served from 2015 to 2018.

In June 1995, I came back home to America to attend my grandfather's 90th birthday celebration in Omaha. It was quite a party. It seemed like one whole floor of a hotel was occupied for Grandpa's birthday. There were Aunt Nadyne and her family, Uncle Frank, and his family—so many of my cousins and my brothers: Juli, Christopher, Gregory, Michael, Phillip, Kristian, Nicholas, Peter, Erik, Patrick, Loeun, and Pasha. We had all traveled from all over the world to be together. All my cousins were incredibly kind and charming, but Pasha, Nadyne's youngest son, and I became best friends immediately. I was surprised to learn that our grandfather was so well-loved and respected in Omaha. Also, I was amazed to see that many of his influential friends were there to wish him well. I was happy for the opportunity to shake hands with many of the wealthiest Americans in Omaha at the time.

* * *

By mid-July 1995, I was on my way back to Cambodia and this time at my own expense.

In Phnom Penh, I was picked up by my very good friend Sam Dara, a famous actor and a police colonel, who brought me to his residence in the city. Out of his kind heart and our friendship, Dara and his family were happy to offer me a place to stay temporarily. Dara was a well-educated artist and very connected to politicians. He was a university graduate and fluent in English. I joined him in acting in some of his movies. We also sang on stage with thousands of people in the audience. The most crowded concert that we performed was a three-day event at the National Olympic Stadium. Many Cambodian artists came together and sang with the famous Hong Kong movie star, who played Chhan Chhao in the movie, *Pao Chen*. He was the trusted bodyguard of celestial Justice Pao of the court of the Chinese Song Dynasty. Tens of thousands of people attended the concert. Among the songs that I sang, one that caused much cheering was *Tos Yang Na* (No Matter What!). The original version is *Et Pourtant* sung by a French singer named Charles Aznavour. The popular Cambodian radio announcer, Ek Monkul, interviewed me on stage which caused much cheering.

I had supporting acting parts in the soap operas, *Koukam Koukob* (A Sinful or True Love) and *Rumduol Torng Meas* (A Golden Jasmine's Stem). Both were directed by Nop Sambath and written by Sam Kol Theavy. Among the new emerging actresses who acted with me were, Chorn Chan Leakhena and Kong Socheat. In addition, I broadcast on the radio and sang with Kong Nary many patriotic songs on the early morning radio program for the National Radio of Kampuchea. In addition to acting and singing as a hobby on weekends, I joined the United Nations Development Program. I assisted the Ministry of Tourism and was an Assistant to the Public Relations for Minister Veng

Sereyvuth, a Cambodian-New Zealander. I also helped with writing grant proposals to the United Nations World Tourism Organization to fund the Cambodian Tourism Ministry.

Investors from all over the world were starting to come to do business in Cambodia in the mid-1990s. All of a sudden, there was a great need for people to know a foreign language. Dara and I decided to establish a language school in Phnom Penh. In August, we opened one of the very first foreign language schools in the whole country. At the school English, French, Japanese, and Thai were taught along with computer skills. Over eight hundred local Cambodians attended the school in Phnom Penh. Because Dara was well-connected and popular, our school was also very popular and attracted all kinds of students, including Buddhist monks, artists, and children of government officials. Our school offered four sessions and one hour for each class. We started as early as six o'clock in the morning and went as late as seven o'clock in the evening. Each classroom could hold up to thirty students of all ages. The fees were low, $30 per month, and as high as $100. Our goal was not to make profits but to provide language and computer skills so the students could qualify for jobs in the newly developing Cambodia.

Our school did well for about one year, but then things started to change. Dara had to leave for Australia on a tour. I had to travel to the provinces weekly to work with village leaders to prepare them for the upcoming national and local elections. We left our secretary to run the school. But as a result, the institution ran aground. On top of that, a local city official began to give me a hard time. He claimed that I had no right to be a sole business owner because I was not a Cambodian citizen. He also claimed that I owed taxes, but he did not produce any documents proving this claim. Sadly, I was forced to close the school.

After moving out of my apartment at the school building, Samnang Siv took me in. Like me, Samnang was a returnee from America where she had escaped after the Khmer Rouge years. She helped promote Cambodian tourism and worked as an advisor to First Prime Minister Prince Norodom Ranariddh. While staying with Samnang, I helped her take care of her antique shop, the Samiti House. After experiencing the devastation of her country and witnessing the living conditions of her fellow countrymen, Samnang decided to resign from her job in a medical research laboratory in Massachusetts to return to her birth country and give back. She was a driving force for the Cambodian government and traveled worldwide promoting tourism. Also, she was the right-hand person of Minister Veng Sereyvuth. Samnang's favorite hobby was hosting her diplomatic friends at home, including ambassadors from the U.S., Canada, Australia, Malaysia, Indonesia, Singapore, Thailand, the Philippines, and some Western European countries. Her dinners were usually spaghetti that she prepared and served.

When Samnang's son Samiti Siv took a year off from college to join his mother in Phnom Penh, we established a travel agency. Sakun In, a Cambodian-American entrepreneur, was our office manager. Samiti and I traveled to Phnom Penh, Sihanoukville, and Siem Reap making deals with hotels and restaurants for our guests. Very soon the twenty-minute flight from Phnom Penh to Siem Reap and the five-hour drive to Sihanoukville became our weekly trips. Samiti and I worked extremely well together. We engaged many trusted business partners.

One late afternoon, Samiti Siv and I drove to Sihanoukville. Approaching the spirit houses of *Yeay Mao* (Black Lady) at Pich Nil Mountain, I asked him to stop so I could worship her with some money or bananas just like everyone would do to travel safely with the blessing from her spirits. Samiti ignored my pleading and continued, passing *Yeay Mao.* All of a sudden, out of nowhere, a rock hit the windshield of our Isuzu SUV and caused a big crack. At first, we thought that it was a gunshot. So Samiti sped up along National Highway 4, heading south. Finally, after realizing that it was just a rock, I tried to have him stop and turn back to the spirit houses. He was not convinced because it was too quiet. But I was concerned that if we continued driving without asking for protection from *Yeay Mao,* chances were that the windshield would break into pieces before we would reach Sihanoukville.

After a few minutes of deep thought, he agreed to take my advice and we turned back to *Yeay Mao's* spirit houses. I put 4,000 riels of Cambodian currency, equal to one U.S. dollar in a bowl in front of the statue of *Yeay Mao.* We apologized for having almost ignored her. We asked for her protection and safety throughout our journey. Along the way to Sihanoukville, we saw soldiers in small groups. We tossed cigarettes to them and thanked them for protecting us. Three hours later, we safely reached our destination and checked into the Krystal Hotel on the beautiful beach of Ochheuteal. To our great amazement, the truck's windshield shattered and fell into pieces at our hotel. It was a miracle. On our way back to Phnom Penh, Samiti did not risk ignoring the Black Lady again.

In April 1996, a week before touring Siem Reap, I spent the whole week reading all about the history of Angkor and the temples. On the day of my trip, I got up early, packed my suitcase, and then went to the port on the Mekong River by the Chroy Changwa Bridge. I boarded a tour boat for an early ride to Siem Reap. I had decided to take a tour boat because I wanted to experience both the famous Mekong River and Tonle Sap or Great Lake. As the speedboat of Royal Express left Phnom Penh and went along the Mekong River leading to the vast water of Tonle Sap, I felt like I was dreaming because the scenery was so breathtaking. I was amazed to see Vietnamese fishermen and their families living on fishing boats and others building their homes in Tonle Sap in the crowded community on the water, known as The Floating Village.

My favorite spot was on the boat's top because it had the best view. At noon, after a five-hour boat trip, I arrived at the port of Siem Reap. I took a taxi to my hotel. Sakun In and I were joined by my friend, the provincial commander of the military police Chea Seila, for lunch at a moderate restaurant in downtown Siem Reap. He assigned his driver to take us around and appointed his older brother, who was also a military police officer, to be our security assistant. For several days, Sakun and I visited the great temples within the Angkor Archaeological Park and other temples in the areas of the first ancient capital of Roluos under Angkor's first ruler King Jayavarman II in the early ninth century.

During the period of an annexation of the Lower Chenla in 708 by Buddhists Indonesian/Malay of the Srivijaya and Javanese of Shailendra, Jayavarman II, a Khmer ruler of the Upper Chenla at the time moved his court from his first capital in Banteay Prey Nokor to Kulen Mountain. In 802, he initiated a Hindu consecration ceremony on the sacred Kulen Mountain to proclaim political autonomy and royal legitimacy. He declared himself god-king, divinely appointed and uncontested. Jayavarman II publicly declared independence from Srivijaya and Shailendra. He then established the first capital of Angkor near the modern town of Rolous in Siem Reap.

Then, Sakun and I decided to spend our last afternoon seeing the forbidden temple, the magnificent Banteay Srei. It was deep in the jungle near the Kulen Mountain in Khmer Rouge territory at the time. After hearing about our risky trip to the temple of Banteay Srei, Governor Toan Chay sent a small group of army men in a pickup truck to prevent us from proceeding. They caught up with us at Badak village on the way to Kulen Mountain. But then the governor decided to have the army men escort us to the forbidden temple, as we still wished to visit there.

This beautiful tenth-century temple of pink sandstone and delicate carvings is dedicated to the Hindu god, Shiva. The walls are covered with deep, intricate carvings, each with superb detail. Banteay Srei Temple was built by the spiritual counselor to King Rajendravarman and later to King Jayavarman V. When we entered the grounds, we saw a small group of Khmer Rouge soldiers come out of the forest and approach us. They were heavily armed with AK-47s and B-40 rocket-propelled grenade launchers.

"Oh, no! We're in trouble," I told Sakun. He turned pale. The government soldiers stayed behind trying to be invisible. It was seventeen years since I had last encountered groups of Khmer Rouge forces. I was so scared. I thought we would be robbed or shot to death and then our bodies would be dragged and dumped in the woods just like they had done to many of my friends at labor camps when the Khmer Rouge controlled the country. So, we pretended to trust them. We exited the temple area and walked toward them with friendly smiles.

"Suo sdei soksabai te mit?" (Hello comrades, how are you?), we said. Instead of praying for my mother's protection as I had done in previous years, this time I also charmed them with money, the power of U.S. dollars. To my huge surprise and relief, I saw them smile and some of them even exchanged their *sampeah* with us.

"That's new," I said quietly. I remembered that when I lived under their control, *sampeah* was prohibited.

As we got closer to them, Sakun pulled out a couple of packs of his 555 cigarette brand and handed them to the one who looked like a leader. I also pulled my remaining U.S. dollars from my wallet and distributed them evenly.

"Are you from America?" one of them asked.

"No, we live in Phnom Penh," Sakun responded. They laughed at us and shook their heads because they knew that we were lying to them. After directing us where to go and not to roam around due to the possibility of land mines, they disappeared into the woods near the temple. After taking a few photos of us in front of the temple, we decided to leave the scene as quickly as possible. From then on, I always had a few packs of cigarettes with me wherever I traveled in the provinces. All local Cambodians knew that even government soldiers expected travelers to give them cigarettes in exchange for security or to avoid being robbed. That night in our hotel room, I was very sick with typhoid fever. My nightmares had returned. My fever spiked and I shook and shivered. I halluci- nated, seeing the sad, innocent eyes of my friends at the labor camps during the Khmer Rouge time. I thought that I was on my way to join them in hell that night. In the morning, I was rushed to the local hospital and had to leave for Phnom Penh immediately for treatment.

My American father Richard and I continued to exchange our monthly letters, and we were always happy to stay in touch. I had been briefing him about the political situation in Cam- bodia, and he would describe how exhausted he was. He was flying regularly to Omaha and San Francisco to visit both his ill father Cecil and brother Frank, and always thinking about me in Cambodia and my safety. He pleaded for me to return home. This touched my heart. But I was not ready to go back.

After living for a while with Samnang at her place, I decid- ed to find my apartment. I found one on a busy road in Phnom

Penh. With Hak Sovanna and Kok An, I became a partner in an import and export business called Cambodia International Cooperation, Ltd. We knew that the country would soon start building new roads, bridges, and buildings. We traveled to Vietnam and Thailand to work out deals to bring construction equipment into Cambodia, such as dump trucks and excavators. This was a perfect time to start this kind of business. Cambodia was just starting to rebuild after many years of civil war. The first contract we signed was with *Oknha* (tycoon) Siv Kong Triv, a native of Sre Ambel, Koh Kong.

However, due to the uneasy political situation in the country at the time, many things did not work out. Both the CPP and FUNCINPEC military tried to woo Khmer Rouge commanders to join their forces, to be the stronger force. Gossip swirled in Phnom Penh's coffee shops and restaurants of potential armed clashes. For my news, I usually relied on the FCCC (Foreign Correspondents' Club of Cambodia), a public bar and restaurant on Sisowath Quay on the Tonle Sap River, where foreigners and journalists from all over the world gathered. Among the regular customers was Eng Roland, the Cambodian Ambassador to Thailand, Malaysia, and Singapore at the time, and then, in 1999 to the United States. The young and charming diplomat stole many hearts. Roland was the younger brother of Princess Norodom Marie Ranariddh, the wife of Prince Norodom Ranariddh. Since he was fluent in English and French languages, Roland would update all his foreign friends on the political situation in Cambodia. I had met Roland on the plane when I was flying from Bangkok to Phnom Penh in April 1994, on my second trip back to Cambodia.

On the morning of March 30, 1997, there was a bloody grenade attack by members of the Second Prime Minister Hun Sen's bodyguard unit. The attack started at a peaceful political rally organized by an opposition politician, Sam Rainsy, in front of the National Assembly building. Sixteen people were killed and over one hundred and fifty innocent people were injured. Immediately, investors in the country began to question their security. The rally was in protest of the corruption and politicization of the judiciary in Cambodia. The morning of the grenade attacks I was having breakfast of *lort cha* (fried noodles with egg and fish sauce) at a food stall by the Royal Palace just across from the bloody scene. But I was not injured.

Cambodia was governed by a coalition government, which was a power-sharing arrangement among political parties at the time of the grenade attack. However, of all the participating groups, Second Prime Minister Hun Sen held the dominant position in the government. With the CPP, he ruled Cambodia with an iron fist throughout the 1980s. Meanwhile, resistance fighters on the Khmer-Thai border waged a guerrilla war against the Vietnamese-installed government in Phnom Penh of Hun Sen, Heng Samrin, and Chea Sim.

In May 1993, there was a general election. Ranariddh's FUNCINPEC, with its allies Son Sann's, BLDP (Buddhist Liberal Democratic Party) and Prum Neakareach, pro-Sihanouk military organization, Molinaka (Movement for the National Liberation of Kampuchea), all three emerged victorious from those elections with sixty-two percent of the vote. However, Hun Sen's CPP received only thirty-eight percent. But Hun Sen refused to give up power and threatened to take up arms and start a new civil war. At this time, in 1993, there were one hundred and twenty seats in parliament to represent the eight million Cambodians. The election results were: FUNCINPEC took fifty-eight seats, the CPP took fifty-one, BLDP ten, and Molinaka one. As a result, Prince Ranariddh and his allies had no other option, but to accept Hun Sen and the CPP into the coalition.

Under this coalition government, the CPP retained control of the ministries of defense and the interior. Hun Sen's appointees dominated these ministries. Also, Hun Sen had a personal bodyguard contingent just for himself of 2,500 thuggish and violent men.

Sam Rainsy was the first finance minister in the new coalition government. He went after tax evasion among business tycoons aggressively and rooted out corruption among government officials. Immediately, he caused strained relations with both Hun Sen and Norodom Ranariddh. In October 1994, Rainsy went after tens of millions of dollars that Teng Boonma, the owner of the Thai Boon Rong Group, owed in back taxes for importing cement to build the Olympic Market in Phnom Penh. Teng Boonma was the richest man in Cambodia at that time. In 1995, both Hun Sen and Ranariddh stripped Rainsy of his government posts and had him removed from the national assembly altogether. Students and teachers took to the streets of Phnom Penh demanding the restoration of Sam Rainsy, but the demonstrators were dispersed by the police force. Shortly thereafter, Rainsy formed the Khmer Nation Party. He quickly became the most zealous opposition politician in the country and gained a strong following among young people.

CHAPTER 15

The Weekend Coup

*T*he tensions within the coalition government finally exploded in fierce fighting in Phnom Penh. On July 5 and 6, 1997, Hun Sen and the CPP ended all pretense of a coalition government by launching a brutal and bloody coup in which Ranariddh and the FUNCINPEC were ejected by force from the government. Hun Sen alleged that the FUNCINPEC was engaged in secret negotiations with the Khmer Rouge.

The CPP had been engaged in negotiations with the Khmer Rouge and had won support from the Khmer Rouge faction at Pailin under the leadership of Ieng Sary in 1996. Hun Sen's negotiations with the Khmer Rouge were meant to undermine the movement by integrating it into the government's Royal Cambodian Armed Forces (RCAF). Ranariddh, on the other hand, used the negotiations with the Khmer Rouge at Anlong Veng to strengthen his faction of the armed forces. According to an eyewitness account, the former top Khmer Rouge commanders named Keo Pong and Phon Pheap had defected to Hun Sen's side. They fought alongside the CPP against the FUNCINPEC during the coup of July 1997.

I usually got up later than most people in Phnom Penh. Most often, I just shut out the noisy morning sounds of cars and motorcycles on a busy street in front of my apartment.

That morning, I got up early. When I checked my watch, it said 5:15 a.m. I did not hear the usual morning noises. I did not look outside. Instead, I just went to the bathroom. Then the phone rang, but I ignored it. A few seconds later, it rang again. When it rang for the third time, I rushed to pick it up.

"Hello? Who's calling?" I asked in English. It was Ky Lum Ang, my former boss, calling to tell me that a trip to the pagoda that morning had been postponed. She also warned me not to go outside and that she was about to turn off her phone and go into hiding.

"Hello? Hello?" There was silence. I wanted to call her back, but I was too nervous and could not remember her number. I walked back and forth in my room trying to remember her phone number. I started to panic and my memory was blocked. But then, I remembered her number. I struggled several times, pounding my finger on the numbers. I wanted to hop on a *moto-doob* (motorbike taxi) to find her at her house in Steng Meanchey, south of the city. But she had said that she was in hiding, so I decided not to go to look for her.

That Saturday morning, three of us were supposed to go to the pagoda on National Highway 3. Ho Sok, Ky Lum Ang, and I were going to donate money to buy soil to fill up holes to build a *kod* (house) for the monks at the pagoda. A week prior, the three of us had planned on going to the pagoda when we were attending an early celebration of the United States' birthday at the Phnom Penh Hotel near the Embassy of the Russian Federation. Lum Ang had called me just the night before to confirm our trip when she was attending a July 4th reception given by U.S. Ambassador Kenneth Quinn at the Hotel Cambodiana. After having a brief talk with Lum Ang, I wanted to call Ho Sok, Sam Dara, and Hak Sovanna, but it was too early. I tried to call home in America, but the government had shut down the international communication line.

I did not hear the usual noises of *tin, tin,* and *tit, tit,* the honking horns of motorcycles and vehicles rushing to cut in front of each other. I started to wonder what was happening. I looked down to the street in front of my apartment; there were only soldiers everywhere standing in position ready to attack. I started to panic again, so I called Dara. But his phone only had a busy signal. I decided to call Nath, a close friend of Sovanna, who was a member of the CPP police force. The call went through. Finally, I would be able to talk to someone who had inside information. Nath gave me a scary warning that a deadly event was about to occur at any moment. He also said, "I'm afraid that Phnom Penh might be burned to ashes if we can't make it over fast." I asked him what he meant and then he told me that Hun Sen's military forces were surrounding the compounds of Ranariddh's top commanders, General Nhek Bun Chhay and General Chau Sambath in the Somnong Dobpi, in an attempt to disarm their security guards. He also told me that if I needed to leave the apartment, I should go east as that would be less dangerous.

After receiving a hint from Nath and seeing Hun Sen's armed forces in front of my apartment, I snuck out the back door and took a taxi motorbike to Samnang's house. The boulevard of Mao Tse Tung heading south was quiet like a ghost town. At that time both Samiti and Samnang were vacationing in the U.S., so I just wanted to make sure the antique shop was safe from being looted. The whole city was pretty quiet. I saw the CPP's armed soldiers standing in pairs at every intersection and street corner.

After paying for my ride, I ran into the courtyard behind the metal and concrete wall. Then, I closed the gate behind me as quickly as possible. The Samiti House was a beautiful wooden house surrounded by a tall and secure fence with pink flowers covering the gate, a garden of jasmines, and a few coconut trees. By the steps up to the house near an Asian apple tree, there was a big vase of lotus. The lotus bloomed all year round. Inside, the Samiti House was decorated with antique furniture that Samnang had collected from Malaysia, Indonesia, and Thailand. She had converted the ground floor into a shop that sold furniture and other items that had been owned by the French.

At the shop, I tried to use the landline phone to call home in America. But I still could not get through. I informed Mohm, the housekeeper, and Mao, the driver to lock the gate and keep an eye on the house and the shop at all times. Also, I told them about the impending attack that I had received warning earlier that morning and what I had seen on the way there. They were scared. At that instant, they wanted to go to their families. Mao took Mohm on his motorcycle to her family; then, he went to check on his own. All of a sudden, I was all alone in the Samiti House and scared. I locked the gate shut all the doors and windows and tried to make phone calls in Samnang's office at the shop.

I called the U.S. Embassy and was told that they were planning to evacuate all Americans out of the country and advised me to go to either the embassy's compound or the Hotel Cambodiana to be evacuated if the marine helicopters came. I also was told that the airport had been closed and the only way to fly out of the country was to go through Ho Chi Minh City in Vietnam. They asked me to make sure I had my passport handy because I needed it to get out of the country. "Damn! I have nothing on me!" I screamed. I started to sweat because everything was in my apartment. No passport, no cash, and no clothes. I wanted to go to my apartment at once, but I could not leave the shop unattended.

While I was in deep thought, my mobile phone rang.

"My friend, where are you?" asked Dara. I felt so relieved. I told him where I was and he said he was helping bring some of his friends from the ministries of defense and interior to safety. I also told him about the situation that I was in. He assured me that everything would be all right, as long as I stayed inside. While talking with Dara, gunfire erupted at the Somnong Dobpi. If I remember correctly, it was around 9:00 a.m. All of a sudden, the fighting became intense. My memories flashed back to the attacks I had witnessed during the invasions by Vietnamese forces in 1978 and 1979. Heavy machine guns and rocket shells landed all over the place in the western parts of Phnom Penh. Dara told me to stay put as he was going home to be with his father and sister.

After Dara hung up the phone, my other trusted friend Saing Odom, a news anchor who worked for a neutral Thai television station, TV3, called from his office to say that his station and Ranariddh's TV9 in Tuol Kork had been shut down. Also, I learned that the state-run TVK and the military TV5 were broadcasting accused Ranariddh and his party of orchestrating a coup to topple Hun Sen and the CPP. The news said Ranariddh and the FUNCINPEC were smuggling heavy weaponry such as tank-destroying rockets into Phnom Penh. Ek Monkul, a broadcaster, had been shot months earlier by Hun Sen's men. He had accused Hun Sen of breaking up Ranariddh's party. What Ek Monkul had discovered was that Hun Sen had funded senior FUNCINPEC members—Siem Reap Governor Toan Chay, Banteay Meanchey, Governor Duong Khem, and the Minister for Transportation Ung Phon—to create a faction within the FUNCINPEC. The Party had been weak since the removal of Sam Rainsy, the popular finance minister, and Prince Norodom Sirivudh, the foreign minister in 1994 and 1995. Also, the corruption and incompetence of its leadership contributed to the Party's weakness. Later, I was told that Ek Monkul had been dragged away from his broadcasting room as soon as the fighting broke out. I also heard that the attractive Cambodian-French woman, Khun Sreypov, the director of TV9, had been gang raped by the CPP's soldiers when they raided the station that morning.

After so many tries, I finally got through to Sovanna. He told me that he was at the office to make sure looters would not take our office supplies. He said that the CPP's soldiers were shooting into the air, chasing everyone and loading up their tanks, pickup trucks, and motorcycles with loot. He suggested that I not return to my apartment because the looting was heavy in that area. Also, he said that only the Khmer Rouge forces under Keo Pong and Phon Pheap were fighting Ranariddh's forces under General Nhek Bun Chhay and General Krouch Yoeum. The FUNCINPEC forces were hesitant to fire back for fear of causing heavy casualties among civilians living in Phnom Penh. That morning, the heavy fighting was in the areas of Somnong Dobpi, Tralork Bek, and Kossamak Hospital.

By evening, the fighting had stopped. Soon Mohm arrived back with her two daughters and sister, Thong. And I went back to my apartment. As I was traveling on Sihanouk Boulevard, some rockets landed near my apartment. Seeing some people starting to head east, my motorbike taxi driver turned around. He sped up Norodom Boulevard and went south, joining the crowd, and dropped me off at the bridge by Kbal Thnal. I walked across the bridge, Chbar Ampov Bridge, toward National Highway 1 and spent the night wandering on the east side of the bridge. My phone's battery died while I was trying to make a phone call. It was dark and the streets were quiet. There were only tanks and military trucks transporting soldiers from National Highway 2 into the city of Phnom Penh. Some believed that those tanks and trucks were carrying Vietnamese soldiers. And that Hun Sen, while he was in Ho Chi Minh City at the time of a coup, had requested those soldiers.

I was alone among strangers and began to regret leaving the Samiti House. That night, in a radio broadcast, Hun Sen said that Prince Ranariddh, who had left for Thailand the day before, and his father, King Sihanouk who was in Beijing, were both traitors and plotting to overthrow him. Hun Sen vowed to crush their networks and bring both of them to justice. By dawn, I walked back to the city and begged one of the brave *moto-doob* drivers to take me to my apartment. As we got to the National Olympic Stadium, the Olympic Market, and shops along Mao Tse Tung Boulevard, I saw many empty stores and businesses. The smell of burning rubber and gunfire was still fresh in the air. After paying a generous fee to the driver, I ran quickly up the steps to my apartment. I was thankful that I was safe and found my apartment was undisturbed.

As I was about to jump into a cold shower, I heard the sound of banging on the back door, near my bathroom. "What's going on? Who the hell is that?" I said to myself. I was scared to come out of the bathroom.

"Hey, Hong! Are you in there? Hong, this is Peter, Peter Swift." Peter was an American friend, who ran a non-profit organization in Cambodia that provided loans to villagers and farmers in the provinces. Also, Peter's family had adopted one of my orphan friends from Khao-I-Dang named Hong Cheng and they lived in Amherst, Massachusetts.

"Good Lord, what the hell are you doing here? Aren't you afraid of being shot at, man," I yelled while opening the door to let Peter in.

As I looked at the bloodstain on his arm, I asked, "Are you hurt? Look at your arm, it's bleeding."

Peter said, "Yeah, a stupid rocket landed right behind my bike! I'm lucky! I'm still alive! I think I'm okay. This bloody mess is from falling off my motorcycle on the way here." He also said that he had stopped by to deliver a letter from my American father, whom he had run into at the airport in San Francisco a few weeks before. In addition, Peter had expected to meet up with Thy Oeu who was supposed to be landing early on the morning of July 5th. Thy was another orphan friend of mine and a fellow band member who was living in Lowell and teaching math at Lowell High School.

I told Peter that there was nothing left at the airport, only empty buildings. He did not say a word, only shook his head in disbelief. Later, I learned that Thy's plane had been diverted to Bangkok on its approach to Phnom Penh on the morning of July 5th, minutes before gunfire was exchanged. Peter and I stayed in my apartment the whole day eating canned food and listening to the news on the radio. We kept switching from BBC News to the local stations. The BBC said Hun Sen was launching a bloody military coup to oust First Prime Minister Prince Ranariddh. The local news channel, on the other hand, said that Hun Sen and the government forces were defending anarchists, attempting to overthrow the coalition government, and wanted to destroy Phnom Penh.

After Peter left around 5:00 p.m., Keo Seila, my police friend, and a tennis partner, came over in his full uniform with a pistol on his hip. He asked me to go with him to check on things in and around Phnom Penh. Out of stupidity, I agreed. I hopped on his motorcycle and held on tightly as we drove down Mao Tse Tung Boulevard toward Tuol Tom Pong Market, then to Kossamak Hospital, and finally, toward Tralork

Bek areas where the heavy fighting had just ended. Although there were still sporadic gunshots throughout the area, we were brave enough, or perhaps just foolhardy enough, to continue our exploration. I saw two destroyed CPP tanks. One of the tanks, near the Kossamak Hospital, had been shot by a FUNCINPEC soldier named Lucky. Later, I was told that Lucky had wrapped his German-made RPG in a straw mat, fired it at the tank, threw the weapon away, and then just walked back home. A few days later, his house was raided and he was killed by some of the CPP's soldiers. Lucky's body was dragged on the road behind an army truck and dumped in an unknown location.

I saw soldiers looting everywhere. They broke into warehouses and dealerships; they stole motorcycles, bicycles, and cars, and then loaded them onto their trucks and tanks. Residents stood at military barricades and watched as their businesses and homes were looted. There were rumors that the owner of the Australian-made VB (Victoria Bitter) beer distribution company committed suicide when he learned that his daughter had been sexually assaulted and all of his cash and products stolen. The CPP's high-ranking officers were allowed to take things like vehicles, while mid-level and low-ranking officers took bicycles, televisions, radios, housewares, clothes, and other valuables. Even the hospital was not spared. Hun Sen's soldiers stole medicine, beds, and blankets. Nothing was left behind for the care of the wounded.

Later on that evening, Hun Sen appeared on the state-run TVK in full military regalia. He broadcast his claim to victory and imposed a curfew after dark. He claimed that he and his supporters were victims. They had to use military force for self-defense as well as to protect the country from chaos. He blamed Prince Ranariddh and his supporters for having started the armed clashes. Again, he vowed to root out their networks and bring them to justice. However, many believed that Hun Sen had launched the coup against Ranariddh. Hun Sen knew that his party would badly lose the 1998 elections to the FUNCINPEC.

Some economists believe that because the crown colony of Hong Kong reverted to Chinese sovereignty on July 1, 1997—which ended 156 years of British rule—the communist Vietnamese pressured Hun Sen to topple Ranariddh. Teng Boonma, a CPP supporter, saw the opportunity to control the entire economy, both in Cambodia and Vietnam. By doing business with Hong Kong, he used his finances to fund Hun Sen and the CPP. Some top CPP officials claim that because Prince Ranariddh sided with Taiwan and recognized Taiwan as a sovereign state, China was upset. This prompted the communist Chinese to help Hun Sen. Thus, Hun Sen launched the coup to oust the prince and to put an end to the FUNCINPEC. Hun Sen became the sole leader until this writing in 2021, and Cambodia became a one-party state, just like Vietnam and China. Ever since his government has grown heavily dependent on economic and military support from both countries, especially China.

That night, all of the western part of Phnom Penh was dark and quiet. Only military vehicles and tanks roamed the streets during the curfew hours. However, Seila and I ignored the law and drove in the dark hoping to see what was happening. I was scared when our motorcycle almost got crushed by a military tank loaded with motorcycles and bicycles near the National Olympic Stadium.

The next day, Ranariddh's royalist government officials, supporters, and journalists went into hiding. However, Hun Sen's soldiers continued to celebrate their victory with massive looting throughout much of Phnom Penh, especially the western part of the city and the Pochentong area. Motorcycle warehouses were emptied of their stock, as were Mitsubishi and Toyota car dealerships. Pochentong International Airport was stripped of everything, including light fixtures, telephones, computers, and much more. Later on, I learned that back home in America, my family was desperately trying to reach me. They learned about the coup in Cambodia from the New York Times and the Washington Post, while they were celebrating July 4th at my sister-in-law Tina's parents' beach house in Rehoboth, Delaware. Everyone was worried about me. They kept trying to reach me by phone for days, but could not get through. Loeun assured our parents that I was safe; he had confidence in my ability to stay alive.

In the days following the coup and overthrow of Prince Norodom Ranariddh, Hun Sen's soldiers hunted down the prince's supporters. Many were imprisoned, tortured, beaten, and thrown into a crocodile farm they were eaten by the creatures. Others had some of their fingers crushed in metal clamps. Some high-ranking officials were executed as they tried to surrender. This included Secretary of State for the Interior Ho Sok, Under Secretary of State for Defense Krouch Yoeum, and deputy chief of military intelligence Chau Sambath. His Excellency Ho Sok, a harsh critic of Hun Sen's close friend—the marijuana king Mong Rithy—was shot twelve times by Hok Lundy at the Ministry of Interior after two days of captivity outside the Singapore Embassy on Norodom Boulevard.

Hun Sen wanted to have a legitimate government even while people were being killed, so he began to look for someone to be the first prime minister within the FUNCINPEC, to replace Ranariddh. First, Hun Sen picked co-minister of Defense, Tea Chamrath. But Chamrath wanted to remain as co-minister of Defense. Finally, the Minister of Foreign Affairs and International Cooperation, Ung Huot agreed to accept the post. Huot became the interim first prime minister until the election of July 1998. His Excellency Ung Huot, the former minister of education, replaced Prince Norodom Sirivudh as foreign minister in 1995. In that same year, Prince Sirivudh was removed from his foreign minister post and exiled to France charged with plotting to kill Hun Sen.

I remember one quiet night in June of 1995 when Dara and I were coming home from a late-night snack of rice porridge (*bawbaw saw*) at Pet Chen on Monivong Boulevard. I was driving Dara's car from Sihanouk Boulevard, and making my way to Norodom Boulevard and Wat Phnom. All of a sudden, Dara screamed at the top of his lungs from the passenger seat because he saw a small group of soldiers pointing their guns at our car: "Stop! Don't shoot! Don't shoot! It's my car! I'm Sam Dara!"

I stepped on the brake to a complete halt in the middle of Suramarit Boulevard in front of Hun San's villa, the oldest brother of Hun Sen.

"What's going on?" I shouted. When I looked to my right, I saw some soldiers walking out from the gate of Hun Sen's mansion. They were pointing their guns at our brown Toyota Vista. I heard someone yelling in a commanding voice, *"P'oun Dara! P'oun eng daeng mean roeung ey te?"* (Little brother Dara! Do you know what just happened?)

A middle-aged man approached us and said, "We had an exchange of fire right here earlier today, and at this moment Prince Norodom Sirivudh's residence is surrounded by our men. Go home now! Don't go out anymore tonight."

"Who was that man?" I asked Dara in a shaky voice.

"That was Huy Piseth, the commander of Hun Sen's body-guard unit," Dara responded. I was sweating and swore that I would never go out late at night again. That night, I stayed at Dara's house.

For days following the coup, I was not able to call home in the U.S. However, I could receive calls from my friends in Singapore, Bangkok, Ho Chi Minh City, Hong Kong, Sydney, and Tokyo. Yuko Yamamoto, a Japanese university student and world traveler, was the first one to call me from abroad to see how I was doing. I met Yuko while she was wandering alone outside Banteay Samre Temple in Siem Reap during her Angkor tour in 1995. Yuko always sent me postcards from every country she visited to update me on where she was. She was kind and offered to wire some money to me knowing that

I must be broke. But I refused to accept it because I did not feel that would be the right thing to do.

One week after the bloody coup, I was still unable to access my money in the Cambodian Commercial Bank. Now, I was completely broke. I was about to go hungry and would be late for my $150 monthly apartment rental. On top of that, my 017 mobile phone company threatened to disconnect my service due to nonpayment. My phone was my lifeline during that time of crisis. I had to do something to keep it going. So, I went to the U.S. Embassy and asked for a loan in cash. But there was no money available to me. At that point, I decided to give up and return home to America. The embassy bought me a plane ticket on loan with the guarantee that I had to pay the U.S. Department of State back in ninety days. Otherwise, I would risk losing my passport. I agreed. I was happy that I would be going back to America, but I was also terribly sad. I could not remain in Cambodia, the land where I was born.

CHAPTER 16

The Farewell

I packed my stuff with mixed feelings of relief and sadness. I was upset to leave my local Cambodian friends including Odom, Vuth, and Toeu who were not as fortunate as others. They had been orphans like I once was. After the fall of the Khmer Rouge, they were placed in the orphanage of Kolab One in Phnom Penh. Odom spoke very often about his father, an officer of Lon Nol's Khmer Republic, who was killed in front of him when he was only three years old. His mother and the rest of his older siblings were also executed by the Khmer Rouge just months before the invasion by the Vietnamese in January 1979. All three, Odom, Vuth, and Toeu, considered me their older brother, and I considered them my trusted advisors. We had spent a lot of time with each other. In return, I gave them English lessons for almost two years. My departure was hard on them.

I paid all my bills and gave most of my clothes, all my furniture, and housewares to friends because I did not plan to come back to Cambodia any time soon. The night before I left, Dara took me out to a fancy dinner at a Cambodian and French cuisine across from the French Embassy. He also paid for a massage for me as our last farewell. Then, he took me to say goodbye to his sister Chan Vy, and her husband, Chan

Savuth, who was Under Secretary of State for Information. We went to their villa by the *Stad Chas* (Old Stadium) near Chroy Changwa Bridge. The stadium was built in the 1920s and had been home to French soldiers during their colonization. Savuth and Vy were incredibly kind and accepted me as their brother; Vy slipped a $20 bill in my pocket. I began to refuse to accept it but changed my mind. Ultimately, I appreciated her generosity. Now I had $90 in my wallet. I was good for my trip to Vietnam the next morning.

That night I could not sleep because I was thinking of all the good and bad times I had during my stay in Phnom Penh for the past three years. I had experienced so much, seeing the development of the country which then devolved into destruction. I had seen the change from a democratic regime to an authoritarian one. I helped to rebuild a once war-torn country by picking up trash on the streets, distributing condoms at nightclubs, and helping government officials make laws for the country. I had started by eating with displaced children on the streets to dining with prime ministers. I had worked hard because I had high hopes for my birth country to become free, prosperous, and respectful of human rights like many developed countries in the Western Hemisphere. Sadly, all my hope, resources, and energy that I had invested in my birth country were gone completely.

Looking back, I am glad that I decided not to join Prince Ranariddh's cabinet. I was safe and had created no enemies because I had stayed neutral. Although I worked for Her Excellency Ky Lum Ang, a key member of the FUNCINPEC and a

Representative from Battambang, I spent a lot of time with Her Excellency Men Sam An, a key member of the CPP, a Representative from Svay Rieng and Deputy Prime Minister.

On the last morning of my stay in Phnom Penh after the coup in July 1997, I woke up early in an empty apartment, with no furniture and no housewares. It was around 5:00 a.m. After washing myself, I went downstairs to turn in the apartment key to my landlord, who lived on the ground floor. Then, I took a *moto-doob* to a taxi depot at the New Market (*Phsa Thmei*). While my taxi moved slowly away from the New Market and went along Monivong Boulevard, my tears began to fall. I greatly missed my family in the village and my friends in Phnom Penh.

In the afternoon, I was dropped off in the town of Bavet in the province of Svay Rieng, on the border of Vietnam. After I had a quick lunch in a small restaurant that I knew in town, I took a motorbike taxi to the crossing gate at the border. At the gate, I was denied a request to leave the country by the Cambodian border police. They said that the border had been closed and no one was allowed to leave the country. I told them that I was a foreigner, but they laughed at me. I assured them that I was not a Cambodian citizen.

"You look Khmer! You speak perfect Khmer! Who are you?" one of the police officers asked. I was so embarrassed by the officer's remarks. I had no choice, but to use my right as an American citizen to get out of my home country.

"Look! Your country is at war! I must leave or you'll be responsible for my safety," I yelled. They ignored me and continued talking to each other. I demanded they call the U.S.

Embassy in Phnom Penh or the U.S. Consulate General in Ho Chi Minh City to confirm who I was.

"Do you have a note from the embassy?" I was asked. I retrieved my American passport and travel itineraries with stamps from the U.S. Embassy in Phnom Penh from my briefcase and threw them on the counter. Now, they took me more seriously.

The most senior official picked the documents up and examined them carefully.

"Okay, please give us some money for coffee and cigarettes and we'll let you go," he said. I did not want to argue so I gave them $25.

"All set, you can leave," said the officer.

"How can I enter Vietnam without a visa, captain?" I then asked.

"Just give them five dollars, you'll be fine," he assured me with a smile.

I thanked them and walked through the gate as fast as I could and then turned around and jokingly said, "Wow! The Vietnamese are that cheap, huh!"

When I walked across the neutral zone, I bought a few packs of cheap cigarettes from merchants there. As I went through the Vietnamese barrier at Moc Bai, I gave one pack to the police and when I entered an immigration building I did the same and gave out cigarettes to the workers. I learned to do this when traveling in Vietnam. The process went much more smoothly than on the Cambodian side. After I paid a fee for an entry permit and then gave a bribe of $5 to the Vietnamese immigration officer, I entered Vietnam once again.

The hard part was over. But I still needed to figure out how to get to the Nguyen family, whom I knew when I came to Vietnam in 1996. While I was wandering around trying to hail a taxi, a young Cambodian man offered to help. He said he was planning to go to Ho Chi Minh City to visit his in-laws and asked me to share a taxi with him. I was delighted. I showed the Nguyen family's address to the taxi driver and asked him to drop me off there. The young man, by the name of Son Phirum, bragged the whole two hours of our taxi ride. He said that he had just gotten married and was a wealthy entrepreneur in Phnom Penh. However, he had lost most of his assets in the recent bloody coup. Phirum also said that he was going to get more money from his in-laws to rebuild his business. First, I believed him. But after a while, I began to feel suspicious, yet I did not say anything. As we got closer to the Nguyen's residence, he began to change his story. He complained that his business and his house had been looted, that his money had been stolen, and that he was broke. Phirum pleaded with me to help him pay for his ride. I was nervous because I did not have enough money for both of us. I only had $50 left.

Around 4:30 p.m., the taxi arrived at the front gate of the Nguyen's residence. It was a very nice three-story home with a tall metal gate. After paying for my ride, I checked my plane ticket again just to make sure it was real. I gently kissed it and then put it back in my briefcase.

"I'm going home," I said with a smile.

Phirum's face lit up and said, "So, you're from abroad?"

I proudly responded, "Yup! I'm from America." He wrote down his address in Phnom Penh and phone number on a piece of paper and gave it to me and said he had a beautiful sister and wanted me to meet her. I told him that I would stay in touch and then I got out of the taxi.

As the taxi pulled away, I opened the gate walked up to the house, and knocked on the Nguyen's door. It seemed like it had been planned. Immediately, Mr. Nguyen welcomed me into his clean, beautiful house. He shook his head and said, "Fighting again, huh? I just don't understand why Cambodians can't get along!"

I felt so ashamed by his comment. Noticing that I felt uncomfortable he added, "I don't mean *you*."

I said, "Oh, no! I completely agree with you, one hundred percent, sir." Mr. Nguyen smiled and then led me into his living room and asked me to make myself comfortable.

"I'm glad you're here. Let me go get your godmother," he said and then went into the kitchen. Mr. and Mrs. Nguyen had asked me to be their godson the minute they saw me when we met in Ho Chi Minh City during my business trip. I reminded them of their youngest son Tuan, who was studying civil engineering in Holland at the time. I thanked him for welcoming me into his home. As soon as Mrs. Nguyen saw me standing in the living room, she gave me a big hug. She then showed me a guest room where I could sleep. I told her husband, Tan, who was the only one of them who spoke English, that I was going back home to America, and that the airport in Phnom Penh was closed. Tan's wife, my godmother, asked her husband to tell me that I was welcome to stay as long as I wanted. I thanked both of them for their kindness.

After I took a nice cold bath, I changed into some clean clothes. My godparents asked their son-in-law to give me a tour of the city. The well-mannered young man did exactly what his parents-in-law asked him to do. After riding along the beautiful riverbank of Saigon, we visited the Reunification Palace, where the Vietnam War ended. The beautiful palace had once served as the residence and office for the presidents of South Vietnam—Nguyen Van Thieu, Tran Van Huong, and Duong Van Minh from October 1967 to the fall of Saigon on the morning of April 30th, 1975. This was when the North Vietnamese tanks bulldozed through the main gate and ended the long and bloody struggle.

After seeing the sites, I craved *pho* a Vietnamese soup with rice noodles, herbs, and beef in broth, and a popular street food in Ho Chi Minh City at the time. When I asked the son-in-law to stop at a busy food stall on the side street, he was reluctant. Although he did not protest, I could read in his mind that he wanted to go to a cleaner restaurant with air conditioning on such a hot evening. I knew what he was thinking, but I quickly told him *pho* was delicious. Also, I knew that street food was cheap. I enjoyed that noodle soup very much that evening, and I was happy that I had insisted on having it. After having two bowls of soup and the Vietnamese popular dessert of a banana with coconut milk, I still had $1 for a tip. Afterward, though, I would be penniless on my first day in Vietnam. I was back to square one, just like my first day as a refugee in Thailand.

Unlike Phnom Penh, every street in Ho Chi Minh City had food and dessert. Despite all the city noise, I slept very well that night. I felt very comfortable being around the Nguyen family. I tried not to think of anything but their kindness for taking me in when I most needed their help. I had not had such a good sleep since the bloody coup of July 5th, so I overslept. When I got up, the sun was shining. It was past mid-morning. When I looked at my watch, it read 11:20 a.m. I quietly opened the door and tiptoed downstairs to the bathroom to wash my face.

"Ahhh! Good morning son," Tan greeted me from the living room.

"Good morning Mr. Nguyen, how do you do, sir?" I greeted him back.

While I was trying to approach the bathroom, Mrs. Nguyen pulled my hand and led me into the kitchen where she introduced me to several women preparing food. I greeted them in English with a bow, bending my body very low. They all smiled but did not greet me back. Among the women, I saw a tall young girl, in her early twenties washing bean sprouts who seemed very shy. She kept looking down but had a little smile.

We had a delicious Vietnamese lunch, of *bun* (beef, rice vermicelli noodles, bean sprouts, vegetables, herbs, and fish sauce). Tan invited many of his friends and construction and trading partners with their families for dinner at his residence that evening. This was a big send-off for me! I was so surprised by their warmth.

Besides hearing the Vietnamese and English languages, it was nice to be around people that evening who spoke Khmer.

Ethnic Khmers began living in this area, where Ho Chi Minh City now lies, centuries before the arrival of the Vietnamese. Beginning in the early 17th century, due to the colonization of this area by Vietnamese settlers, Khmers gradually became a minority in their land. To this day, Khmer people in this area still maintain their Khmer identity, practicing Theravada Buddhism and speaking a dialect known as Khmer. Mrs. Nguyen spoke in Vietnamese and her friend, translated it into Khmer. She said she and her husband were delighted to have me at their home and to be part of their family. Then, she asked if I wanted a Vietnamese wife. Everyone applauded and encouraged me to say yes. So I said, "Yes" because I felt I had to.

Then Mrs. Nguyen continued, "I have a beautiful niece! Will you take her with you to America? She wants to study over there." My godmother was referring to the girl that I had seen in the kitchen that morning. I was stunned.

"I don't think she wants to go with me because we haven't met yet," I responded nervously. In my mind, I remembered that Khmer King Chey Chettha II had given some eastern land to Vietnam in exchange for the hand of marriage to a Vietnamese princess. In 1623, the king allowed Vietnamese to settle in the area of Prey Norkor, presently Ho Chi Minh City, and to set up a customs house there. Due to the increasing waves of Vietnamese settlers, the area slowly fell into the hands of the Vietnamese. Prey Norkor was the most important commercial seaport to the Khmers at the time.

That night I could not sleep. I kept thinking of the agreement I had made with Mrs. Nguyen that I would take her niece to America. I felt guilty. I did not mean what I had said. I had no intention of marrying her. I still did not know what to do with my life. I had no job and no future. Their kindness made me feel ashamed. I desperately wanted the morning to come, so I could go home.

On the day of my departure, there was another big feast. Many family members came to share the Vietnamese traditional dishes of *banh xeo* (crisp pancakes filled with pork or chicken and bean sprouts), *goi cuon* (spring rolls), and my favorite kind of *bun.* Everyone encouraged Ha, the girl I had seen the day before, to practice her English language with me and to serve me lunch. To my great surprise, her English was good. She introduced herself and her family to me and asked about life in America. Also, she explained the meaning of her name, "Ha." It meant "sunshine," in Vietnamese. She asked what my name meant. I told her that Hong meant "papaya," in Khmer. Everybody laughed.

"Do you like papaya?" Ha asked me. I told her that I did. Everyone was very polite, giving her a chance to practice her English. However, the conversation did not go well. Ha was very shy and I was afraid of getting into a serious relationship with her.

Around 3:00 p.m., I was ready to leave for the airport. I carried my briefcase out of the bedroom and walked through a room full of people saying goodbye. My heart beat with mixed feelings of sadness and joy. I was sad to be leaving the Nguyen family. They had given me incredibly warm hospitality during my two-day stay. However, I was happy to go home to America to see my parents and the rest of my family, all of whom I missed dearly. Soon, we all squeezed into Tan's blue station wagon and headed to the Tran Son Nhat International Airport. On the way, we stopped and took some pictures of the Museum of Vietnamese History and the beautiful garden of the Reunification Palace.

Before I checked in at the airport, I thanked and hugged everyone. Walking to the gate of Cathay Pacific Airways, I saw Mrs. Nguyen crying. At that moment, I thought of *Paa* when I said goodbye to her in Lum Puk to live with Nan.

"I'll come back to visit you, ma'am," I assured Mrs. Nguyen with a heavy heart.

"Have a good trip and don't forget to write us," said Tan.

I assured him that I would stay in touch. Sadly, however, I have not since set foot on the soil of the Socialist Republic of Vietnam.

Six hours later, I arrived at Haneda International Airport in Tokyo. I had a brief reunion with Yugo and her sister at the airport. Then, I continued my journey on a Japanese Airline, crossing the Pacific Ocean, and heading back home.

CHAPTER 17

Home

*A*t the Los Angeles International Airport, I made a 1-800-collect call to my parents in Providence. Although I felt blessed to have returned to America safely, I felt ashamed of my failures and for not accomplishing as much as I wanted to while working overseas. I checked into the Marriott Hotel near the airport.

That evening in the hotel room, I spent a long time in the bathtub thinking about what I would do back in Massachusetts. I was ready to start a new life in the land of opportunity and freedom for all. The following morning, my Southwest Airlines flight landed at Logan International Airport in Boston. It was so wonderful to be back home. For years, I had been missing everything about Boston. After having a nice breakfast of *pho* at the "Best of Boston" Vietnamese restaurant in Chinatown, I took the Bonanza Bus Lines to Providence, Rhode Island to see my parents.

After spending a few days with them at their new home in Rhode Island, I was on an adventure again. I decided to move to Washington, D.C., and stay with my brother, Nicholas, and his family who had just moved from North Carolina and bought a house in Silver Spring, Maryland. My intention for moving to Washington, D.C. was to do an internship on Capitol

Hill. During my three-week stay in Maryland, I participated in protests at the White House and the Capitol denouncing Hun Sen and his bloody coup which had ousted the first popularly elected prime minister of Cambodia. Also, I visited the National Democratic Institute, the International Republican Institute, and various congressional offices to give updates on the political situation following the recent events in Cambodia from my perspective. Then, I moved back to Massachusetts and applied to law school; but first, I worked as a consultant for Hermes Enterprises selling ergonomic computer products out of Nashua, New Hampshire. Also, I helped a friend to run his temp agency in Lowell, Massachusetts. On weekends, I taught immigration and citizenship classes to Southeast Asian students at the Cambodian Mutual Assistance Association in Lowell.

In November 1997, I met Thavra So in Boston at a birthday dinner for a friend, whom I knew from my days in Phnom Penh. When I first saw her on the corner of Tyler Street in Chinatown, I hid behind a Chinese restaurant to take a peek at her while she was talking with her friends. I do not understand why I was so shy at that time. After a long wait, we all decided to have dinner at Weylus restaurant, in Saugus on Route 1. Because I was seated across from Thavra, we had the opportunity to talk. We seemed to have a lot of things in common. Our conversation was mostly about Phnom Penh and the political situation there. That evening after dinner, I escorted Thavra home.

The next day, I called Thavra at the suggestion of her close friend, Kourou Chhoeuy. I had also met Kourou the night before. I was surprised that Thavra answered my phone call and seemed happy to talk to me. Although it was our first call, the conversation was quite lengthy. After learning that her student visa was about to expire, I offered to sponsor her to stay in America. She did not refuse but asked me to give her time to think it over. After consulting with her family back home and learning about the political situation in Cambodia, she agreed to let me sponsor her as a friend. But I was hurt because I was hoping to be more than that. One day I asked her out and she said yes. I borrowed Hai and Lorraine's car to pick her up from the house that she shared with her second cousin in Revere. I stopped at a florist on Broadway to get a bouquet. When Thavra opened the door, she seemed happy to see me. As we were about to leave, she asked if it was okay for her second cousin to come along. I was a little disappointed but understood that she did not trust me yet. We had only met one time.

Thavra was born in Phnom Penh, in one of the most prestigious private hospitals in the country, two months before the Khmer Rouge entered the capital city in April 1975. Her family was bourgeois and resided in the exclusive, Section Six in the Chamkar Morn district. Her parents named her Nech Thavra. But at home everyone called her Sreyneth and all her close friends called her Ahneth. And they still do to this day.

Thavra's father Hok Sinech was a prominent businessman. He owned an airline company that did business in Phnom Penh, Bangkok, Hong Kong, and Singapore. He was out of the country on a business trip and not with his family when Phnom Penh fell into the hands of the Khmer Rouge. Thavra's mother Uong Samon was born in Kampong Speu on

November 1, 1934, and was also in the military, as a captain. She was in charge of special intelligence for President Lon Nol from 1970 to 1975. She was one of only two female military personnel who held the position of captain in the country at that time. Her mother's father, Uong Sok, was the village chief of Chres in Kampong Speu province.

Thavra was the valedictorian of her high school class at the well-known and prestigious Lycée Sisowath. It was the first high school in the country, founded in 1936. The high school was in the former residence of King Sisowath Moni-vong, who had given the school its name. Lycée Sisowath produced the best and brightest students in Cambodia at that time. After graduating from Sisowath, Thavra attended the Royal University of Law and Economics in Phnom Penh and majored in pre-law. In November 1996, her parents sent her to America. First, she attended a private school in East Boston. Then, she enrolled in Bunker Hill Community College to study Liberal Arts.

When the Khmer Rouge entered Phnom Penh, Thavra and her mother became separated from their family. She and her mother went to live in Battambang. Like many other babies, Thavra's survival was a miracle. Her mother was forced to work in the rice fields while Thavra was left in the care of a village elder. She was fed only the water from rice porridge. She was always very sick with diarrhea just like my brother Mouch had been. Her mother cried every night when she returned from the rice fields. She mourned the loss of her other children and was sad watching her sick newborn girl. She was

exhausted from laboring for the Democratic Kampuchea of
Pol Pot for twelve to sixteen hours a day. She had only a little
rice porridge to eat.

After the Khmer Rouge was overthrown in January 1979,
Thavra and her mother returned to Phnom Penh to search
for her surviving relatives. She went to claim back her villa
but found it occupied by a Vietnamese government official.
So, her mother decided to clean up an abandoned home she
found in another part of the city. After claiming it as her own,
Thavra's mother sold the gold that she had hidden during the
Khmer Rouge. She opened a small restaurant on the street at
Pet Chen. A few months later, in the summer of 1979, Thavra
and her mother reunited with all of the surviving family members in Phnom Penh.

Thavra's stepfather, Chun Lun, who married her mother
in 1979, was the first businessman in Cambodia to import automobiles and export steel to Taiwan. By the 1980s, his business was very prosperous. Within a few short years, Lun and
Samon were considered the most successful business couple in
the country. In Cambodia at that time, there were no banking
or credit transfer systems. Lun and Samon would transport
great amounts of cash in the trunk of their Mercedes-Benz.
They would drive for six hours to the port of Kompong Som
to pay for products and to pay their workers. From the mid-
1980s to the mid-1990s, the family was considered among the
elite in Cambodia.

Thavra was a very kind person. She always bought books
and study materials for her fellow students who could not afford

them. She was well-liked among her peers and her close friends who were the sons and daughters of high-ranking government officials and business entrepreneurs. Besides the Khmer language, Thavra studied English, Chinese, and Thai. She joined a swim team and earned black belts in both Karate and Tae Kwon Do at the ages of sixteen and seventeen respectively. People saw her more as a tomboy because she always fist-fought with boys after school.

I remember one beautiful evening when we first met. I was 28 years old and she was 22. We were walking at Revere Beach. All of a sudden, Thavra did a spin kick. I saw one of her legs go straight up in the air. I turned away pretending not to see it. But I knew from then on that I had to be nice to her. Also, on weekends, Thavra worked for various private companies in Phnom Penh. All of her salary went into treating her nephews and nieces to dinners and entertainment.

I took Thavra to meet my parents for the first time on Christmas Day of 1997. She received a warm welcome from them. On New Year's Eve, Vuth Pich and Kourou Chhoeuy invited us to join them to see the ice sculptures in Boston. Instead, I decided we would drive to Philadelphia to visit my brother Loeun and his family. That New Year's Eve was a very cold night and the temperature reached far below zero. Thavra wore the lovely black leather jacket that she had brought with her from Cambodia. She was freezing, but she did not admit that she was cold. A few weeks later, the doctor found that she was severely ill in her lungs. Since neither one of us had health insurance, I paid the doctor $150 with a credit card. When

I took Thavra back for a follow-up and tried to use my credit card, I learned it had been canceled. So, we went to Lowell General Hospital to apply for healthcare. But we were rejected.

One day, Prince Ranariddh came to Massachusetts looking for international support. Kong Vibol, chief of the prince's office, invited me to his hotel room at the DoubleTree in Lowell. He asked me to help them prepare for national elections in July of 1998 and return to Cambodia. I was ready to go and help them. But first, I needed an answer from Thavra if she would allow me to sponsor her.

One night, when we were parked in front of the Robert Frost Library at Amherst College, I told Thavra that I would be going back to Cambodia to help some people run for office. Also, I let her know that I would be joining the FUNCINPEC because I believed that only Ranariddh and his party could make Cambodia a truly democratic country and win support from the international community. After hearing what I had to say, Thavra started to cry. She agreed to accept my offer to sponsor her stay in America but said she was not in love with me. Still, after that, Thavra and I went out every weekend.

However, after consulting with her family back home, she accepted my hand in marriage. We were married in Lynn, Massachusetts on Valentine's Day, February 14, 1998, a beautiful Saturday morning by a justice of the peace, Joanne M. Sullivan. Soon after our marriage, Thavra moved in with me to start our new lives. We rented a bedroom in a house that we shared with friends on Pine Street in Lowell. For the first year of our marriage, it was challenging for us. We lived without savings and health insurance. I worked off and on. When I went to work, Thavra would hide in our bedroom playing video games on my old computer, waiting for me to come home. But when her school started, we would leave home at 7:00 a.m. and return at 11:00 p.m.

While I worked during the day in the North Shore area, Thavra would wait for me in our car, a red two-door Nissan NX that I had bought cheaply in Long Island, New York, while doing her schoolwork. She waited from 9:00 a.m. to 5:00 p.m., and we only saw each other on my lunch break. When she attended evening classes at the North Shore Community College, it was my turn to wait for her from 7:00 p.m. to 10:00 p.m. Thavra was often sick and we were completely broke. When we got together with friends, everyone would take turns lecturing us about the struggles of life. Sometimes, all we did was just admire other couples who we adored for their success. Although we felt bad about ourselves, we never lost hope that someday we could be like them. But some friends were sensitive to our situation.

In September, Thavra and I planned to have a formal marriage ceremony and wedding reception. The ceremony took place at the Saints Anne's Episcopal Church in Billerica, Massachusetts and my mother, Rev. Johnson, married us. Many of our close friends and family members attended. They gave us their blessings by putting their hands on top of our heads and wishing us good luck and a long-lasting marriage. For the reception, we had invited two hundred guests to the restaurant, Park Cafe, in a historical building in downtown Lowell.

However, I got a surprise phone call from the restaurant owner informing me that my check had bounced. I did not believe her because it was the company's check, a friend's temp agency I managed. I did not tell Thavra the bad news because I did not want her to panic. I cashed out my retirement from my previous employer, paying a big penalty. Luckily, the check arrived in time and the reception went smoothly. It was so wonderful to see some of Thavra's relatives come from France and other parts of the United States to celebrate our special event with us.

However, our honeymoon was an unusual one. We went to visit Thavra's uncle and cousins in Baltimore, Maryland. But we did not go alone. We took along with us Thavra's uncle Kunsaky, aunt Sarasy, sister Phomary, and niece Sreya. After one week in Baltimore, we came back home on a Sunday afternoon. On our way, the back tire of our car blew out on I-95 North and the rim was crushed as we passed the New York Turnpike entering Connecticut. I was given a citation by the state police for allowing six passengers to ride in a five-passenger car. The tow truck towed our car to the nearby town. Since all the garages were closed, we decided to look for a place to stay for the night. I called a taxi to take us to a nearby hotel. The taxi driver assured us that he knew a nice place at a reasonable price. We were happy to hear that, but it turned out to be a big disappointment. He dropped us off in front of a luxurious hotel, Marriott located in the woods, and then took off very quickly after receiving his fare. We checked into a nice room with two beds. However, both beds were occupied by our family. The newly wedded couple who were supposed to be on a honeymoon sat in an armed chair and watched our family members snore in comfortable beds.

The next morning, a Monday, I was due to report to my new job in the Lynn office on Union Street. Because I was stuck in Connecticut, I called the office manager and told her everything about my situation. But it did not go well at all. When she heard that I could not show up for my first day at work, she assumed that I was at a new casino that had opened. When I showed up to work the following day, she had a long talk with me in her office. I had to do all kinds of explaining to convince her that what I said was true. She said her boss in downtown Boston gave her a hard time hiring me.

After living for one year in Lowell, I found a good-paying job in Lynn. We moved in February 1999. My job was at the South Cove Community Health Center and Thavra worked at the Gregg House preschool. Every day, she walked to work one hour each way, while being pregnant with our first child. We shared a two-bedroom apartment on the third floor with other family members. In November, we moved to another apartment and Thavra's sister and niece moved to Lowell. Although our new apartment was still on the third floor, it was our home. Thavra got another job, working for the Cambodian-American Community of Massachusetts. And I got a new job working in the Massachusetts Department of Revenue.

Our first child was about to be born. This was a happy time for us. Our lives were going well and we started to save money. We were also able to send money to my family in Chi Kha and to Thavra's parents in Phnom Penh, Cambodia.

We also bought a second car so that Thavra, who had learned to drive, could drive to work and attend classes at night. On March 26, 2000, our first child was born; we named her Anna. Our daughter came into this world a perfect baby at six pounds fifteen ounces and twenty inches long. She had a lovely face. During the pregnancy, Thavra ate lots of pomegranate fruit to help with the baby's birth and have a clean baby. It seemed to work. Our baby came out so beautiful and so clean. Also, during pregnancy, Thavra had craved Sushi so she often sneaked out to a sushi bar. Thavra went into labor at the Salem Hospital on Friday evening, after work. Our daughter was not born until early Sunday morning.

That day was one of the happiest in my life. When it was time to cut the umbilical cord, I shook. It took me several tries to get the cord cut. I was afraid of hurting our precious baby, whose eyes were wide open, staring at me, ready to cry. At that moment, Thavra and I shed tears of joy. Taking our baby home was a challenge. I was so afraid to drive. I sat in the car holding on tightly to the steering wheel. I forced myself to shift the car into gear and stepped on the gas. Slowly, the car moved away from the hospital parking lot and we headed home. A friend came to help us, knowing that we were inexperienced new parents. Our daughter's room was full of baby stuff and her crib was full of stuffed animals.

Since daycare was too costly, Thavra took our baby to work every day. I had to leave early for my work, so Thavra had to carry the baby carriage herself. One day, Thavra and baby Anna fell on some ice. It took Thavra a long while to regain her strength and put our daughter back into the carriage. Thavra and I were brand new parents and had much to learn. A year later, Thavra got a job at the Lynn Community Health Center (LCHC) as a case manager. Our lives began to improve.

Two years later on March 19, 2002, our second child was born and we named him, William. On Tuesday morning, Thavra felt that she needed to go to the hospital. While we were taking care of our daughter, Thavra's water broke. I ran to get Ngon Chum at the Lynn Buddhist temple and brought her to our place to watch Anna. I then rushed to take Thavra to the hospital. By mid-afternoon that day, Thavra's obstetrician came and our baby boy came into this world. Thavra had a very scary labor. William was a big baby, nine pounds six ounces and twenty-one inches long. Our son was born at 4:20 p.m. Just like his sister Anna, William was a perfect baby. The only difference was that he was hungry right away and started to look for milk. After a second child, I was a pro.

In 2001, after three and a half years of marriage, Thavra applied for U.S. citizenship. After waiting for more than a year, she went for her naturalization interview in Boston. It was the same day, March 19, 2003, that the American-led coalition forces (Operation Iraqi Freedom) launched tomahawk cruise missiles against Iraq. Also, it was our son's first birthday. Thavra had her naturalization interview and passed easily that same day. After Thavra was sworn in as a U.S. citizen on May 1, 2003, we began to fill out papers to sponsor Thavra's parents. This was the same day that President George W. Bush declared "Mission Accomplished" in Iraq. Less than one year later, Thavra traveled to Cambodia and brought her parents to America. She also helped her sister Phomadin and her three children come to the U.S. They arrived a year later and went to live in Minneapolis, Minnesota.

In May 2004, we bought our first home in a residential area in Lynn. We still reside in this home. It is an old house, but perfect for us. It is a two-story single-family home with four bedrooms, a spacious kitchen, a living room, a dining room, and two bathrooms. I felt blessed to have been able to have my own home and know that my children would not have to experience homelessness like I had been through in Cambodia and refugee camps in Thailand.

CHAPTER 18

Big Dream

I have always been passionate about politics and community work. So, in April 2006, I helped create a new political movement, Khmer Mchas Srok (KMS). I was elected vice president and was responsible for its mission in the United States. We lobbied at the UN in Geneva and New York asking the international community to continue to monitor human rights abuses in Cambodia and to strengthen democracy and justice there. The movement's mission was to educate the public about the various problems in our country—such as land-grabbing by powerful people and government officials, corruption, the lack of social justice, and other violations that the Cambodian people faced daily.

Thavra and I participated in KMS conferences throughout the U.S. I gave speeches in Washington, D.C., and New York to explain the political situation in Cambodia. I appealed to the international community to pay close attention to the many abuses that the Cambodian government was committing on its citizens. Since I set foot in America, I wanted to do something to help Cambodians in Cambodia. I understood the differences between living under oppression versus living in a free society.

The KMS was formed in October 2006 in Massachusetts when Dr. Chak Sakhon, an economist educated in France, came to America to seek support for a new Cambodian political party. After three nights of meetings in Lynn, she was convinced that a political movement was needed. This movement would be a check on the government in Cambodia. For instance, the Cambodian government at the time had no intention of holding regular free elections. Finally, a resolution was adopted at the KMS's convention at UMass Lowell. There was full coverage by Radio Free Asia, the Voice of America, the KI Media, and local news. Many states throughout the country sent representatives to attend the KMS's convention. KMS asked its members to contribute only $1 per month. The funds raised would be used to hire international lawyers to represent the KMS and its president Dr. Chak Sakhon at the UN.

The method for raising funds was successful. After a few short months, the movement expanded, with branches not just in the U.S., but also in other countries, such as Canada, France, and Australia. I worked hard to help us build our reputation among members and supporters. We held meetings until late at night, every weekend. Sometimes our young children slept under the table because we were so deeply involved in the new movement.

Thavra and I also helped to promote and preserve the Cambodian culture in Lynn. Since moving to Lynn, we have been on a planning committee to organize the Khmer New Year. First, we had just a small crowd at the North Shore Community College. Then, we expanded to the Lynn Vocational

Technical Institute and then, to the Lynn Buddhist Temple. Finally, we were able to expand to Lynn Commons in April 2011. The Khmer New Year event has attracted several thousand participants each year. It has become the biggest public event that Lynn has ever held. Government officials and elected officials at all levels show their support and attend the annual event. On this particular occasion, we were able to lobby our city officials to fly the Cambodian national flag in front of the city hall during April to honor the Cambodian New Year. Also, we ran a very successful food pantry at the Lynn Buddhist temple, which has served several hundred Southeast Asians on the North Shore for many years.

In May 2011, I decided to participate in the local elections by running for public office. Although I had always been interested in politics, I had never yet run for office myself. I always worked for other politicians, helping to get them elected. My interest in politics dates back to 1991 when I campaigned for the Democrat, U.S. Congressman John Olver, in a special election to succeed the seventeen-term Republican Congressman Silvio Conte, who had died in office that year.

In 2007, I helped form a committee to recruit candidates to run for offices locally and statewide from the Asian community. In 2010, Kirirath Saing was the Southeast Asian Liaison in the office of Lynn's Mayor Judith Flanagan Kennedy. Our committee's goal was to groom him to run for political office someday. Although he talked often about wanting to throw his hat in the political ring, he kept saying that he was not ready. The committee was interested in having my wife, Thavra, run for office, but she vehemently refused. Her goal was to get through graduate school. We tried to convince Posan Ung and Sokheang Hong, but they both refused. Therefore, I began to play a lesser role in the committee because I was afraid of being appointed, as they had tried to do several years earlier.

One day in April 2011, Harry Schnur, Thavra's colleague at the LCHC approached me and asked me to run. But I refused. I had been hiding from him for weeks. After Harry convinced me that the city needed diversity in its government, I agreed to run for office as a city council representative. I called to consult with Kirirath to be sure that he was not planning to run. I submitted a copy of my resume to Harry who gave it to Robert Fioccoprile, a well-known community and political activist. One evening, I met with Gardy Jean-Francois (then the mayor's aide), Kirirath, and Robert at Gardy's residence in Lynn. After reading through my resume, Robert assured me that I was qualified. Both Robert and Gardy were mutual friends and knew the politics in Lynn inside and out. Robert himself was a veteran political operative who had been helping people get elected for more than forty years.

One day in May, I gathered my close friends and family together for a meeting in my backyard. I announced that I was considering running as an at-large councilor and that I wanted to get their opinions about my interest. After getting their approval and encouragement, I called the local newspaper, The Daily Item, telling them that I was going to run for councilor at large. I had an interview with Chris Stevens to announce my candidacy and had my picture taken by Paula Muller, who worked for The Daily Item at the time. After I officially announced my candidacy, I pulled out nomination papers from the election office. I was the last one to sign my name on the sheet that listed the candidates for the at-large councilor position. My hands and knees were shaking when I signed my name to be on the ballot. This was only the second time that I had walked into Lynn City Hall. The first time was a year earlier when I had attended a community meeting in the council chambers organized by then Ward 5 Councilor Brendan Crighton. Immediately, after I signed my name to be on the ballot, I began to receive phone calls from friends expressing their confidence in my candidacy. They had seen my name on the front page of The Daily Item. Their enthusiasm for my candidacy motivated me.

The first person that I asked to sign my nomination paper was someone standing alone waiting for a soccer game to start at Hood Park. He refused to sign it. I asked him to give me a chance to have my name appear on the ballot for the election; he continued to ignore me. I felt so disappointed. Then, I walked over to join my family to watch our son, William, play soccer. Then and there, I thought of giving up. At the same time, Robert Fioccoprile called to remind me about an event that evening. At first, I ignored his phone call, but finally, I decided to take it because he kept on calling me. That evening, I joined Robert at the event and was well-received by many residents. It was a great night and it was the first time that I had the opportunity to engage in conversations with some of Lynn's elected officials. To my surprise and relief, everyone was kind and seemed to know me.

When I got home, it was great to see KMS officials, including Dr. Chak Sakhon and Sean Masavang, having a meeting at our dining room table. Our good friends and community leaders, Sophor Chhour, Sokheang Hong, and Kosal Nou were kind to support my candidacy and encouraged me to be brave. After knowing that I had the support of the Asian community, I began to reach out to different leaders in all the communities throughout Lynn. I was well received by so many non-Cambodian people. Then, I started to form my inner circle team to help me run a successful campaign. I appointed Harry Schnur and Michael Ouk, young college graduates, as my co-campaign managers, and Elaine Press, another young college student, as my treasurer. In addition, I appointed Socheath Toda and Joanna Sese, two technological-savvy young women for the social media component of the campaign, and Robert Fioccoprile and Gardy Jean-Francois as my political advisors. Also, Thavra played an important role as my everyday advisor and in organizing all the campaign volunteers.

We worked very hard day and night for months throughout the election season. The committee chose our campaign slogan, *For All Voices*, symbolized by three stars to represent my journey in life. The smallest star represented my life in Cambodia, the medium star represented my life in Thailand, and the largest star represented my life in America. The campaign colors were blue, yellow, and white. On June 10 that year, I launched my campaign kickoff at the Old Tyme Italian restaurant on Boston

Street in Lynn. Before launching my kickoff, I wrote letters to all the elected officials in Lynn. Also, I wrote to the state delegations from Lynn and the surrounding communities. I wanted to introduce myself and explain why I was running for city council. Among those to whom I wrote were State Senator Thomas McGee, State Representatives Lori Ehrlich, Donald Wong, Steve Walsh, Robert Fennell, and Mark Falzone.

I thanked Robert Stilian, the Old Tyme restaurant owner, and Diana Chakoutis restaurant manager. These were names on the paper that Harry handed to me before I gave a speech. I had no clue exactly who they were. I thought that they might be husband and wife. Two years later, Diana ran for Ward 5 councilor to fill the open seat. Although she was the last one to announce, Diana's popularity and her charm attracted Ward 5 voters. She was elected to the city council, and she represents her constituents to this day.

Diana and I are close allies in the council. Because Mayor Judith Flanagan Kennedy and Charlie Gallo, the Lynn school committee member, are both out of politics, I always search for Diana when there is going to be a group picture. Also, we are about the same height.

In election year, 2011, ten candidates were running for the four at-large seats: Four incumbents and six challengers. The four incumbents seeking re-election were Daniel Cahill, Paul Crowley, Stephen Duffy, and Timothy Phelan. The challengers were Calvin Anderson, Buzzy Barton, Miguel Funez, George Meimeteas, Clay Walsh, and myself. The campaign was very intense; each candidate campaigned hard—campaign signs blanketed the city, big ones, and small ones. Pickup trucks and flatbed trucks sporting big signs moved around to different locations for better visibility. There were constant phone calls and door-knockings which drove voters crazy.

My very first political debate on July 13 at the Ahabat Sholom Congregation on Ocean Street was nerve-wracking. I sat between Timothy Phelan and Miguel Funez. I noticed that all the candidates had prepared notes in front of them while we sat at a long table patiently waiting for an order from Mary Trahan, the president of the East Lynn Community Association at the time. When I looked around the room, I was frightened to death at seeing half of the room wearing Buzzy Barton's campaign buttons and the other half with Daniel Cahill and Clay Walsh's stickers. I was shaking like a little kitten. I kept drinking water the whole time. I almost finished one bottle before the debate even started. When I looked at Thavra, who was sitting directly across from me, I saw her face was pale. She knew that I was scared.

When we were about to start the debate, Timothy Phelan walked in carrying a yellow notepad. When he sat down on his assigned chair, between me and Clay Walsh, his leg accidentally kicked mine. He turned to me and said, "Sorry!" I said, "That's okay, Mr. President. How are you?" He responded with a smile and then said, "I'm great! I've heard a lot of good things about you. Everyone told me that you're a good guy!" I thanked him for the compliment. Stephen Duffy leaned into me from the other side of Miguel Funez and said while rolling up his sleeves, "Don't worry, just enjoy yourself and you'll be fine."

That evening would be the first time that I met Paul Crowley and Buzzy Barton in person, as well as Timothy Phelan. Each of us was asked to give an opening statement. I read every single word on my paper. I saw Thavra shake her head. Everyone in the room listened quietly to me. After sensing the quiet environment, my nervousness got worse and I started to sweat. My voice was low and soft. Thavra and Harry made all kinds of hand signals to try to make me speak louder.

When it came to Timothy's turn to speak, he pushed the microphone away and stood up, speaking without a mic. His voice was loud and crystal clear and he was using dramatic hand gestures right over my head. This made me shake even more. I felt intimidated by his powerful arguments. During the whole two hours of debate, I began to lose my focus and kept praying for the end. When it was finally over, Alex, my best friend from UMass, came over to me and said, "Wow! You did it! You survived, Hong." I thanked him and then turned to ask Thavra and Harry how I did. Harry said I did well, but Thavra disagreed and told me to do better next time. "You did okay! But I couldn't hear you. You have to watch me when you speak. When you see me rub my throat that means you need to speak louder," said Thavra.

To my pleasant surprise, I finished fifth with a very strong showing in the primary election on September 20. When all the polls closed, many candidates gathered outside the election office at city hall waiting for the totals. Everyone pushed their way to the front to get a closer look at the final results from each polling station. But I stood quietly sweating nervously in the background, holding my hands together and waiting anxiously to hear the results. When the counting ended, Angela Owens, a young photographer from The Daily Item, snapped a few pictures of me. She aimed her camera at me and waited for me to smile when I found out that I was assured a spot for the November election. Chris Stevens interviewed me about my position. I praised my team, supporters, volunteers, and the residents of Lynn for placing their trust in me that day.

That evening, two candidates were eliminated. This left only eight to compete in the November general election. When I entered the reception room at the Mitapheap Restaurant on Western Avenue to greet my supporters, I cried with joy in front of a room full of family, friends, and supporters. I could not imagine that thousands of people voted for me! After seeing me cry, Thavra tried to comfort me and then she joined me in crying. It took me a few minutes to gather my emotions to be able to deliver a speech. The next morning, Daniel Cahill published some very nice words on the front page of The Daily Item. He said that I was the star of the night; voters thought that I was endorsed by a rising star attorney and a popular local politician at the time. Soon enough my campaign started to be recognized by the Lynn voters and surrounding communities.

While my campaign was strong and raised a fair amount of funds, Thavra and I faced financial hardship with our family. We had used up all our savings and had maxed out our credit cards to help pay for the KMS expenses and activities. Also, we used our money to pay the salaries of twenty local employees who worked for us in Cambodia and to pay for

Thavra's graduate school. Besides paying for the KMS and Thavra's education, the majority of our money went to investing in our agriculture venture in Cambodia. We invested in cassava and paper tree plantations. Unfortunately, when it came to harvesting, we always lost money. The buyers always paid us less than what the contracts stipulated. It is fair to say that the market in Cambodia was based on the buyers' words. The court has always been in favor of the rich and powerful. In addition to spending hundreds of thousands of dollars on three hundred acres of land, our families in Cambodia needed money constantly for medical reasons causing us always to be late in our mortgage and credit card payments. It seemed that every Friday or holiday, the constable would come and hand us court papers threatening to take us to court for late payments. This made us stressed. Although we faced financial difficulty, we kept it to ourselves. After some of our lands in Cambodia were sold, we caught up with all our payments.

Besides having a hard time collecting three hundred and fifty certified signatures to place my name on the ballot in the September and November elections, I was faced with some negative reactions during my campaign. Some people said that I had no chance of winning. Others would tell me to take my signs down. A few times, people called the police on me and some of them threw my campaign palm cards into their trash barrels in front of my family and me after we had handed them out. Sometimes, people would stick their heads out of a car window and spit at me. Some people would put their thumbs down when I held up my signs for visibility. Other people would tell me to go back home. Although I felt hurt, I forced myself to smile and to thank them. But most of the time, I just simply told them that I was already home and asked them to give me a chance to prove myself.

On top of that, my lawn signs kept going missing and some of them were burned. I cried, feeling bad for myself. However, Thavra felt more hurt inside than I did. She kept begging me to quit. But I convinced her that I had gone too far and that I must continue to put up a good fight. Robert and Harry stuck around and spent a lot of time with me strategizing for the campaign and reminding me to stay positive. "Mr. Net, I've been in politics for forty years and I know what I'm doing. Stay positive and trust me, the people of Lynn will remember the name of Net for a long time," Robert would often remind me.

I was somewhat hopeful because many people accepted me warmly. Every day for six months, we worked very hard. Thavra and I and some of my team members spent time in people's living rooms and at their kitchen tables. We spent countless hours registering them to vote and explaining the voting process to them. We educated people about their rights to get involved and why they should vote. A few spat at me, called the police when I was in their neighborhoods, gave me the thumbs down, slammed their doors on me, and told me to go back to where I came from. The whole time, I reminded myself to be even more respectful, and that I might eventually earn their trust.

There was also unfair treatment toward our children at the schools. This compelled me to get involved. The school tried to have our daughter stay back in first grade because she was too quiet. There was no warning or alert from the school at the time about her academic performance. After testing her ourselves and knowing that she was capable of doing everything like the other students in her class, we started to fight hard to make the school test her. Also, we took the case to the school superintendent's office. Finally, the school promoted our daughter to the next level. She has been one of the top students throughout her twelve years in school.

On November 8, 2011, I was elected, one of the four councilors at-large, defeating two incumbents. Buzzy Barton finished third and Timothy Phelan topped the ticket. Daniel Cahill finished second. That election night, I made history becoming the first Asian-American ever to be elected to a public office in Lynn and the second Cambodian-American to be elected to a public office in America. During the LCTV broadcast live coverage of the election, I could not bear to watch the results rolling in. While I was neck and neck with Paul Crowley, the whole room of my supporters became quiet. When Michael Ouk asked me to follow him outside, I heard Kosal Nou jump off the ground and scream with joy. I did not pay attention. After learning from Michael that it had been confirmed by the election office that I was elected, I was still not convinced. As I walked into the reception room, everyone cheered. At the same time, I saw Robert Fioccoprile walk into the room. His tie was hanging off his neck and half of his shirt was unbuttoned. He told me that he had been in the emergency room having IV liquid. He was so nervous that I would lose the election. It had almost caused him to have a breakdown.

The next morning, both The Daily Item and Lynn Journal wrote that Buzzy and I made history by opening up the door to city hall. Buzzy became the second African-American elected to the city council after Matthew Will, who had been elected two decades earlier. Since my first successful election, I have been going around encouraging people to step up and get involved in the civic and political processes. I appeal to the younger generation to come back to Lynn after graduating from college to help build the city. "Elected officials and city leaders, like myself, are here just to keep the seats warm for you. We need to be replaced someday," I have often said to them. In addition to my inner circle, a dynamic campaign team, the social media and press such as The Daily Item, Khmerican, KhmerPost USA, Lynn Journal, KI Media, and Lynn Community Television, played significant roles in promoting my candidacy and helping me get my message to voters. Chris Stevens from The Daily Item, Vandy Pan from the Khmerican, Soben Pin from the KhmerPost USA, Cary Shuman from the Lynn Journal, Thavry Ung from the KI Media, and Cassie Vitali from the LCTV interviewed me and wrote wonderful articles about me and my candidacy. This attracted voters and prompted many to throw their full support behind me.

Two days before election day, my brother Nicholas flew up from Maryland to campaign with me. He suggested that he must have gotten the extra votes to make me win.

CHAPTER 19

Politics

The morning of election day, I ironed my American father's old blue shirt that my mother had asked me to pick out the day after my father's funeral ceremony. I put my father's shirt on, along with a campaign tie. After giving it a gentle kiss, I asked my father for his blessing because I knew that he had always loved politics and that he would have been proud to see me running for public office. I whispered, "Dad, I know that you are looking down on me from above. Please help me win this election to make you proud. I miss you and will always miss you." At the same time, I sat in front of my computer and wrote an acceptance speech, just in case I needed it.

Some weeks before my father passed away, he and Mom visited Nicholas and his family in New Zealand, where Nicholas was working for a non-profit organization. Although my father was cancer-free, he became sick while in New Zealand. He and Mom rushed back to America for medical attention. Before he went to the hospital, my father went shopping for new clothes because he always liked to look sharp. That same day, he also bought some presents for his granddaughter Anna, our daughter, for her sixth birthday. After mailing them out, my mother took him directly to the hospital. Shockingly, the doctor told my mother that the cancer had spread all through my father's body and that it was too late to treat. My mother refused to believe the doctor because they had just gone shopping that day. Besides, my father was strong and he believed he was cancer-free. But the doctor told my mother that my father could not go home. The bad news caused my father to lose hope and he immediately went into a coma.

He had been diagnosed with multiple myeloma, a type of cancer where white blood cells do not produce antibodies. The day that my parents were supposed to come to see our newborn baby at the hospital, I received a phone call from my brother, Nicholas telling me the bad news. My head was spinning in the hospital room after hearing the news, but I did not share it with Thavra because she was in the middle of recovering from delivery.

Two days before my father's passing, I received a call from Nicholas briefing me on his advanced condition. Immediately, I purchased a plane ticket and then went to the Buddhist temple in Lynn. I asked for some holy water from the head monk, put it in a bottle, and then left for the airport, flying to Washington, D.C. Dulles International Airport. I went straight to the hospital in Bethesda, Maryland where my father was. Patrick was on his way from Amsterdam, Holland, and Loeun from New Jersey.

That evening, I asked to be alone to sit beside my father in his hospital bed. First, I sprinkled a little holy water on him to bless him. Then, I took the opportunity to tell my father how much I loved him. I told him how much I appreciated the new life he had given me and thanked him for all the love he continued to give to me and my immediate family. I took the half-hour as an opportunity to be with him and tell him about all the things he had done for me. I also told him that Thavra and his grandchildren, Anna and William, had wanted very much to come and that they loved him very much.

After hearing my voice and knowing that I was choking and about to cry, I saw my father manage to move his fingers just a little bit, and then, his tears came rolling down his cheeks. I leaned in and kissed my father's cheek gently. Then, I whispered in his ear and told him one last time that I loved him. Also, I promised that I would be a good father and husband and always kind to others. I told him that he was my hero and everything that I had ever wished for. At that moment, I heard his voice speak softly; he tried to open his eyes a little and then more tears came down. I believe that he must have known that I was right beside him.

Loeun also took his turn to talk to our father as I had done. That night my mother and I spent the night with my father in his hospital room. My mother slept on one side and I on the other side of my father holding his hands tightly all night long. Although his fingers were cold and turned blue, I was not scared at all. That night, I flashed back to the time when I had comforted my birth mother, Muoy, as she lay dead on a straw mat in our hut. I was right beside my mother. I held on to her the whole time until she was taken away by the villagers to be buried in an unknown location. That night in the hospital room, I asked Lord Buddha and God Jesus Christ to allow me to be a part of my father's life again, if there was a next life.

The following morning, Sunday, the doctor came into the room and told us to prepare for Dad's funeral. Then, a counselor came to counsel us. Lastly, a priest came and with holy water blessed our father. I sprinkled some holy water on my father. We all cried. Our mother took it the hardest. "Oh, Richard! What can I do without you?" asked Mom, while crying. It was so painful for my mother to see the love of her life leave her after forty-six years of a happy marriage. Their love had been harmonious and strong. Ever since I came into their lives, I had never witnessed my parents yell at each other. When they fought, they would go to a separate room quietly, but it would not last more than an hour for them to start talking to each other again. At that moment, we all took turns comforting our mother telling her that we would call and visit her often. Although my mother had always been strong both physically and mentally, that day she looked as fragile as a broken champagne glass.

That evening, I flew back to Boston with a heavy heart. My eyes were blurred and my chest was pounding with pain. I was saddened to have not been able to have my last conversation with my father or hear him say goodbye. But I was glad that I had had the opportunity to tell him everything I had always wanted to. When I got home, I saw that my father's presents for his granddaughter had arrived right on her birthday. It was very painful to see his handwriting on the gift boxes. This made me and Thavra cry even more. Just minutes past midnight, the phone rang and when I picked it up, I heard my

mother say, "Hong, Dad just passed away." I could not say anything only thanked her for letting me know and then hung up
the phone. It was Monday, March 27, 2006, that our beloved
father passed away at the age of sixty-eight. In my mind, I
thought that he must have waited for his granddaughter's sixth
birthday knowing that she had received his presents. A few
minutes later, my brother, Nicholas called and also shared the
sad news. I went into our daughter's room crying and Thavra
went into our son's and cried as well. Our children woke to the
sounds of our crying. They asked us why we were crying. But
we did not tell them what was happening until the next day.

My win for the city council was a sign of hope that Lynn
was ready for a positive change. Being a councilor, I served as
an elected official in the legislative branch of government. I
would create laws and ordinances for the city, approve bud-
gets and tax rates, as well as have a say in all of the mayor's
appointments. The city council is where the public is allowed
to speak in support or opposition to laws and where the councilors listen and then, discuss or debate the issue before taking
a vote. Usually, the non-profit groups speak the longest and
make the most noise. When I came to the full council meetings
in the council chamber, I would bring the letters that I had received from constituents and concerned citizens. I would wave
the letters to the public when I had voted in support. When it
came to a discussion or debate, I would cut the introduction
and go straight to the heart of the issues. I kept my speaking
brief, usually around four or five sentences. All meetings, including sub-committee meetings, are televised.

Vesna Nuon had been elected to the city council in Lowell after multiple attempts. He finished seventh and was the second Cambodian-American to be elected. Rithy Uong had been elected a decade prior. Local newspapers and The Boston Globe wrote beautiful articles about Vesna's and my victories, highlighting that I had made history by being the first Asian-American elected to a public office in the city of Lynn. My campaign materials were put on display in the Lynn Museum for the public to view.

Daniel Cahill and Brendan Crighton taught me and Buzzy a lot about the council's work. One day, Daniel told me that the first vote I would take, half of the people in the city would feel affected, and the other half would feel benefited. "As we are all aware, you can't make everybody love you. You stand your ground and vote for what you believe is right. Do you hear me?" Daniel said. Brendan, on the other hand, gave Buzzy and me copies of the Lynn City Charter and Robert's Rules of Order to study. I took the opportunity to read every page of both publications and tried to memorize the rules and laws.

I first met Brendan when he was a ward councilor and chief of staff for then-State Senator Thomas McGee. This was when I was emceeing for the Khmer New Year at the Lynn Buddhist Temple in 2000. He was young and single in his early twenties when he was first elected to the city council. This young man moved up the political ladder very fast. After two terms as a ward councilor, he was elected as councilor at-large. Then he became a state representative in 2014, replacing Steven Walsh, who had resigned to become an executive director of the Massachusetts Council of Community Hospitals. Then, Brendan ran unopposed for state senate in a special election after Thomas McGee was elected mayor of Lynn. McGee defeated two-term incumbent, Judith Flanagan Kennedy in 2017.

I first met Daniel on the campaign trail in the summer of 2011. After his mother Jane Cahill introduced me to him at his fundraiser, held at the Lynn Museum, we quickly became friends and have been allies in the council until he moved up to become a state representative in the special election of 2016. Daniel, like Brendan, ran unopposed to fill a vacant seat that State Representative Robert Fennell had held. But then, Robert Fennell left to run the Lynn Water and Sewer Department after Robert Tucker retired from the department. Later on, Robert Tucker was appointed by me and approved overwhelmingly by the city council to chair the newly established Lynn's Human Rights Commission. Earlier, the commission had been founded by me and Robert Fioccoprile.

For the past four years in the council chamber, I have often been a breaker of tie votes. Two groups always vote differently. For a long time, I was pulled between the two sides of the aisle. But most of the time, I sided with Daniel Cahill and Brendan Crighton because they usually informed me of the issues ahead of time. Besides, I tried to act as a unifier. I never yelled or showed any anger toward anyone if I did not get my way. I worked to strengthen public safety, the local economy, and public education. Also, I cared about a unified city. I worked with my colleagues, the mayor, and community leaders to make sure that external politics did not affect the community of Lynn.

One day when a few of us local and state delegations were standing together participating in the Khmer New Year celebration on the Lynn Commons, then-Republican U.S. Senator Scott Brown approached us. In attempting to shake our hands, some of the councilors tried to walk away. But I grabbed one of the councilors' hands and asked him to stay. I said, "Please stay. No matter what, he's our senator and we have to accept the people's choice." Later that day, I received a text message from the councilor thanking me for stopping him from walking away from the senator. The text message read, "Thank you for making me a better person."

Scott Brown, a former state senator, ran in a special election to fill a seat that had been held by the late Senator Edward Kennedy in 2010. He defeated former Massachusetts Attorney General Martha Coakley, with a slogan of "It's The People's Seat." A charismatic Scott Brown attracted the people of Massachusetts of all ages. He ran for re-election to a full six-year term in 2012 but lost to a Harvard University professor and Democratic challenger, Elizabeth Warren. Later, he was appointed by President Donald Trump and approved by the Senate in June 2017 as U.S. Ambassador to New Zealand.

One year after my election to the city council, I resigned from the KMS to focus on my family and serving my constituents. The KMS movement had consumed a lot of time and resources. Thavra also decided to resign to focus on school. Thavra worked full-time during the day and went to school full-time in the evening. She came home at midnight every night. I have seen her arrive home and cry from exhaustion and loneliness. The children and I were always sound asleep. She wanted to quit many times. But Thavra was determined to have a better future for her family and to break the cycle of Cambodian women being housewives for generations. This compelled her to continue. After receiving her bachelor's degree in social work from Salem State University, Thavra went on to graduate school. She finally graduated with a master's degree in mental health counseling from Cambridge College in 2015. Following our resignations to focus more on our new careers, the KMS did not do as well as we expected because many of its members began to question the direction the movement was heading.

After I had been sworn in for my fourth consecutive term as councilor at-large in Lynn City's government in 2018, I threw my hat into another political ring. At-large councilors usually become mayors or state representatives. To follow in Lynn's tradition, I tried to run for state representative, the seat vacated by Brendan Crighton, representing West Lynn and Nahant in Massachusetts' eleventh district. Many people thought that I was qualified for the job because of my experiences with government and community involvement. But as soon as I announced my candidacy, I received a few phone calls from people I knew, asking me not to run. They gave no specific reasons. But many other people did want me to run. In the end, I ran.

Deciding to run for the state representative position in 2018, I was reminded of the 2015 election, when I ran for my third term as councilor at-large. That year, I had run against many big names in Lynn. Everyone on my team had warned me that I would face a tough election for challenging such well-known and powerful candidates as the former president of the union of firefighters, Buzzy Barton, the council president, Daniel Cahill, the former council president and mayoral candidate, Timothy Phelan, the top ticket-getter for school committee member, Richard Starbard, and the director of the teacher union, Brian LaPirre. In that election year, many members of my campaign team had suggested that I should not run against these men and that I would face a bad defeat. I, too, was afraid of being defeated. But I trusted the residents of Lynn and I was convinced that the voters would give me another chance to continue serving their city. And they did! On election night in 2015, the voters in the city of Lynn placed me among the three top vote-getters.

In 2018, I was one of three candidates running for state representative. We campaigned, focused on issues, and not on questioning any candidate's character. Our campaigns were admired by everyone who watched us closely. Many people said it was a clean and honest campaign. Many agreed that the campaign set an example for others to follow. As James Walsh, chairman of the Nahant Democratic town committee described it, "Democratic Candidates for State Representative, those three gentlemen, Peter Capano, Hong Net, and Drew Russo showed us that a candidate can be principled without calling into question the character of the other person."

Peter Capano was the president of one of the biggest unions in Massachusetts and has been in politics longer than me, so he was able to get all the union members and their families to back him. Drew Russo was vice-chair for the Democratic city committee in Lynn and was a special aide to former U.S. Congressman John Tierney; he was able to have all democratic leaders and their allies back him. I was left with the support of only SEIU, MassAlliance, and ordinary citizens.

People spoke highly about me and my candidacy. But it was not good enough for me to emerge triumphant. I was proud to know that my good friend, Rady Mom, was elected to represent his district in Lowell at the State House. He was the first Cambodian-American to be elected at the state level. Post-election, I learned that my desire to help others and my desire not to hurt others were viewed as weaknesses on my part. My willingness to help others, honesty, and integrity will always continue because that is what I believe in.

CHAPTER 20

Then and Now

While she was alive, Thavra's mother, my mother-in-law, often told us that when she passed away, she wanted to have her ashes spread on the mountain near the village where she was born. Also, she told us that my American father had appeared several times to her in a dream. He asked to be set free because he was bored living in a box. At first, she ignored his requests because she did not know that we had put my father's ashes in a box in our house. After my father had been cremated, my mother shared his ashes with her children to keep.

After Thavra's mother told us about her dream, we decided to take my father's ashes and spread them in the Atlantic Ocean at East Point, in the town of Nahant, Massachusetts, near the Northeastern University College of Science. We thought that it would be the most suitable place for him to rest because my father had always been passionate about education. When he was in college, my father had fought bitterly with his father, who had wanted him to become either a medical doctor or a lawyer. My father went against his father's wishes and instead became an educator. This caused a lot of tension between him and his father. My father did what he wanted to do and was happy with his decision throughout his life. By contrast, his brother, Frank became a psychiatrist as his father wished. However, Uncle Frank was never happy. He died of cancer in 1998.

One day in July, Thavra's mother died unexpectedly. After eating a dinner of rice with chicken soup at our home, she fell in the bathroom and became unconscious at once. Thavra's stepfather and I carried her to the living room. Michael Ouk happened to be at our house and he called 911 immediately. Thavra cried and talked to her mother in the ambulance to the hospital. Her mother never regained consciousness. At 8:00 p.m., Friday, July 1, 2016, Thavra's mother was pronounced dead. She never had a chance to say her last words to any of her loved ones. When we left the hospital, it poured rain and there was thunder. On our way home, tree branches fell in front and behind our car. It seemed like we were being asked not to leave the hospital. When we had come to the hospital, the skies had been clear and the sun had been bright. That night, Thavra's stepfather saw his wife in a dream. She said that she was scared and felt lonely in the hospital. Thavra's stepfather woke up and burned a stick of incense asking her to rest in peace.

One week later, on Saturday, we had a big funeral ceremony for Thavra's mother. Hundreds of people attended. Our son, William, along with his two cousins, Rattanak and Sophanouc, all ordained as Buddhist monks mourned the death of their beloved grandmother. Their heads and eyebrows were shaved and they were draped in saffron robes. It is a Cambodian tradition to have either the son or the grandson shave his head and eyebrows and drape himself in a white or saffron

cloth to mourn the death of a family member. Thavra, Phomadin, Phomary, Sreya, Anna, Thavra's cousin Phichara Chou,
Thavra's stepfather, and I were draped in white cotton clothes,
the color of mourning. Thavra's mother was bathed, dressed
in her favorite silk long-skirt and long-sleeved shirt, and had
her makeup and hair done beautifully by the Solimini Funeral Home's staff. In addition, beautiful jasmine flowers were
draped around her neck and on her right wrist. Her hands
were joined on top of her chest and she held three unburned
sticks of incense and some candles. She lay in a coffin chosen
by Thavra.

The funeral procession was escorted by a few police cruis-
ers and many vehicles followed the hearse. Cars carried family
members, Buddhist monks, and priests lined the whole way
from the Lynn Buddhist temple to the Puritan Lawn Memorial
Park in Peabody, Massachusetts. To honor Thavra's mother's
wishes, everyone in the family flew to Cambodia. We took her
ashes to spread on the famous mountain of Srong in Kampong
Speu province, southwest of Phnom Penh. Again, we had another big ceremony. It seemed as though everyone in town and
surroundings attended. A few weeks after my mother-in-law's
passing, our beautiful white Maltese dog also died. Everyone
was sad about the death of LouLou.

While in Cambodia, we attended the funeral of Dr. Kem
Lay, a beloved political commentator, who was gunned down
in broad daylight in the middle of Phnom Penh ten days after
Thavra's mother had died. Kem Lay was well known and respected for his political commentary, including his trenchant

criticism of the current government of Hun Sen and the CPP. His project, "100 Days With Khmer Families," attempted to search for the truth of political and social justice in Cambodia. However, this project made the ruling party nervous. He was the third notable activist to be killed in recent years, after the union leader Chea Vichea in 2004, and the environmental activist Chut Wutty in 2012. Many Cambodians and the international community believed that Kem Lay's assassination was a setup by the CPP authorities. After the assassination, many believed that the government refused to release the photos to the public showing the real killer. While in the country, we witnessed over two million of Kem Lay's supporters joining the funeral procession from Phnom Penh to his hometown in Takeo province. On the day of the funeral, the government ordered all gas stations along the route to close their pumps to dissuade motorists from joining the procession. However, nothing could stop petroleum vendors along the route who were able to provide motorists with gasoline to fill up their gas tanks.

While we were mourning Thavra's mother and Kem Lay's assassination in Cambodia, my birth father was very sick with multiple complications. It was emotionally draining for both me and Thavra to travel between Phnom Penh, Kampong Speu, and Koh Kong to juggle my father's illness and Thavra's mother's funeral and to think about my father's enormous medical expenses. A few months later, he passed away in great pain. However, I was glad that I had had the chance to see my father for one last time.

After our children graduated from middle school and earned their black belts in Tae Kwon Do, as a reward for their accomplishments, Thavra and I took them to see their grandfather, my birth father, and to visit some memorable places in Cambodia. We spent a few days in the busy, noisy capital city, Phnom Penh, then went to Angkor, to visit the exquisite temples. We saw a sunrise at Angkor Wat and admired from the top of Phnom Bakheng a late afternoon sunset which painted treetops golden and illuminated the reservoir, Baray. Angkor Wat is the world's largest religious monument. It was built by King Suryavarman II as a Hindu temple in the early 12th century, but it was converted into a Buddhist temple towards the end of that century. The lotus-like towers represent Mount Meru, home of the gods. It has become a symbol of Cambodia, continuing to appear on the national flag regardless of regime. The central complex has a base of 717 by 620 feet, surrounded by galleries measuring 5,000 by 4,000 feet. The outer walls measure 2.5 miles bordering moat for 200 yards wide. Its galleries tell the struggle between good and evil.

Today, Angkor Wat is the country's prime attraction for visitors. Also, together we enjoyed the beauty of the enchanted forest from the Elephant's Terrace, the mysterious smiling faces of Bayon Temple, the giant trees on top of Ta Prohm, and the great city of Angkor. All were built by King Jayavarman VII, the Khmer's master builder. Under the reign of Jayavarman VII, the Khmer Empire was at its peak, covering much of what today is Cambodia, Thailand, Laos, and southern Vietnam. We also visited the magnificent architecture of Banteay Srei Temple.

To refresh the sweet memories of my childhood, and evoke the time I had gone on vacation with my birth family three decades earlier, we took our children Anna and William to Kampot to eat in a noisy and hot market, *Phsa Chas,* swim in Tuek Chou, eat popular Kampot's durians, taste famous seafood and sweets that were sold by food-vendors at Kep, and enjoyed the blue-water beaches of Kompong Som. Seeing Thavra smiling at our children's admiration of all that we showed them, even the view while riding on National Highways 3 and 4. I was reminded of my birth mother's affectionate smile when she watched me as a child quietly admiring the beauty of Cambodia, my birth country.

About the Author

*H*ong Net was born in a remote village west of Cambodia, was raised Buddhist, and spent his childhood in labor camps in Cambodia, teenage years in refugee camps in Thailand, and his young adulthood in western Massachusetts. In 1979, Net fled to Thailand as a refugee, escaping the Killing Fields of communist Khmer Rouge and the invasion of communist Vietnam. At the age of fifteen, Net was given a second chance at life in America living with his foster family in western Massachusetts. After receiving his college degree in political science, Net returned to his native country to help the newly democratic government rebuild a war-torn country. During the bloody coup of 1997, he returned to America and worked for the Department of Revenue. In 2011, Net ran for politics for the first time and was elected to the city council. He is the first Asian-American to be elected to a public office in Lynn, and the second Cambodian-American in America. In 2012, Net authored Lynn's first Human Rights Commission, where he serves as an advisor. In 1998, Net married his wife Thavra who is currently a mental health counselor and director at the Rainbow Adult Day Healthcare Center, where Net is a business partner. Today, Net lives with his wife and children Anna and William in Lynn, Massachusetts.

9 798822 944749